THE SOCIOLOGY AND POLITICS
OF CONGRESS

THE SOCIOLOGY AND POLITICS OF CONGRESS

by Lewis Anthony Dexter

Currently Visiting Professor, State University
of New York (Graduate School of Library Science),
and Canada Council Visiting Professor of
Political Science, Dalhousie University; sometime
Visiting Professor, University of Puerto Rico,
Ohio State University, University of California
(Berkeley), Michigan State University,
Massachusetts Institute of Technology, Howard
University, Lowell Technological Institute,
University of South Florida, St. Anselm's,
and Talladega College

with a chapter by KENNETH KERLE
HAGERSTOWN JUNIOR COLLEGE

RAND M^cNALLY & COMPANY · *Chicago*

RAND McNALLY POLITICAL SCIENCE SERIES

Advisory Editor

MORTON GRODZINS

Late of the University of Chicago

Dedicated to

JAIME BENÍTEZ, Chancellor and President,
University of Puerto Rico (1942-1971)

and

CHARLES O. PRESS, Chairman, Political Science,
Michigan State University

political scientist–administrators who make the experience
of being a visiting professor a stimulating one

ACKNOWLEDGMENTS

As *always,* my chief acknowledgments must be to:

(*a*) The numerous people who have been kind and patient enough to be interviewed by me. I am particularly grateful to former Congressman Victor Knox of Michigan, who has permitted me to quote the material on pages 233–36.

(*b*) My colleagues Raymond A. Bauer, Harvard Business School, and Ithiel de Sola Pool, Massachusetts Institute of Technology, with whom I worked on *American Business and Public Policy* (Atherton, 1963).

(*c*) Massachusetts Institute of Technology, Center of International Studies, for stimulating and supporting me in the study of Congress, both in the Bauer-Pool project and in a later study of Congress in the field of military policy. I am also indebted for help to several other organizations that aided me in studies of Congress, especially the American Enterprise Institute of Public Policy, the necessarily unnamed client for whom I prepared the sketches that appear here in Appendix C, and the Carnegie Corporation.

In connection with this particular book, I have several additional and specific obligations:

1. To Dr. Kenneth Kerle of Hagerstown Junior College, for letting me republish herein the paper that appears as Chapter 5 below.

2. To Randall Ripley, Ohio State University, for helpful suggestions and comments.

3. To the late Morton Grodzins, University of Chicago, for insisting that I undertake this book—which, in the first instance, I did only with great reluctance.

4. To Arthur Maass, Harvard University, for the idea and occasion for Chapter 10 below, and other suggestions.

5. To the Society for Applied Anthropology, for transferring to me the copyright of Chapter 8 below, which originally appeared in its journal, *Human Organization,* in 1957.

I am also under obligation to the Atherton Press and to the Massachusetts Institute of Technology for permission to reproduce several paragraphs from *American Business and Public Policy* and, more profoundly, for not interposing any obstacles to my using the material in the second chapter below.

I must express my warmest thanks to Professor James A. Robinson, director of the Mershon Center (now provost), Ohio State University, for his valued assistance; and to Anne Trupp, Theresa Loffredo, and Gloria Werth of the Mershon Center for typing this manuscript, and for their helpful cheerfulness in many other respects.

LEWIS ANTHONY DEXTER

Rio Piedras, Puerto Rico
June 16, 1969

TABLE OF CONTENTS

Introduction

I

This book is organized around three major questions: (1) How far can citizens affect legislative outcomes and actions by the voting choices they make and by the part they take in election campaigns? (2) How can citizens affect legislative outcomes by means other than election activity—such as lobbying? (3) In interpreting and trying to influence Congress, what ideas, conceptions, and images are most useful for what purposes? Each of the three parts of the book concentrates on one of these questions.

1. What effect can the interested, involved citizen have on congressional policy-making and legislation? How does voting or participation in election campaigns make a difference?

The general conclusion is that under some specified circumstances voting and elections can make a great deal of difference in what Congress does; the cynical and frustrated view that legislation is uninfluenced by elections is simply wrong. On the other hand, it is naïve to assume or believe that most issues are directly decided on the basis of election results and calculations about electoral consequences. There are so many interests and so many issues that members of Congress do not find it necessary to follow constituent views on any given issue, provided that in general they create the impression of doing a satisfactory job. A Republican leader in the House of Representatives used to be often quoted as saying, "I never heard of any man being beaten on an issue."

This is both correct and incorrect: a Congressman or Senator may and can differ quite sharply from such constituency concerns as there are on nearly any issue, precisely for the reasons indicated in the words "such concerns as there are." It will be extremely unusual when any large proportion of the voters is committed to give priority to any particular issue—and unless voters give priority to an issue, they will by definition cast their votes on some other basis. For instance, it is entirely possible that the majority of Arkansas citizens have never sympathized with Senator J. William Fulbright's stands on international relations; but so long as he does not seriously offend them on race relations and so long as he helps the utility interests and the textile producers of the state and so long as he conforms to their general notion of what a Senator should be like and takes an acceptable stand on some other matters, he has as an incumbent a considerable advantage over most challengers. Occasionally Congressmen and Senators may take a position that is effectively dramatized by an attractive opponent and which loses them a significant proportion of their supporters; but this is a consequence of either ill luck or miscalculation. There are many parliamentary devices and offsetting procedures by which a Congressman or Senator can go through the motions of doing those things that please his constituents without in fact materially contributing to what they believe in; Senator Sparkman of Alabama has symbolically supported the southern position on race matters but in fact has actually done a good deal to contribute to equality for the Negro. And there have been Republicans from industrial districts who have symbolically appeared to support labor without in fact doing much for its program. No doubt the majority of serious segregationists in Alabama have generally opposed Sparkman, and the majority of involved trade unionists have generally opposed Republicans of the sort mentioned; but in both cases opponents have been unable to make a sharp and convincing campaign issue, and the incumbent has been reelected partly because of things he has done on other matters—in Sparkman's case, for instance, on the TVA and rural farm housing and small business.

In the nature of the situation, some small businessmen in Alabama may be violently segregationist; but nevertheless the same men may support Sparkman and even contribute to his campaign because they believe he has done more to get federal aid for small business than almost any other member of the Senate (and far more than any of his opponents would have been likely to do). This, of course, would be particularly true if their own firms have benefited from such aids secured by guidance from his office.

Nevertheless, some Congressmen and Senators have been beaten or have failed to seek reelection because it became *clear* that their position *in general* was contrary to what their district wanted or desired. Southern liberals such as Frank Smith of Mississippi (after redistricting) or Hugo Sims of South Carolina would fall in this category. Claude Pepper as U.S. Senator profited from certain special circumstances ("lucked in") in his early campaigns; but by 1950, when anticommunist feeling had developed more strongly, he was obviously tagged with an image too leftist for Florida. (Still later, of course, he was able to return to Congress in the House from a relatively liberal Miami district—although he probably could never again be elected statewide.)

That is to say, Congressmen and Senators are rarely, if ever, beaten on just one issue. But they may be beaten because they have offended potential supporters or aroused otherwise apathetic opponents on a series of matters. Had they been wiser, they would have retrieved their support or disarmed their opposition by choosing to go along on some issue about which they cared little or by casting about for some issue on which they did in fact see eye to eye with those who might otherwise cause them trouble and emphasizing it. In Kenneth Fry's interviews for the *American Business and Public Policy* project with Farm Bureau leaders in the Illinois district of the late Congressman Noah Mason, they told Fry that they emphatically agreed with Mason's self-estimate of himself as "stubborn" on many matters such as reciprocal trade. (In earlier reports about Mason, while he was still alive, I, accepting this view, called him Congressman Stubborn.) But they pushed on reciprocal trade, nevertheless, with the hope of making him somewhat uneasy, so that on some other issue of less moment to him, or on which he even agreed with them, he would go along or do more, as the case might be—for instance, taxation of cooperatives. Or, as I point out in my discussion below of the Javits-O'Dwyer-Buckley three-cornered race for the U.S. Senate in New York in 1968, it is conceivable that under certain specified circumstances, a threat of defection from either Javits or O'Dwyer by supporters of environmental defense programs could have led either of these men to stress measures in that field more than they would if left to themselves. They would not give up basic convictions, but they would change emphases, or possibly sacrifice preferences.

Looking at all this from the standpoint of the voter means that, granted certain kinds of circumstances, he can help to influence his Congressman, or other Congressmen for that matter, to change emphases or to shift positions on matters *relatively* minor to the Congressman. And what is relatively minor to the Congressman may be absolutely major to the voter; important as some of us think the deployment of MIRV is, there are probably some members of the House and Senate who regard it as a mere matter of preferences, and there are probably some members who still regard ecological balance as minor.[1] (The voter can help influence other Congressmen by campaign contributions, by working in a campaign for a man or his opponents, etc.)

However, all this, so far, omits what, in the present state of the Congress, is the most significant respect in which alert and hardworking (or lucky) voters can influence Congress. Most of the work of the Congress is done in committee; this is especially true of the House. The committees generally pose the questions and frame the bills; the membership as a body can only say yes or no, or make one or two amendments to legislation of many kinds. The committees are, by sixty years of custom, organized on the basis of seniority; the member with the longest service in the majority party is chairman, and so on down. Senior members, in general, have much more influence than junior members. On many committees, there are only one or two or three effective members. Their election or defeat may make all the difference in how certain legislation is handled; and so may a shift in the chairmanship or the composition of the committee. If, for instance, Robert Kean, fourth-ranking Republican on Ways and Means, had by luck become chairman of that committee in 1953, or even ranking Republican in 1955, his ascendance would have helped Eisenhower's administration get several

---

[1]In 1956 a former Congressman, then governor-elect, for whom I was helping to prepare an inaugural address, commented scornfully on the suggestion that we say something about cleaning up the rivers. "That's only of interest to those women," he said. He meant the League of Women Voters, clearly a politically trivial bunch from his standpoint.

of its programs through, especially reciprocal trade, particularly as under those circumstances Hal Holmes of Washington, also a "liberal" Republican, would presumably have become third-ranking member on that side. The other four top-ranking Republicans were basically opposed to many Eisenhower programs; one, Daniel A. Reed, was elderly and just might have been persuaded to withdraw if faced with a really strong primary opponent; the second, Thomas A. Jenkins, was beatable, in my judgment. To be sure, the third, Richard M. Simpson, was unbeatable and youngish; in fact, he died quite young, and such accidents are always possible. Or, at the present time, a shift in the composition of the Senate Armed Services Committee in 1970 might affect the outcome of proposals to deploy MIRV; even a shift on the House Armed Services Committee might do so. Whether the most recalcitrant (from the anti-MIRV standpoint) of the senior members are vulnerable, I do not know; but opponents of MIRV might well inquire. Vice versa, some of the Democrats on the Senate Armed Services who have opposed ABM and presumably would oppose MIRV are certainly vulnerable in 1970, and it is to be presumed that hard-liners, defense contractors, etc., will try to defeat them.

2. The second question is: How can voters and citizens affect legislative outcome and policy-making, other than by participation in elections? And this means, of course, concern with the reverse question: How are Congressmen affected by demands and requests and petitions and what the journalists call "pressures"?

Here again the answer is that the voter and the concerned citizens are semisovereign. Granted willingness to spend some time on a matter, granted some resources of expert knowledge or funds or persuasiveness, granted, of course, willingness to learn to think in political (rather than in strictly ideological or professional) terms, citizens can make a good deal of difference on an issue of moment to them, *sometimes*. Few people, in fact, have the kind of patience and perseverance and willingness to think politically, so that they acquire such influence. But it is possible to do so, as I point out below, especially in the discussion of how ecological legislation might be affected. The more aware serious people are of what might be done, the more people, we may hope, will (*a*) learn how to exercise such influence and (*b*) see the legislative optimum as securing a tolerable and workable, but not necessarily an ideal, result, for instance. On the other hand, efforts of this sort take as much time and skill as the effort to be, say, a first-rate tennis player or a good musician. The person who simply makes demands or suggestions to Congressmen without knowing the background and without canvassing the situation is not very likely to be influential. Politics, in other words, takes thought and persistent work—which of course may still be fun and satisfying to some temperaments.[2]

Basically, Congressmen and Senators must generally choose between a multiplicity of interests and demands from many sides. They cannot react effectively to all or even to most of them. Furthermore, a great many real demands are inarticulate, subconscious, waiting to be mobilized. Some of the demands to which a Congressman is exposed are self-created—from his own conscience or his doctrine of politics. A good many come from his colleagues on committee or in the House or from those whom he respects anywhere rather than from his district. On many issues, all he can see, really, is that some people want something done. But there is no way to find out exactly what they want, because they have not thought through the problems carefully enough. In general, voters want to eat their cake and have it too, but, always, Congressmen must realize that an improvement here is likely to involve cost and trouble there, and must try to balance the two against each other.[3]

In any case, Congressmen, like other people, interpret and choose to attend to matters in accordance with their own predispositions, situations, and experience. So one Congressman may hear a demand for more unemployment insurance while another hears a demand for imposing quotas on foreign textiles and shoes—even though the complaints are couched in similar language by the same sort of people. The most important difference between Congressmen in many cases is the kind of persons they are; Mr. X, because of a series of predispositions, is likely to hear one sort of message—or, more carefully put, to interpret a given set of words

---

[2]Since 1960 my own life has happened to exclude any systematic effort along these lines; before that, I had some relevant experience. If I could push a button and find myself in the thick of a campaign to defeat ABM and MIRV or to support legislation for ecological balance, I probably would do so. I am certain that I would not push a button to change to my present academic life if I were actually running such a campaign. The main disadvantage of activity of this type is the almost chronic absence of minor administrative and clerical aids, which cumulatively make life pleasanter for professionals.

[3]A very illuminating discussion of the general theory of choice is to be found in Philip Wicksteed, *The Common Sense of Political Economy*, ed. Lionel Robbins, vol. 1 (London: Routledge, 1938). Just as Wicksteed applies choice to household administration, so it can be (and should be) applied to politics. I hope someday to be able to do this, with special reference to *the making of choices about what to attend to*, particularly the determination of the bounds of "bounded rationality."

in a certain way—while Mr. Y, because of other predispositions, will interpret the same sort of message in another way. Two Congressmen from very similar districts might indeed hear quite different demands. This is partly because of differences in attention and interpretation and partly because the *effective* constituency of one man is different from that of another. A man whose enthusiastic campaign workers are officers of the American Legion, whose contributions come from members of the National Association of Manufacturers, whose personal friends in his district include a number of conservative physicians, perceives and indeed represents a different constituency from that represented by a man whose enthusiastic campaign workers are college teachers of social sciences, whose campaign funds come from liberal millionaires and labor unions, and whose personal friends are largely husbands of members of the League of Women Voters. The first man is in danger if he loses one sort of support that the other can never hope for. Perhaps more significant, their pictures of the audience to which they play, of the "real" district, are different. And they of course actually hear from different people. Yet districts can and do switch from men of one type to men of another by what seems the merest chance; as Congressman Herman Eberharter of Pennsylvania told me, a man could come up from his district who voted against everything he stood for, and it wouldn't make much difference. This is not always true, because here and there there are occasionally effective interest groups that really switch votes on an issue; and here and there, on matters of religion and race, for instance, there is widespread voter sentiment. Nevertheless, when Senator Robert M. La Follette, Jr., was beaten by Senator Joseph McCarthy in Wisconsin, the state was represented by a different kind of man, attuned to different audiences; and after McCarthy's death, he in turn was replaced by William Proxmire, still a third type of man. Yet the constituency—the state—did not change very much, if at all.

The second part of the book is therefore largely concerned with the personal, political, and structural factors that influence attention, communication, and interpretation in politics. Without making any pretentious or even systematic effort to state a methodology, I have tried to present these issues in terms of the transactional model of behavior as developed by Arthur F. Bentley.[4]

---

[4]Arthur F. Bentley, *An Inquiry into Inquiries* (Boston: Beacon, 1954); also John Dewey and Arthur F. Bentley, *The Knowing and the Known* (Boston: Beacon, 1949).

3. The third question I have addressed myself to is: What ways of thinking about Congress are useful? And vice versa, what are the dangers of the ways of thinking about Congress which are now familiar? For reasons indicated in Chapter 9, I have tried to devote considerable emphasis also to the dangers of exaggerating my own approach to Congress, as developed, for example, in *American Business and Public Policy*, or in the earlier chapters of this book. In the course of discussing these questions, I believe I suggest unfamiliar ways of looking at Congress in particular and at policy-determining systems in general which may be useful either to the imaginative and creative citizen, concerned with understanding or influencing what goes on, or to the research scholar.

II

This book is, in fact, one of a series on Congress and political action. *American Business and Public Policy* (Atherton, 1963; senior authors, Raymond Bauer and Ithiel Pool) discusses a particular legislative struggle in Congress and the nature of the congressional job. *How Organizations Are Represented in Washington* (Bobbs-Merrill, 1969) shows the part that lobbyists and Washington representatives play in influencing policy outcomes and legislative actions. A book in manuscript, as yet untitled, but perhaps to be called *Community and Political Action* (Rand Mc-Nally, forthcoming), deals with the problems of bringing about institutional change from the standpoint of the concerned citizen who wants to do something about a given social need. (This was originally prepared as a manual for minority-group strategy, but is being revised in broader terms.)

Taken collectively, these books will, I hope, offset some misinterpretations that could conceivably develop if this present book stood by itself. Here I have more or less assumed that influencing Congress is a matter of primary significance; the other books, I believe, make clear something that is only mentioned here, that on many legislative and policy matters there are better ways of trying to secure results than seeking to influence Congress. On many matters, for instance, as Arthur Maass[5] in particular has made clear, the President and the executive are the initiators of legislative proposals, and it may well be that, on numerous issues, the choice of a President affects legislation as much as or more than the composition of a congressional committee. It is also frequently the case—as both *How Organizations Are Represented* and *Community and Political Action* try to show—that the first or most significant way for a given individual to exert influence is to form a voluntary organization or to affect those already in existence. It may also be the case, as I point out in those books, that some individuals may contribute more to their purposes by working through the courts or through state governments or through the United Nations, and so on. Simply because Congress is formally the chief legislative body by no means assures us that Congress is the only or the most significant policy-making unit. I have here merely started with the proposition that it is an important policy-making unit and that there are many occasions when sensible men will see that to secure their purposes they must influence it.

One other qualification should be stressed as to what is said in this book: I am talking, of course, about influencing the Congress as it is and has been, at least since about 1920. It happens, however, that the structure of decision-making in Congress has remained fairly constant for fifty years, despite the adoption of some proposals for what was supposed to be far-reaching reorganization.

There is nothing in the nature of reality that guarantees that Congress will continue unchanged for another fifty or, for that matter, ten years. If, for instance, Bauer, Pool, and I had made a study of some state governments in 1953–55 comparable to our study of Congress, it is conceivable that our work would be regarded now as, practically speaking, out of date. In the state I know best, Massachusetts, quite consequential formal changes in the distribution of authority have been made since 1959, and even more far-reaching ones are scheduled to go into effect in 1971. In the jurisdiction I know second best, Puerto Rico, a Commonwealth Act and a new constitutional order have modified practices and procedures very materially in the last twenty-five years; and

---

[5]See statement and testimony by Arthur Maass in *Hearings Before the Joint Committees on the Organization of Congress,* 89th Cong., 1st sess., S. Con. Res. 2, pt. 6 (June 10–23, 1965), pp. 940–57, and also his statement and testimony in *Hearings Before the Subcommittee on the Separation of Powers, Committee on the Judiciary,* U.S. Senate, 90th Cong., 1st sess. (July 1967), esp. pp. 193–201.

possibly the results of the introduction of a new two-party alignment there, beginning only in 1969, may lead to equally substantial
alterations.

As Richard W. Bolling,[6] for instance, makes clear in a vivid and
readable account, the congressional system did change a good deal
when Thomas Reed of Maine became Speaker, and again after
the overthrow of "Cannonism" in 1910. It may be that Congress
will again undergo significant or revolutionary changes. If so, some
of the practical points made in the following pages would no
longer be valid. If, for instance, the seniority system were abolished
or seriously modified, the particular approach to influencing committee action here suggested would of course no longer be workable. In most state legislatures, where committees are appointed
new each session, such an approach would not work now. If, too,
a "responsible party system," as some desire, following the British
model, were adopted in the U.S.A., of course the processes of influence would change greatly.

But the general underlying way of tackling problems of influence
exemplified in this book would, I believe, be likely to remain valid,
even granted great change. First: the specific people or position-
holders within the new institutional system who can most profitably
be influenced would still have to be identified—and to identify them,
one would have to understand the major processes of formal and
informal decision-making within the new system. Second: the ways
in which individuals can effectively choose to influence these
position-holders would have to be examined, and therefore the
channels of communication and the nature of attention in the new
system would have to be reflectively observed. Third: in order
to evaluate any theories or proposals about influencing or communi-
cating to the Congress under the new situation, the metaphors,
analogies, figures of speech, frames of reference in which it would
then be seen ought to be critically analyzed in the manner suggested
in Chapter 10.

So far as I can see, the generality of the point of view just put
forward could be tested by making a similar analysis of the sociology and politics of a state legislature (preferably in some state like
Florida, where the institutional structure by no means resembles
the federal model; in some respects Florida is more like Uruguay
as it was, or Switzerland), or the sociology and politics of the

---

[6]*Power in the House* (New York: Dutton, 1968), pp. 53–105.

Canadian Parliament, or, for that matter, the sociology and politics of the U.S. Congress in, say, the 1880s or 1890s. Some of the studies on these bodies or that period could be reorganized to supply at least a partial basis for such comparable analysis.

III

In very brief terms, members of the Congress are both free *and* constrained: but they have considerable freedom to choose where they will be free and by what they will be constrained.[7] They must please or at any rate appear acceptable to a reasonable proportion of their constituents and they must keep their names known to their constituencies (many members of the House are probably reelected for no better or worse reason than that they have been heard of, whereas their challengers' names are unknown).[8] They must avoid violently offending significant numbers of groups in their constituency.

Most Congressmen and Senators are aware of the point made and illustrated in Appendix A—that in any future election, they may run well ahead of or well behind the ticket. This awareness itself may make some men freer and some men more constrained.

---

[7] I am speaking here of freedom and constraint from constituency or public demands. Of course, there are constraints imposed by the party in the House or Senate and by the members of one's committee, and perhaps also, in some state delegations, by the fellow-members of one's delegation. But these constraints are surely far less in the congressional than in the parliamentary system—and again a member has the freedom to choose an inside or an outside role, to decide whether he will be most effective as an educator, agitator, and gadfly or as a collaborative colleague. As regards the Senate, Ralph Huitt has made this point explicit in his description of Senators Morse and Proxmire (see Ralph Huitt and Robert L. Peabody, *Congress: Two Decades of Analysis* [New York: Harper & Row, 1969]). It is more difficult for a House member to be an effective gadfly, but probably not impossible. (Despite all his weaknesses, Adam Clayton Powell, in a way, has occupied that role; and a modern John Quincy Adams might play the part of a Morse in the House.)

It is also necessary for most members, unless they are lucky, to please some interests or public-spirited citizens sufficiently so that they can get campaign funds. Here again, the brave and ingenious man will see competing possibilities, and is not by any means bound to his previous contributors, while the timid man will fear risking anything. Also, the man who adopts a position and sticks to it—who takes an identifiable stand—probably has a better prospect of raising funds in case of a tough campaign. (I am talking here about an incumbent's prospects of raising funds; for challengers, especially Democratic challengers, fund-raising is often incredibly difficult.)

[8] Hence the great advantage that any relative of a well-known figure has or anybody who has become famous in any way. Hence also the advantage of an ethnic name or identification in many districts.

The man who fears and apprehends that he may lose some support here or there may make an effort never to offend anybody, never to take an identifiable stand. (There is not, incidentally, the slightest evidence that this attitude is any safer electorally than a bolder approach.) But the man who wants to do something, and believes in it, will see that so many factors influence any given election, and that there are so many ways of making gains to offset losses, that he may be encouraged by this very variation[9] to feel that he can work on those matters to which he attaches priority.

---

[9]On secondary matters, too—those that do not get in the mass media repeatedly or do not affect primary group sentiments—a member probably does strengthen himself more than he weakens himself by taking an identifiable stand, simply because of the limited amount of attention paid to public issues, and the specialization of communication channels. If he does something that helps a given group in his district or conforms to their notions of proper public policy, they are more likely to hear of it, and to talk about it, than are those who would be opposed to or hurt by the stand. The best-known example here is that helping a producer group get some special advantage often is not noticed much by consumers who are hurt by the same legislation; this is simply a particular case of the specialization of attention. In general, taking a stand on clean water, say, or budget procedures, or some other issue favored by the League of Women Voters, is more likely to be noted by League members (and even their husbands) than to be clearly identified as hostile by the *smaller* interests in the district that might be hurt by such action.

Indeed, in general, the importance of specialized channels of communication in permitting politics to operate as it does in this country is great. Frank Kent and other political writers of the 1920s tell of politicians who gave speeches to faddist groups of one sort or another which they would have been embarrassed to have had reported; the tape recorder and the increased newspaper coverage of campaigns makes such blatant hypocrisy more difficult now; but a Congressman can still sympathize with the plight of small manufacturers or garbage dumps forced to stop polluting rivers (or even try to get compensation for them) while acting to put into law the requirements they are afraid of—and get credit from both sides. I do not regard this as necessarily hypocritical; the Congressman may profoundly believe in cleaning up rivers but also believe the cost of the cleanup should be borne by the community rather than by individual businesses—and may, as a matter not only of politics but of kindness, see no point in rubbing rawer the already inflamed feelings of the affected interests.

Part One

WHAT EFFECT DO CITIZENS HAVE
ON LEGISLATION THROUGH ELECTIONS
AND THROUGH COMMUNICATIONS?

CHAPTER ONE

What Difference Do Elections Make in the Congress?

I

From the standpoint of the citizen, how much difference do elections make? Can he reasonably hope to influence policy by taking part in the choice of Congressmen? Always? Sometimes? Occasionally? Under what circumstances? How, if at all, can a group of interested and alert citizens—or, for that matter, a single alert and interested citizen—increase support in the Congress for some proposal in which they believe? Granted that, in a world of scarce resources, time and energy are always short, is taking part in congressional elections the most useful, the optimum way of affecting public policy? Or is trying to influence the way in which Congressmen legislate, appropriate, and investigate the wisest investment of time and energy for the concerned and dedicated citizen? Or are there alternative methods of trying to determine public policy which are wiser than either?

Anyone accustomed to the complexity of human life—or at least to the complexity of academic writers about human affairs—will not be surprised to learn that (in my judgment) the only general answer must necessarily be: Sometimes it is one thing; sometimes it is another. It is, however, hard to find clear statements that even begin to tell us how and under what circumstances elections to Congress may actually affect public policy. Of course, there are hundreds of articles and books dealing with Congress and the legislative process, and there are probably thousands of accounts of political campaigns and of why people vote as they do. But on the key issue—*Under what circumstances does it make a difference which candidates are chosen and how people vote?*—on that key issue, little light is available.[1]

With this question in the back of my mind, I studied the Reciprocal Trade Extension Acts of 1954 and 1955—acts the purpose of which was to authorize the executive branch to negotiate liberalized trade agreements and reduce tariff barriers reciprocally. I

---

[1] I would like to reassure the reader: this is probably the longest and most technical footnote in the book. After I had completed the main text of my manuscript, Randall Ripley told me I should read John C. Wahlke's *Public Policy and Representative Government: The Role of the Represented*, Laboratory for Political Research report no. 9 (Iowa City: Department of Political Science, University of Iowa, September 1967; originally prepared for the Seventh World Congress of the International Political Science Association). Wahlke's work raises some very significant questions related to the subject of this book of mine. In pointing out how his focus fundamentally is on a different question, I think I may suggest what my book is about, and also I may suggest some significant questions about the notion of representative government in relation to the current concern with participatory democracy.

Wahlke's exceptionally comprehensive and brilliant review of findings *could* be read as implying that the representative process has little to do with the specific content of legislation and policy decisions. Of course, Wahlke is here concerned with the represented viewed, in some sense, as a collectivity making collective demands, and he is primarily evaluating the demand-input model, which postulates that the majority of (or all) citizens make effective demands. He is quite aware, of course, that special groups do indeed make demands, which may be heeded; but since, as his subtitle indicates, he places his major emphasis upon the represented *taken as a (unitary) collectivity*, he necessarily finds that in fact the represented have little to do with what legislation or policy is reached, most of the time. However, I have looked at the matter from another standpoint: Can (*some of*) the represented have effective influence on policy, if they choose to do so and act effectively? What kind of knowledge is useful in increasing chances of effectiveness? Furthermore, I am concerned with the question: From the standpoint of the representative, when and in what sense is representing someone or some group of someones likely, desirable, necessary, or, in terms of electoral prospects, rewarding?

Of course, one way in which my question differs from Wahlke's and therefore in which my answers differ from his is indicated by the italicized words "some of" in parentheses above. The restrictions of the capacity for attention on the part of officeholders and others with the formal or informal authority to "make political decisions"—the limitations of the channel, in a familiar phrase—mean that, although *some* demands and *some* demanders will be heeded, if everyone makes demands or even if a large number of people make demands, many demands must be ignored. The channel—the capacity for attention of the officeholders—is not capable of infinite expansion or anything approaching it.

Practically, therefore, it is extremely fortunate that, as Wahlke's survey makes particularly clear, a large number of citizens do not make demands. The whole slogan of "participatory democracy," if literally interpreted, would, and will, involve alterations in our political system which it is hard for me even to envisage because it would be so different from any political system of any size of which I have heard. Indeed, one could argue, if one were inclined to describe political systems as inherently functional, that, just as there is an "invisible hand,"

wrote a report on which Congressmen heard what from whom about reciprocal trade extension and related matters.[2] In writing this report, I found that I had to consider what Congressmen heard about other matters also—because the amount of interest and attention they paid to reciprocal trade was in fact a function of other issues to which they paid attention, and of frames of reference. Other issues matter because attention and interest, as forms of time and energy, are always in short supply, especially for the working politician,[3] so that a major factor in influencing the amount of attention paid to any one issue is the amount of attention that either is free or can readily be diverted from other issues. Frame of reference determines how an issue is seen: one Congressman from a northeastern state may hear messages about unemployment as calling for tariff barriers against foreign imports, whereas another may interpret approximately identical messages as demanding a reduction in "unfair" advantages of southern producers, due to tax breaks, etc., while a third may, for the most part, see the same messages as supporting proposals for a more comprehensive and equitable social security system. I found, of course, that I had to consider such matters as procedure; the techniques by which Con-

---

in Adam Smith's term, which makes the free-market economic system operate functionally, so there must be in modern representative democracies some kind of functional invisible hand that makes most people refrain from making significant demands on government while at the same time leading a significant portion of the people—enough to stimulate more or less adaptive change—to make demands on government. (In terms of Wahlke's presentation, perhaps it would be preferable to say that the demands that most people make are merely for symbolic reassurance or for continuance of established practices—and such demands do not require nearly as much attention or reflection from officeholders as do explicit *institutionally adaptive* demands made by articulate minorities.)

[2]This report, "Congressmen and the People They Listen To," was dittoed and distributed twice by the Center for International Studies, Massachusetts Institute of Technology, 1955. Since the second dittoed form was copyrighted, it is available from the Library of Congress (and other libraries also). The report was also issued later, with significant omissions (mostly of the historical part, and also of the materials contained in the second chapter of this book), as a Ph.D. dissertation in sociology at Columbia University, 1960.

A greatly condensed version of the report appears in Raymond A. Bauer, Ithiel de Sola Pool, and Lewis A. Dexter, *American Business and Public Policy: The Politics of Foreign Trade* (New York: Atherton, 1963), chiefly in pts. 3 and 5. Other articles of mine contain other ideas from the report; so far as I can judge, the two significant parts that have not yet been published are (1) a history of the reciprocal trade extension acts and (2) a discussion of time as a scarce resource in congressional politics (the latter is not in one place but scattered through the report).

[3]Perhaps time is an equally scarce resource for all professional men, but to me the ratio between what a man might do, if he had all the time in the world, and what he can do, since time is limited, appears lower in percentage form for working politicians than for almost anyone else except virtuosos and scholars who would like to take all knowledge as their province. Ultimately, of course, time would become a limiting factor for everyone, but most people are limited in their ambitions and desires by other things (such as strength, imagination, lack of access to necessary physical resources, etc.) before time limits them.

gress handles legislation and its own internal organization affect what is heard and heeded, and how what is heeded is interpreted.

It became obvious to me, as I reflected about the matter, that from the standpoint of supporters of either side, elections could in some instances be important. The reciprocal trade extension acts that we studied, those of 1953, 1954, and 1955, were likely to be followed by three-year extensions in 1958 and 1961 (or at any rate by efforts at such extensions).[4] On the one side were those who wanted to see more liberal opportunities for foreign trade, including the admission of foreign imports into the United States. On the other were those who wanted to see greater opportunity for domestic industries to protest against and obtain reductions in the "unfair"[5] importation of foreign goods and/or wanted to prevent "unfair" liberalization of current trade laws and agreements. A section of my report showed what the best election outcomes in 1956 and 1958 would be from the standpoint of each group. Whose defeat would most profit opponents of liberalized reciprocal trade? Whose defeat would most benefit supporters of liberalized reciprocal trade? Where could either side hope plausibly to affect election results?

Several of my co-workers on the trade-study project felt (if I understood them correctly) that this portion of the report should not be distributed. The feeling was that this statement, naming names and suggesting tactics, could prove embarrassing both to the foundation that had financed our study (the Ford Foundation) and to the institutions that had received the grant and/or were directly responsible for the study (Massachusetts Institute of Technology and the Bureau of Social Research, Washington). I did not object strongly to the veto of such publication for practical reasons, and I also felt that, for the intellectual reasons stated below, publication of the statement in 1955 would have been inadvisable. It may be

---

[4]Reciprocal trade extension acts have extended the grant of authority to the executive to negotiate agreements for varying time periods. On the whole, however, three years was the most likely period; members of the Ways and Means and Finance Committees find hearings on reciprocal trade every Congress quite boring and to some degree time-consuming, but at the same time they do not wish to grant authority to the executive for "too long" a period. The executive is apt to try to insist on at least three years because the process of negotiating an agreement with the foreign country involved is long and time-consuming (agreements are apt to take account of many commodities, each one of which is considered separately by the negotiators), and, granting a period of preliminary preparations, two years may be rushing the process of negotiation too much, whereas the executive can live with three years.

[5]In the climate of the 1950s (and I believe this was still true in the 1960s) few people around Washington, at least, were any longer overtly opposed to reciprocal trade. People whom their critics called "protectionist" were, in terms of their own statements, merely opposed to "unfair" liberalization of trade barriers.

that it would have been unwise to try to publish this material as late as 1963 (when the main book resulting from the project, *American Business and Public Policy,* was in fact published). By this time, however, the passage of the years has made it safe enough to publish the statement (which in effect is Chapter 2 below). Our sponsors cannot now be hurt, so far as I can see, by its publication;[6] but even more important, the passage of time has made it less likely that there will be undue emphasis upon personal details and illustrations and consequent inattention to general analytic issues.

Such a danger always exists so long as an academic document can be used as a weapon in ongoing controversies.[7] Had the material that is published here as Chapter 2 been issued in 1955, it might well have been used in election campaigns. At any rate, individual Congressmen or Senators might well have regarded the report as a personal attack. Now, however, several of those mentioned by name are dead, and the situation of some of the others has changed so much that what is said here could have little bearing on their future prospects.[8]

---

[6]It is relevant—to show the general atmosphere of apprehension with which such studies were conducted years ago—to mention that in 1953, after Ithiel Pool had already made a contract with me, some officials of our sponsors urged him to withdraw me entirely from Washington: interviewing Congressmen seemed to them altogether too dangerous a business. Partly, of course, they were influenced in that particular year by apprehensions created by Senator Joseph McCarthy, who had terrorized many intellectuals. Partly, however, as a Ford Foundation executive said, their reluctance stemmed from the certainty that anything I reported would be on subjects about which many of the trustees of Ford knew a good deal; whatever I reported, it could only appear obvious or wrong, as the case might be, and so would perhaps cast discredit on the whole research effort.

This timidity was by no means confined to our sponsors: I myself was very timid about interviewing Congressmen.

[7]Put another way, it is not safe intellectually to publish academic reports including personal details until they have ceased to be newsworthy!

[8]We did include a (possibly watered-down) chapter on "The Tactics of Congressional Control" in the final copyrighted version. Although as late as 1964, according to what I have been told (I have not checked since), the report was on almost continuous loan to congressional offices, we did not, to my knowledge, receive any complaints at all from anybody on Capitol Hill about this material.

However, the fears of our sponsors were not at all ill grounded. My experiences on a similar project show this. Under a Carnegie Corporation grant to Massachusetts Institute of Technology, I later (1955–57) made a study of Congress and military policy. The general findings of this study appear in my article "Congressmen and the Making of Military Policy" (initially published in *New Perspectives on the House of Representatives,* ed. Robert L. Peabody and Nelson W. Polsby [Chicago: Rand McNally, 1963; 2nd ed., 1969]; several times republished, most readily available in *Readings on the Politics of American Democracy,* ed. Marian D. Irish, Robert L. Lineberry, and James W. Prothro [Englewood Cliffs, N.J.: Prentice-Hall, 1969], pp. 371–84). I read a preliminary version of this paper at a meeting of the American Association for the Advancement of Science in December 1958.

Within the following week, I have been told, Massachusetts Institute of Technology received at least five accusatory long-distance phone calls, I believe from the Air Force, wanting to know, in effect, what business I had to present Congress as suspicious of the defense departments, and professing to welcome controversy between them (the attitude expressed in the

So far as I can see, in order to show how elections can influence legislation, it is necessary to name names and discuss specific personalities. Consequently, I have decided, now that the passage of time has made it safe, to publish the bulk of this statement (with, of course, some revisions to clarify it). I am, in a way, sorry that I do not have as specific knowledge of any current legislative issue; I have not been engaged in this kind of research on Capitol Hill recently. On the other hand, my very ignorance, as regards present members of Congress, permits me to do something much closer to what the average interested citizen can learn to do anyway. In Chapter 3 I show how, *using information and materials accessible to any politically alert citizen,* without dependence on the sort of specialized research and interviewing I did on reciprocal trade legislation, judgments can be tentatively made about which elections can influence legislation, and how. I have chosen as my example policy about environmental defense; and I show what kinds of questions the politically alert citizen can reasonably try to answer for himself about the ways in which the congressional elections of 1970 and 1972 may affect legislation and policy in this ecological area. Obviously, I cannot write with the same clarity or certainty here as I can when talking about elections and reciprocal trade in 1956 and 1958; but I believe putting the two discussions together will help interested citizens see what they need to find out in order to participate in election campaigns in a way useful to their purposes. In the fourth chapter, I then proceed to show how interested and alert citizens can exert influence on Congressmen in the environmental defense field, through communications, lobbying, personal contacts.

In many ways, I would have preferred to choose for my current example the issue of the Multiple Independently Targeted Reentry Vehicle (MIRV); but this is not as good an example of the general tactics and strategy of dealing with Congress, because it appears entirely possible that sometime in the near future a great debate

saying "It's only when thieves fall out that honest men can find out what's going on" was frequent among Congressmen). Now, a report of my paper had been rather prominently printed in the *Washington Post,* and the Air Force is, of course, a big M.I.T. contractor. No such publicity, to my knowledge, was ever given to anything in our trade study till long after the event, and M.I.T. does not have such close relationships with any particular participant in the trade-tariff controversy, as far as I know. (It is interesting also that I personally received a phone call from a man who described himself as a personal assistant to the then commandant of the Marine Corps, requesting permission to circulate forty copies of my paper at Marine Corps headquarters, and saying, "We are all your disciples." The Marine Corps generally welcomed congressional participation in defense policy- and budget-making because it had been closer to Congress than to the other defense departments or services.)

will take place on this matter which will dramatize and sharpen divisions on military policy in a manner that rarely happens on issues. It is also the case that this is an issue about which it is hard to feel detached, whichever side one is on. For these reasons, I reluctantly decided against choosing this as my current example.

But, in fact, on almost any *general* issue with which the Congress may be concerned—MIRV or reciprocal trade or environmental defense or medicare or aid for higher education or the Commonwealth Act in Puerto Rico or foreign aid or the laws about narcotics or celebration of the two hundredth anniversary of the Battle of Yorktown or labor relations programs or whatever—the same kinds of questions must be asked and the same kinds of considerations must ordinarily be taken into account. To be sure, some issues—for instance, medicare or the slaughtering of wild horses, about which Congressmen received more mail in one session, I believe, than on any other matter except postal pay raises—are matters in which thousands of people have an interest, whereas other issues concern only a very few. Some matters will be handled entirely in committee, whereas on others a floor vote and debate can make a difference. Some matters will, in fact, interest only a few members of the Congress (as would, I think, be true of any legislation or appropriations regarding the two hundredth anniversary celebration of the Battle of Yorktown), whereas some matters will concern a good many. Some are simple in a way, because one committee will handle all of the relevant legislation, whereas others (like environmental defense) are complicated, because they involve many committees. Granted that all these differences exist among policy areas and pieces of legislation, there is a general approach suitable for any citizen who wants to understand how to influence congressional action. The answers may be different, but he ought to ask questions of the same sort, based upon the same awareness of how Congress operates.

II

The Pure Democratic Theory of Elections: The discussion below contradicts *both* the pure democratic theory of elections and the pressure-group notion (*in its popular form*) of legislative policymaking. Let us consider, first, the democratic theory. Followers of

Rousseau—or American progressive democrats, of the sort who in the eighteenth century believed in "direct instructions," and in the early twentieth in referendum, recall, initiative, and the direct primary—maintain that elections ought to make all the difference in the world. According to them, the voters speak, and the office-holders should then obey.

It is worth remembering in this connection a story attributed, I believe, to more than one of the early New England legislators, who as democratic followers of Samuel Adams were supposedly committed to "direct instructions" (instructions given by the town meeting, usually at its annual session, as to how the town's representative in the legislature should vote). When challenged on the matter by some practical-minded man, the canny legislator is supposed to have explained, "Oh, as to that, I take very good care to write the instructions myself."

In ideological moments, many Americans still talk as though Congress should—and can—follow the direct instructions of the public will. Many who, if directly asked, would not make such an assertion nevertheless profess bitterness and resentment when they find Congress seeming to ignore some public sentiment or opinion.

Actually, it is utterly impossible for the Congress to follow public will or public sentiment on most issues. The legislative task is very complicated, both in substance and in procedure. On most matters, it is impossible to identify any clear public will.[9] Even when, at the moment, a public will can be identified, the experienced Congressman knows that the public's great will is to eat its cake and have it too. That is to say, the public will wish such incompatibilities as a tremendous program to relieve misery now, but no taxes now or later. The Congressman must weigh incompatible desires against each other; and he must also balance the conflicting demands of influential publics. Faced with the task of balancing (in technical terms, satisficing),[10] the Congressman can find no public

---

[9]On this, see the interview with Samuel Jacobs in Appendix B. See also my "What Do Congressmen Hear: The Mail," *Public Opinion Quarterly*, 20 (1956): 16–27, reprinted in expanded forms as "What Do Congressmen Hear?" in *Politics and Social Life*, ed. Nelson W. Polsby, Robert Dentler, and Paul A. Smith (Boston: Houghton Mifflin, 1963), pp. 513ff. See also my "Communications—Influence, Pressure, or Education," in *People, Society, and Mass Communications*, ed. Lewis A. Dexter and David M. White (New York: Free Press, Macmillan, 1964), pp. 395–412. See also Wahlke, *Public Policy and Representative Government*.

[10]See Herbert Simon, *Models of Man* (New York: Wiley, 1957), p. 261, for a definition of this term, and Bauer, Pool, and Dexter, *American Business and Public Policy*, pp. 407ff. and 129ff., for a discussion of its relevance here.

mandate telling him how to balance—that is, what the best satisficing solution is. In a sense, the public does not like politics because politics involves making hard choices; even selecting the least unsatisfactory path means giving up many desired and desirable goals. And later on, if things turn out wrong—go worse than expected—it is likely to be the Congressman, the legislator, or some other politician who gets blamed for the outcome, no matter whether at the time the initial decision was made he appeared to be following some sort of constituency demand.

The legislative system is constructed in such a way as to make it possible for the legislative task to get done, for Congressmen to balance and satisfice. And the more experienced the Congressman, the more he comes to see that most measures must be worked out in committee. No large number of people can balance and satisfice. (Nor can any large number of people draw up a bill with clear legal meaning.)

But, once granted that measures must be worked out, more or less quietly, in committee, it is quite difficult for constituents to control their Congressmen and Senators. Constituents can, in the broadest terms, say, "On those measures that actually came to the floor, *which we have heard about,* where he had to vote yes or no, we are satisfied [or dissatisfied]." They can, certainly, say, "On those matters of personal service that we know about, he has [or has not] done a good job."[11] But it is extremely hard to follow the man's work where it counts most—in committee, in the leadership, etc.

How can one evaluate the Congressman (and there are some) who will generally be consulted by a good many of his colleagues on matters that his committee considers, and who will make a prudent, sensible, public-spirited judgment on these matters, yet who on some other issues votes for reasons of party or faction or simply because he is doctrinaire in a way that, for instance, many teachers of political science would regard as quite wrongheaded? Con-

---

[11]As an example: I suspect that the man who has been my own Congressman since my town was subject to reapportionment several years ago is a rather ineffective legislator. I am certain that his office ranks near the bottom of any I have happened to encounter in helpful constituency service. Yet in order to find out what his impact really is, I would have to go to Washington and interview quite a few people. In 1964 and again in 1968 I voted against him in the general election, but I had little evidence as to his opponent's capacity; in 1968 I also contributed $75 to a primary opponent who did not appear to have much chance of victory (and in fact did not do very well). Now, the significance of this is that, over the last thirty-five years, much of my time has been devoted to the Congress. I am accustomed to reading the *Congressional Quarterly* and numerous news magazines and newspapers. And yet I have only an impression about my own representative, who has served in the Congress

gressman R. Walter Riehlman of Syracuse, New York, as ranking Republican on the Military Subcommittee of Government Operations, did, I believe, an outstandingly prudent job—the facts and the situations convinced him and he knew how to analyze them—yet his votes on some major issues probably offended and upset many teachers of public administration at the Maxwell School in Syracuse, who had no knowledge of his committee work. Or the late Senator Guy Cordon of Oregon as a member of the Senate Appropriations Committee made an unusually serious and careful effort to find out what he was doing and to balance various aspects of government expenditure against each other; few of the enthusiasts who backed Richard Neuberger to succeed him in the Senate had any reason to understand this aspect of Cordon's service. How is one to judge a Republican—if one is a liberal Democrat—who votes with his party on the record votes, but in preparing reports in his committee may push for liberalization, or within the Republican party may exert some small influence in the direction of liberalization? Or—if one is a conservative—how can one judge a Democrat who, when the chips are down, votes the party line, but in fact in committee and in the Democratic party pushes against liberalism? (These terms, of course, are quite vague, but for our present purposes will do.)

There are, in fact, Congressmen and Senators like John Sparkman of Alabama whose influence is apparently sometimes directed against something that most of their constituents hold dear. Senator Sparkman has now served in the Congress for thirty-four years; during much of that time he has pushed for and played a part in activities and measures that have helped Negroes and other minorities—the

---

for fourteen years. (To be sure, I have never heard that he has made the slightest effort to be noticed or attended to in my town, which is in a sense orphaned from the major city in his district, but even so!) If this is true of me, what can be expected of people who have never professionally been concerned with Congress? (As a personal excuse, I may say that in 1962 and 1964 I was engaged in gubernatorial election campaigns, so there was no chance for me to do anything about congressional elections—but again this shows a deflecting factor of importance among the politically active—and in 1966 and 1968 I happened during the election season to be handicapped by illnesses. During the next election period, I shall be out of the district!)

I should add that I have had, until recently, little occasion to be concerned with the work of his committee, and that I am told by responsible people that he has been one of the more careless members about being available when he should be, and that I have reason to believe he does not handle his staff very well. For some further background on the character of the district and why I know little about him, see my discussion of this district in "Standards for Representative Selection and Apportionment," in *Representation*, Nomos X, ed. J. Roland Pennock and John W. Chapman (New York: Atherton, 1968), pp. 155–66.

GI Bill, the Tolan Committee investigation of migrant labor, the improvement of rural housing, many aids to small business. My guess (and it is a guess, not a certainty—but part of the point here is that, realistically, in evaluating candidates we have to do a good deal of guessing) is that John Sparkman of Alabama may have done more to better the lot of the Negro than almost any other member of Congress (more by far, by the way, than any Negro member of Congress so far, and more, possibly, than some great champions of civil rights).

But he has not run *directly* counter to the rhetoric and symbolism of his southern white constituents.[12] Much that has benefited Negroes has, of course, in fact also benefited many Alabama whites. They too, particularly around Huntsville, where Sparkman comes from, have been helped by the Tennessee Valley Authority. They too have benefited from rural housing and, in times past, from the GI Bill. Sparkman is, in manner and bearing, an attractive man, with definitely southern manners and accent. Some who may even have had a feeling or knowledge that what Sparkman was doing in the

---

[12]It is relevant, both to my integrity as a citizen and to the issue under discussion, to raise this question: Have I, a strong advocate of complete integration and equality, the right to call attention *in print* to Sparkman's record? After all, someone could quote this against him.

I can answer first: In 1944, when I taught at a Negro college (Talladega) *in Alabama,* some of my associates *at that college* wanted to say or do something to encourage the reelection of Senator Lister Hill, who (like Sparkman, though less so) stood for policies that, on the whole, benefited Negroes, as against his reactionary opponent in the senatorial primary that year. I urged them to say nothing whatsoever because *at that time* any statement by anybody, white or Negro, associated with a Negro college, or any contribution, could only hurt the candidate it was intended to help, if it came to the ears of some white Alabamans.

But in 1972, when Sparkman comes up for reelection again—if, indeed, he decides to run—the situation will, I think, be totally different. It will then be important that southern Negroes in general, and Alabama Negroes in particular, realize that Sparkman has been their friend all these years. The movement for George Wallace having been what it was in 1968, it will no longer be possible for Sparkman to soft-pedal the fact that he has been of tremendous help to Negroes. However, there is a possibility of a substantial Negro vote in 1972, which of course did not exist seriously in 1944. The danger now is that Sparkman in 1972 may be opposed even by the Negroes for whom he has done so much!

It is natural, of course, that many Negroes should not realize that men like Sparkman have been their friends. Probably they will be more convinced by personal facts, if these can now be made credible, such as that Sparkman as long ago as 1943 was decently respectful—a rare thing then—toward a Negro who was then working with the Tolan Committee (whereas in the 1954 Democratic primary in Alabama such a fact would have hurt Sparkman, not helped him).

The general issue here is, of course, that a detailed knowledge of a man's career and actions may show that he stands for something quite different from what one would suspect from his superficial rhetoric and appearance. Of course, such a difference between appearance and reality is important chiefly in the case of men of outstanding ability like Sparkman. It would have made little difference in the case of the late Congressman Adolph J. Sabath of Illinois, at one time chairman of the Rules Committee, whether he was or was not as liberal as he appeared, because in fact he never had any particular influence in the House as a whole, and he very rarely, indeed, had much influence on his committee, which quite systematically was willing to override him—he seemingly lacked the skill to use the advantages that chairmanship might have given him.

long run was undermining "white supremacy" were nevertheless pro-Sparkman in particular senatorial contests, because for factional and historical reasons they were hostile to his opponent or potential opponents. And once committed to him, and feeling that he is a nice man, and wishing to avoid intellectual discomfort, in accordance with the psychological tendency to reduce cognitive dissonance, they persuaded themselves that really he must be for the things they believed in. His willingness to adopt the appropriate rhetoric of the old South on occasion has, of course, helped perpetuate such a feeling.

Of course, this is an extreme case. In general, the way in which men get elected to Congress means that, on the whole, they will sympathize with their constituents, and no doubt on most matters Sparkman does. Fortunately, too, the way in which they are selected and elected and reelected means that, on the whole, they will be or will become a bit more farsighted than their constituents. *Their experience before and after being elected does usually result in one very important difference: most Congressmen are not very intolerant or doctrinaire;* they hear too many sides of a situation. They have to balance too many principles and interests against each other, so that they come to see that principles are only a special kind of interest.

III

Preliminary Remarks on "Pressure," Persuasion, and Influence Through Communication: It is argued sometimes that it is better to try to influence a man *after elections* than to stress getting your own kind of man elected. Some lobbyists feel strongly that taking part in election campaigns is dangerous. If advocates of a particular cause defeat or help to defeat a well-liked Congressman or Senator, they may provoke ill will from his former associates. If they try to defeat—but do not succeed in defeating—an influential Senator or Congressman, they rarely find that they have endeared themselves to him when he comes back to Washington.

Besides, there is the typical experience illustrated by a friend of mine. He was for many years in the business of raising money for candidates for Congress and the Senate. He told me at one time that he was going to get out of that field. "These people," he said (that is to say, the candidates whom he had helped to elect), "are so damn ungrateful." More broadly put, a successful candidate has so many reasons to be grateful to so many people that he is not as responsive to particular groups as they expect and hope. Furthermore, two things happen once a man gets to Congress, even when he gets back to Washington after a reelection campaign:

1. Things look different. He is on a committee; he is briefed by older members about their committees. He meets experts and government bureaucrats. He sees things differently. So he changes his mind. Sometimes—frequently—he grows.

2. He starts thinking about the next election, rather than the last one. Now, it is usually the case that an incumbent Congressman can get all sorts of help that is not available to a mere candidate in his first campaign. Party officials and the leadership will introduce him to all sorts of important people. Even the President may help him. He serves on a commitee; through that committee he meets people who share his views and will do a good deal for him. But they would not have helped him when he was a first-time candidate, with no committee assignment. He discovers, too, that he can do many services for his district which get him support from business and labor. So past obligations fade, and future opportunities grow in importance. The more senior he becomes, the more outside contacts of importance are available to him.

For these reasons, from the standpoint of the Washington lobbyists, it is ordinarily a mistake to try to defeat enemies. But there are occasions when Washington lobbyists should make a great effort to get friends reelected.

However, the typical "good citizen" is not, of course, a lobbyist. What can the college student do who wants to help in a congressional election, the way some students helped Eugene McCarthy in 1968? What should the well-to-do businessman do who feels he should contribute money in politics? What can the good citizen do, back home in his district, who has a chance to influence congressional nominations and elections? (It is important to underline the point that, in some districts, so few people really take part at all in congressional nominations and elections that it is possible to get influence in them just by hard work.)

Of course, such a citizen, such a student, such a well-to-do businessman could help some organization hire lobbyists, rather than take part in campaigns. Such a student or businessman or citizen can also, of course, write to his Congressman or go to see him.[13] But, by and large, in order to write effectively, one must become something of an expert on a subject, or one must acquire personal influence with one's Congressman or Senator. *A particular letter may by good luck be very important in influencing a particular Congressman, so it is always worth trying.* But it is a chancy, hit-or-miss thing, unless one knows something about the Congressman and has some special, meaningful experience or knowledge of the issue. Even then, many Congressmen will disregard completely experts or expert knowledge, because of preconceptions and preferences. It is probably true that League of Women Voters groups give more careful attention to what they study with reference to legislative action than any other organization in the country. Yet the late John Taber, chairman of House Appropriations for two terms, and ranking Republican, read into the record an extremely critical attack on them as "ignorant women."[14] In fact, during my interviews more Congressmen spoke disparagingly to me of the League of Women Voters[15] than of any other organization. A number of the Congressmen I talked with seemed to me to resent *women* concerning themselves with budgetary issues, for instance (one of the League's projects emphasized study of the budgetary process). And one can find many other identifications that lead this or that particular Congressman to close his ears.

Indeed, a great deal of mail does not get through to particular Congressmen or Senators; a good example of this was the late Senator Thomas C. Hennings, Jr., of Missouri. His legislative assistant told me that they heard nothing about reciprocal trade; his administrative assistant did not attach any particular weight to constituency concern with the matter. His mail clerk, however, told me that this was, at that time, the biggest producer of mail in the state. Yet, between Senator Hennings and the mail clerk, the issue got lost, because, in

---

[13]Congressmen are much more experienced in evading issues or expressing general sympathy without specific commitments than *most* constituents and visitors are in being sure a Congressman has really heard the point they want to make. This is simply part of the nature of the system; Congressmen cannot afford to attend seriously to all the inputs that come to them. As a measure of personal survival and self-protection, they have to learn how to avoid and evade issues. (There are many ways of avoiding an issue, and one way is to turn a political discussion into an academic one.) There are just too many interests and problems struggling to be heard.

[14]See my article on "John Taber: Watchdog of the Treasury," *Zion's Herald*, 126 (August 1, 1948), for an explanation of why Taber may have disliked the League. As an analytic article on the Congress, the article is emphatically *not* to be consulted; it is polemic.

[15]See Bauer, Pool, and Dexter, *American Business and Public Policy*, chap. 27, "The Ladies of the League," pp. 388–96, and Lewis A. Dexter, *How Organizations Are Represented in Washington* (Indianapolis: Bobbs-Merrill, 1969), pp. 69–71.

large part, the Senator and his staff were so busy with the numerous committees and subcommittees on which he served. Constituents got replies in the Senator's name, sometimes saying, "We have referred the matter to Senator Byrd, the chairman of the Finance Committee," or something like that. When I asked, "Have you?" the answer was "No, but I think that's perfectly honest. If it said anything new, we would."

Another Senator—and he is not untypical—really could not tell me what he had heard about reciprocal trade matters, although both he and his obviously very acute assistant were seriously endeavoring to remember. He gave me an off-the-cuff list of all the other matters in which the Finance Committee—the committee that considered reciprocal trade legislatively and on which he served—was engaged and commented that it was simply too difficult to follow all these matters.

So if an individual or interest tries to communicate, petition, exert pressure, he cannot be at all sure of being heard or being heeded. Congressmen can and do select, consciously or unconsciously, what they will pay attention to, and since there are so many different interests and concerns, and since it is extremely rare for any of them to be able effectively to control large sections of the vote, Congressmen can and do disregard quite articulate interests. After all his huffing and puffing, the great and powerful labor leader John L. Lewis of the United Mine Workers was not able to do President Roosevelt and his supporters any great harm in 1940; and similarly, in 1938, after all *his* huffing and puffing, Franklin D. Roosevelt's attempt to purge a number of members of the Congress, such as the late Walter George of Georgia, was an almost complete failure. Now, if Lewis and Roosevelt could not accomplish very much in affecting elections, what can the ordinary interest group, the ordinary business corporation do *by pressure,* or by the threat of electoral retaliation? It is wiser and safer, most of the time, to try to persuade, influence, convince, or soften opposition rather than to threaten. Certainly, when one can influence an election favorably, well and good—but it is usually unwise to conduct a campaign so bitter and so intense than one loses one's chance at some subsequent time of influencing one's opponents, if by chance they are elected or reelected. Roosevelt was fortunate that he did not entirely alienate Walter George in 1938; because, during the war years, Walter George's support was actually or potentially of some moment to Roosevelt's programs. Lewis did, in fact, lose influence because of his bitterness in 1940.

Although Lewis was by no means an amateur at politics, Roosevelt still less so, neither of them had the attitude that distinguishes the professional in politics from the amateur: Today's enemies may be tomorrow's allies, so never make it impossible to convince or get access to today's enemies.[16]

Of course, wealthy interest groups can withhold campaign funds from an enemy or buy him off by giving him campaign funds, but such efforts may sometimes boomerang, and are sometimes ineffective.[17] In any case, the ordinary good citizen does not have sufficient financial resources for exerting influence through campaign contributions.

So, all things considered, to be politically influential, ordinarily the good citizen must determine what is persuasive and effective with what politicians, or with what people to whom politicians listen. But every two years there may be an opportunity to exert some influence through participation in political campaigns. The college professor or student who is fairly mobile and has contacts in various parts of the country may be able, if he wishes, to be of some help in an important congressional contest far away from his home state. But those who are not mobile, especially those who live in sparsely settled states, may sometimes find there is nothing much they can do of significance in congressional races. In any election, a number of incumbents are almost certain to be reelected;[18] and in some cases there is little that most outsiders, unfamiliar with the politics of the state or district, can do to help local candidates for Congress or the Senate.[19]

---

[16]This statement is put in normative terms. It can equally well be phrased: If you wish to succeed over a period of years in a variety of political enterprises, you may have to collaborate in the future with or influence those who are currently your opponents or enemies. In order to keep open your options and make it as easy as possible to collaborate in the future, it is well to avoid extreme bitterness or what your present enemy will regard as unfairness toward him. This means, for instance, that a strong advocate of civil rights or a strong opponent of MIRV is well advised not to become so prominently identified with bitter opposition to incumbent Congressmen that the latter will not heed him if he comes around on some other matter or on some compromise stand on MIRV or civil rights.

Not incidentally, Roosevelt made the same mistake in his purge effort in 1933 as he did in his emphasis during the latter part of World War II on total victory. On the latter point, see Wallace Carroll, *Persuade or Perish* (Boston: Houghton Mifflin, 1948).

[17]On this point, see the interview with Secretary of State (of Florida) Tom Adams about his experience in that office and in trying to mount a gubernatorial campaign on pp. 1 and 12 of the *Miami Herald,* sec. A, June 15, 1969.

[18]Although, if this book also included some discussion of election tactics and possibilities, I would try to show that sometimes incumbents win because everybody thinks them unbeatable; occasionally (not very often) the story of the emperor's new clothes may apply to their alleged strength.

[19]Of course, people willing to run mimeograph machines, or type, or do errands, if reasonably competent, are always very useful in campaigns! But ringing doorbells, writing speeches, etc., sometimes demand some local knowledge before they can be done effectively.

In speaking of the weakness of pressure and of threats, I am, to reiterate, specifically not talking only of the weak and helpless, or of ordinary amateur citizens. On the contrary, in interviews with seemingly well-heeled and highly prestigeful interest groups, business firms, and trade unions, we repeatedly encountered the theme "Our opponents are powerful but we are handicapped." Biggish businesses speak with envy and longing of the influence and cunning they attribute to big labor; and big labor speaks with jealousy and longing of the influence and cunning it attributes to big business. The truth appears to be that, generally, in a pluralist society and in a world of vast and rising aspirations, very few groups get most of their demands heeded in the way they hope for.[20]

IV

What Is the Dynamics of the System? The Semisovereign People: Later interviews with representatives of interest groups in other fields have done nothing to change our initial impression, derived from the trade study, about those who wish to influence Congress and the government. "Each side . . . in full good faith . . . depicts the other as well-heeled professionals, whereas we are amateurs operating on a shoestring." (Sometimes the outsider may think the shoestring is made of gold and pretty thick to boot, but nevertheless the attitude is approximately correct in that most interest-group representatives have to spend much of their time raising money, dealing with internal matters, or diverting their energies to what from a Congress-influencing standpoint are irrelevancies.)[21] "The public and the sound arguments are portrayed as 'on our side' but the other side (frequently) suceeds because it is rich, unscrupulous, and conniving."[22]

Elmo Schattschneider, in a much appreciated review of our book *American Business and Public Policy,* concentrating particularly on my discussion of Congress, raises a problem. He says that the book "slays a choice collection of political dragons; economic determinism

---

[20]On this point, see my *How Organizations Are Represented in Washington.*
[21]See *ibid.,* especially chaps. 1 and 8.
[22]Bauer, Pool, and Dexter, *American Business and Public Policy,* p. 399.

is manhandled; myths about lobbyists and businessmen and a lot of folklore about Congressmen are destroyed. It kills off or wounds a small army of pressure boys and groupists." (Mr. Schattschneider means, of course, not that we do anything physically detrimental to lobbyists as such, or to interest groups, but that we cast great doubt on the whole set of explanations of public policy which emphasize pressure, interest groups in the narrow sense, etc.) He continues: "It torpedoes at least a boatload of public opinionists. All friends of democracy will applaud the slaughter." (He is talking, or course, about all friends of Burkean representative democracy. Disciples of Rousseau and of the referendum and recall were not so pleased; in fact, a few such were irritated.)

> Perhaps, however, the authors have been too successful in driving away the wolf-packs which assail Congress, because they seem to have left themselves without an·adequate dynamics of politics. One is reminded of Thurber's mother, who admonished him not to "go driving around town without any gasoline in your tank."
>
> The image of Congress that emerges from this study differs substantially from the common impression of it. It is much freer from external pressures, has more latitude, and is much less reluctant to surrender its burdens to the executive than it is usually supposed to be.

The last statement is an absolutely correct report of what we implied; however, in 1959 or a little later, the situation began, I think, to some extent to change, and since 1966 Congress has tended to reassert authority that in 1956 it had surrendered or was tending to surrender.

> There is great wisdom in the book about the nature of legislation and about the way in which Congress legislates, the extent to which it acts on the basis of confidence in its own specialists, for example; also the care with which it avoids final decisions, and how it tends instead to work out the rules of the game under which contests can be continued. . . .

Essentially, this is why true believers of all types tend to despise Congress and American politicians; the latter purposefully avoid finalizing things!

> So far, so good. The trouble is that the authors leave Congress floating through space, rotating on its own axis, like the moon. Do we

really want to leave Congress there? The reviewer regrets very much that the authors did not go on to study the influences that *do* move Congress. . . . Why did they omit the big one, congressional elections? A study of congressional politics that omits congressional elections is like an omelet without eggs. . . . Surely, public policy is not merely the responsibility of businessmen and Congressmen. . . .[23]

Now, as I have already explained, an unpublished portion of this book, as originally written—the portion I am in essence about to publish for the first time—dealt with these matters. In a technical sense, I could have defended our book by saying, "It's all there. But we couldn't take the risk of publishing it." However, the real point is more significant than this.

Professor Schattschneider's review goes ahead to argue:

> Maybe political scientists ought to be required to reread Article I, Section I of the United States Constitution, wherein it is brought about that once every twenty-four months Congressmen sweat blood on Election Day. To be sure, Congressmen ought to be free, and are free, to do their work without excessive public interference, but when they have done their work, they go back to the people and stand trial for their political lives.
>
> As far as it [*American Business and Public Policy*] goes, it is a great book.

My inclination was to comment, "As far as it goes, it is a great review." For I think the subsequent discussion will show that elections do not—and in the nature of the case cannot—settle most things. *There is the issue of priorities.* There are a number of other issues. But, on the other hand, elections do make a good deal possible and a good deal impossible.

So, in a term that Schattschneider himself has made prominent in another connection, "the people" taken as a whole are *semisovereign* at elections. And an individual citizen with some energy and ability or free time or money, and some skill, who wants to make a difference through participation in elections, can sometimes—not always, but not infrequently—do so. The best way to demonstrate the limits on popular sovereignty, and the best way to show what an individual citizen can and cannot hope to do, is to discuss a specific situation.

[23]E. E. Schattschneider, review of Bauer, Pool, and Dexter, *American Business and Public Policy*, in *Public Opinion Quarterly*, 29 (1965): 343–44; used by permission, gratefully acknowledged, of the author and the publisher.

V

The Situation in Regard to Reciprocal Trade in 1955: The problem to which I addressed myself was: What difference can a person or group that wishes to affect what Congress does about reciprocal trade make *through participating in elections* starting in 1955? Several matters of fact had to be taken as background.

1. A reciprocal trade extension act, good for three years, had been passed in 1955.

2. Any serious modification of the Reciprocal Trade Extension Act would be considered, first and most carefully, by the Ways and Means Committee of the House of Representatives. There was not, practically speaking, any way out or around or through this. Barring a very surprising, almost revolutionary, development, the Ways and Means Committee would claim jurisdiction on such a matter.

3. Similarly, in the Senate, the Finance Committee would consider any such extension.

4. It would, in principle, be possible to take up modifications in the act prior to 1958. In practice, the Ways and Means Committee has so many things to occupy it of urgent importance—taxes and social security, to name just two—that it would be extremely unlikely that it would reconsider the matter until the existing act expired. Of course, some really pressing national or international situation could change this picture.

5. When reconsidered, the new act might provide somewhat more opportunity for escape clauses or quota provisions than prevailing practice allowed; but by and large, since the United States had actually made agreements with other nations under previous acts, and no doubt would make more agreements between 1955 and 1958 under the authority granted by the 1955 act, any radical reversal of established agreements would be unlikely. Protectionists could hope to nibble at the edges in 1958; in the case of some commodity particularly hurt by foreign imports, some change might be imposed. But the *system* of agreements would not be done away with.

6. The Ways and Means and Finance Committee members, in particular—and any other particularly influential members, for that matter—may persuade administrators to encourage action against for-

eign imports. "Voluntary quotas"[24] are a case in point. And, of course, vice versa, any particularly influential member or group of members can help persuade administrators *not* to take such action.

Reciprocal Trade, the Idea and the Policy. Involves a Lot More Than Reciprocal Trade Legislation: So Other Committees Enter In. The point to be made here is true, as far as I know, of any important policy or program. It also serves to illustrate one way members may seem to be supporting a policy, but actually can undercut it, or vice versa. Sometimes they deceive themselves; sometimes they only deceive their doctrinaire constituents.

Reciprocal trade as an idea and a policy means essentially that foreign trade shall be encouraged, and that governmental barriers shall to a minimum feasible degree interfere with the free manufacture and sale of products and services. Protection, of course, as an idea and a policy, means that, on the whole, preference shall be given to domestic manufactures.

Reciprocal trade legislation permits the administration to negotiate agreements for the freer flow of goods with specific countries or a group of countries. In fact, however, much other legislation may interfere with or regulate such a free flow of goods.

Holbert Carroll, in a significant discussion of the House of Representatives and foreign economic policy,[25] shows how much legislation involves foreign economic policy and how many committees get involved in such matters. For instance, the House Committee on Agriculture may recommend a bill imposing a quota on many foreign agricultural products—wool, for example, or dairy products. And members of the Committee on Agriculture who are very active in

---

[24]A "voluntary quota" means that foreign manufacturers (or governments) agree that only a certain amount of their product will be sold in the United States, but the agreement is an informal one, without the force of law—a "gentleman's agreement." Such quotas have been proposed or agreed to when there has been a considerable increase or threatened increase in the importation of some foreign product. The advantage of such voluntary quotas from the standpoint of the foreign producer is that they avoid the possibility of legal action (invocation of an escape clause or congressional legislation) and that they are definite—whereas it may take some months or years to be sure what legal action will lead to. From the standpoint of the domestic producers threatened by foreign imports, they are also definite and immediate. The general tendency is to propose a base year and to agree that only a certain percentage of the imports of that year should be sold in the United States. Voluntary quotas also presumably tend to encourage domestic producers to get out of uneconomic lines, or to change manufacturing techniques, but, for the time being, protect jobs.

[25]Holbert Carroll, *The House of Representatives and Foreign Affairs* (Pittsburgh: University of Pittsburgh Press, 1958), chaps. 4 and 5, pp. 38–89. One of the great weaknesses of Bauer, Pool, and Dexter is our inadequate attention to Carroll's point. I herewith recommend that everyone who reads our book then read Carroll.

supporting or opposing such quotas may vote quite differently on reciprocal trade legislation as reported by the Ways and Means Committee. Yet what they do on the Agriculture Committee may be more important, so far as their influence goes. The Committee on Merchant Marine and Fisheries may push measures requiring that various sorts of goods be shipped in American bottoms, rather than in much less costly Norwegian shipping, or it may bitterly resist measures to open up coastal shipping in the United States to foreign bottoms. (As a matter of fact, if foreign ships could freely serve American coastal waters, it would be as much of a service to the consumer as the import of some cheap physical product; of course, there are all sort of objections in terms of labor standards, national security, etc.) Committees concerned with labor or minerals may try to protect American miners from being thrown out of work by the importation of foreign minerals, produced at lower labor costs. It is possible for legislative or appropriations committees to specify that all or a part of some particular government purchase be domestically manufactured. Obviously, "Buy American" provisions protect American industry, raise the price to the taxpayer, and keep out foreign goods.

At some particular time, or for some particular country, it may well be that some of these other pieces of legislation are more important than general reciprocal matters. For example, during the 1950s, it is probable that Norway was more interested in and affected by the Merchant Marine and Fisheries Committee's insistence that goods be shipped in American bottoms than by reciprocal trade legislation; perhaps, right now, Norway might benefit more from a relaxation of coastal shipping regulations than from any change in reciprocal trade matters.[26] And very possibly, in terms of the overall politics of trade, such relaxation in coastal shipping regulations would be more significant than any change likely to take place due to reciprocal trade legislation. Carroll suggests that the action of the Merchant Marine and Fisheries Committee in insisting that 50 percent of all mutual security goods be shipped in American bottoms tended to make it more difficult at that time to persuade some French trade unions to abandon Stalinist ties.[27]

Similarly, in the past, it has probably been true that, from the standpoint of international sentiment, more ill will has been created

---

[26]This sentence and the next are speculations; I have not studied this issue.
[27]Carroll, *The House of Representatives and Foreign Affairs*, p. 68.

by so-called health restrictions on Argentinian meat than by any barrier to manufactured goods from that country.

Effective Members of a Committee. As Carroll also points out:

> *The efficient part of a committee consists of a core of members, usu-ally only a handful of men, representing both political parties, [who] actively participate* . . . [and] shape legislation. . . . They write part of the committee's report . . . [and] then take the bill to the floor and fight for (or against) it. . . . The efficient element of a committee is rarely composed of a majority of members, even though it must carry a majority with it. . . . Indeed, in some instances, the efficient element may be just one man.
>
> [However] the efficient element may change from one piece of legislation to another. . . . That is, some capable men may not re-gard certain pieces of legislation as interesting, relevant, or signifi-cant, and may ignore them, but may pay great attention to others. *The fruit of [the] efforts [of the efficient part of a committee] is embodied in statutes, and not merely in bills.* The men who compose it are the leaders who determine [what the House will do].[28]

Now, the Ways and Means Committee probably had a higher proportion of efficient members than any other committee in the House.[29] Yet, on such a matter as the tariff and reciprocal trade, some members were not particularly interested, and others were. Those who were not interested in trade may have been interested in taxes or social security.

The general points are two, assuming that one is particularly in-terested in a given policy. First, it is especially important to reelect those committee members who stand on your side, and are *efficiently* committed to it. They pose the issue on which the House and Senate later vote. In the vote, the House and Senate as a whole often do little more than say yes or no.

Second, it is probably more important to reelect those members who are effective on any committee that in the next session might

---

[28]*Ibid.,* pp. 27–29 (italics added).

[29]I am speaking of my impression of the period 1953–55; I make no attempt to judge the relative number of effective members on Ways and Means now, as compared with other committees. There is a possibility that the extraordinary effectiveness and competence of Chairman Wilbur Mills (see the sketch of Mills in Appendix C) have over the years led Mills himself and the leadership to be less concerned with placing able men on Ways and Means than was the case in earlier years.

consider matters of interest than it is to reelect members of a major committee, such as Ways and Means, who, although they vote on your side, do not care very much.

A third point is more debatable. The general tendency would be to say that it is equally important to *defeat* an effective member who is opposed to one's position. I am not sure how far I would proceed on this basis. Of course, that depends partly upon how urgent and how important one thinks an issue is. If the issue is really one of life or death, so important that nothing else comparatively matters, then, of course, one would be correct to try to defeat effective enemies first. Perhaps some matters in the field of ecology and conservation are of this sort. Perhaps MIRV is. It is hard to conceive that reciprocal trade is a matter of this sort.

One reason for not defeating effective congressional enemies is obvious: men who are effective on one matter are *likely* to be efficient on other matters. There are not enough effective members of committees anyway; the congressional system might break down if a lot of effective members were to leave and not be replaced. Even if one disagrees with a particular Congressman or Senator very strongly on some issue, if he is effective, he may do more on other important issues than the typical inactive member, and do it better. For instance, Congressman Aime Forand, of Rhode Island (see Appendix C), was probably the most active and aggressive semiopponent of reciprocal trade policy *on the Democratic side* on the Ways and Means Committee during the 1950s. But nevertheless, he did, according to all accounts (I have not studied this myself, and of course if one were faced with the issue practically, one would want to study it), do a good deal to promote what we now know as medicare. Now, a good many supporters of reciprocal trade, who support it as a liberal measure, also supported medicare. Medicare was also within the jurisdiction of the Ways and Means Committee.

This case, and numerous others like it, indicate why it raises questions to try to defeat incumbent members on any single issue. How can priorities be weighed against each other?

The second reason why I suspect it is frequently unwise to try to defeat an effective incumbent is this: Legislation in sum is usually a compromise. As we pointed out in *American Business and Public Policy*, legislation frequently is passed so as to bring about an incremental change in one direction or another, but so couched as to permit all sides to the conflict to continue fighting about what the next change will be. For this kind of legislative process to continue—

for compromises to be made by which both sides can live—the people who speak for the different sides when the measure is hashed out and marked up must know their own side very well; but they must be able also to understand the other side's arguments and viewpoints. They must, that is, be able to understand what their opponents can compromise on as well as what their supporters can compromise on.

That means that it is desirable for a good many members of a committee to be both efficient and experienced, so that they have learned the other side's view quite well. Such men are less likely to insist upon an unbearable sacrifice from their opponents and more likely to try to invent something acceptable to everybody. (Of course, on some committees there are not enough such men, and in these cases either undesirable or unworkable legislation is passed, or the actual legislation is worked out elsewhere, by committee clerks, by lobbyists, or by people in the executive department.)

So my present feeling is that, where I can tell the difference, I would tend to work rather for the defeat of politically ineffective committee members, of two types: (1) The most important person to defeat is the opponent who is doctrinaire and uncompromising in his opposition. Few such men get elected to Congress, and most of those who are elected do not get reelected. But there are some: Senator George W. Malone (see pp. 51–52) of Nevada was an extreme case of this sort in opposition to reciprocal trade. (2) And it is, if my viewpoint here is correct, more desirable to defeat those members, especially members with some seniority, who are ineffective committee members and are strongly opposed. If they are reelected enough times, they may become committee chairmen, or, almost as dangerous in some instances, serve on conference committees.

Conference Committees. A word on conference committees is in order. When, as often happens, the House and Senate differ on a measure, a conference committee is appointed to reconcile the differences. By long tradition, the senior members of the committees that considered the legislation are appointed to the conference committee—usually three or four members of the majority party from each of the committees, and two or three from the minority. Now, of course, it can happen that the majority of these men—ten or fourteen—have different views on a matter than the majority of the committee or of the Congress. Yet they can in some cases modify a measure toward their preferences, and, because time is always short and conference reports come at the end of a session, when time is especially short, get their version accepted, rather than that of either house.[30] For this reason, the conference committee has been called "the third house of Congress." Most often, this is what happens: One body passes a measure stressing one position, the other another. But the conferees from one house happen to sympathize more with the other, so they immediately accept the latter's version. Under such circumstances, it is difficult to get a conference committee report rejected. As an example, it might be that the House, let us say, would pass a measure more acceptable to supporters of reciprocal trade than the Senate—one having, for instance, less opportunity for escape-clause action. Now, suppose that the Democrats are in control of both houses, but that two of the senior Democrats in the Senate and one in the House sympathize with the relatively protectionist views on escape clauses. Suppose there is a conference committee of ten, and all the senior Republicans want stronger escape clauses. Then it is likely the Senate version will win out. It could well be that most of the members of the House and most of the members of the House committee and 49 percent of the members of the Senate and a majority of members of the Senate committee favor the House version. Yet the conference committee will probably have its way.

---

[30]For a discussion of conference committees, see George Galloway, *The Legislative Process in Congress* (New York: Crowell, 1953), pp. 316–25, or almost any general description of the Congress. Conference committees may be larger than indicated in the text; but they usually are rather small. For one reason or another, some senior member may not serve, and a more junior member of the legislative committee be appointed. But the tendency is as I have indicated.

Conference committee reports are usually adopted, despite any uneasiness or discontent, for two reasons: (1) It is difficult procedurally to work out differences between the two houses, other than through a conference committee, and it would be a threat to the customary operation of the Congress, with its emphasis on seniority, to appoint conference committees on some other basis. (2) Shortage of time is always a great problem in the Congress; one thing most members are agreed upon is that they do not want to reconsider something that has already been discussed and passed. Sessions would never end, issues would never be disposed of if such reconsideration became customary—and, in the nature of the case, time is especially short toward the end of a session, which is when most conference committee reports are made. Therefore, grumble though they may (as seen in the speech by Senator Fulbright, twice quoted by Galloway, first on p. 321 and again on p. 601), members prefer to accept conference committee reports.

CHAPTER TWO

More About the Difference Elections May Make:

RECIPROCAL TRADE EXTENSION

I

Suppose, for the sake of illustration, one had been in 1955 a strong supporter of reciprocal trade. Or that one had been an opponent of *extended,* liberalized reciprocal trade. One would have to take all the ideas mentioned in the preceding chapter into account. The basic points would be: (*a*) legislation is largely processed in committee; (*b*) the *opportunity* for influence on committees is in considerable degree a matter of seniority. Seniority is dated from a member's appointment to the committee; the man who has served on a committee longest, and belongs to the majority party, is its chairman (unless he personally chooses not to be).

At that time, in 1955, the majority party in the House, because of the special importance of Ways and Means, insisted upon a 15–10 ratio on that committee. In the Senate, however, where the parties were closely balanced, the Democrats had a majority of only one on Finance. If either party won a more substantial margin, its proportion of members on committees would go up. This could well have the effect of forcing some members of the minority to quit important committees like Ways and Means or Finance and serve on less important committees. Representatives James B. Utt (California) and Victor A. Knox (Michigan), who had served on Ways and Means in 1953–55, when the Republicans had a majority, were dropped from that committee when the Democrats took over in 1955. But, by custom and tradition, they had a right to return to Ways and Means, if they chose, ahead of any other Republicans not on the committee. Both did later return, and Representative Utt is now (1969) second-ranking member on Ways and Means.

Now, within this framework it is important to note that it does not always make much difference *in legislative terms* if a new member of the House has a strong devotion to some particular cause. There is no particular reason to suppose that he will be assigned to a committee that deals with the issue with which he is concerned. In the case of Ways and Means, it is quite rare to assign a new member to that committee; the House leaders wait until they know a man, and have seen that he can get himself reelected, before he is put on a committee as important as that.

To be sure, there are occasions when it may be worthwhile to elect a man who is dedicated to one's own particular cause, even if he is a new member. But, in general, the important thing legislatively is: Who are the senior members of the committee? And particularly, who are the senior members *of the majority party* on the committee?

On some issues—in general, issues that are regarded as party issues or on which the administration takes a stand—the views of the leadership matter. The House leadership consists of the Speaker, the majority leader, the whip, and possibly one or two others, on the majority side; the minority leader and his associates on the minority.

On reciprocal trade, it happened that Speaker Rayburn was, according to many indications, *personally* committed. He regarded it as one of the vital reasons why he was a Democrat. Although an elderly man, he was in seeming good health in 1955, and looked likely to remain Speaker for some time; and in fact he did not retire for almost seven years. He was, also and relevantly, perhaps the most influential Speaker the House has had since 1910. On the other hand, if anything happened to him, his natural successor, the majority leader, John McCormack of Massachusetts (who did ultimately become and is still Speaker), was not believed to have any such concern with reciprocal trade; and, on the whole, groups to which McCormack was close in his constituency would probably have tended to lead him to be lukewarm about it. However, several of the younger men who in 1955 were talked of as possible future Democratic Speakers were strongly committed to reciprocal trade.

Among them was Wilbur Mills of Arkansas, who was, at the time, although not chairman, the most effective member on the Democratic side of Ways and Means. In this position, he could and did work for reciprocal trade, and was able to do so still more effectively when, later, he became chairman. Being years younger than the two men senior to him on Ways and Means, and being safely established in his district, he was certain to become chairman, unless instead he was chosen Speaker. (Actually, later on, civil rights and the Southern Manifesto weakened his prospects for the Speakership.)

The then chairman of Ways and Means, Jere Cooper, was in all probability even more strongly committed to reciprocal trade than Rayburn and Mills. He was not, however, as outstanding a leader as they. An instance of his lack of qualifications for chairmanship was an extreme reluctance to be interviewed by reporters—a real handicap in a national politician!

The second-ranking Democrat on Ways and Means, John Dingell, of Michigan, in general followed along with the party on trade matters, but he apparently possessed the sneaking sympathy for protection that a good many old-time trade unionists had, and here and there (for example, on the importation of beer) there were matters on which he was distinctly unsympathetic with the Democratic low-tariff line; as chairman, had he succeeded Cooper, he might even have tried to obtain special exemptions on such matters. (In fact, he predeceased Cooper.) He was not, in any case, highly regarded as an effective member by those connected with the committee. (It is fair to say that his son, who succeeded him in Congress, although not on this committee, is held to be a man of greater ability.)

On the Other Hand, the Republicans: Joseph Martin and Charles Halleck, the two most important leaders in the Republican party, followed the Eisenhower administration in supporting reciprocal trade extension. Republican opponents of extension told me, "Joe and Charlie are worth at least twenty-five votes to reciprocal trade, but in their hearts they know it's wrong. They're just doing it for the White House." Certainly, had a Democrat been elected President in 1956, and in 1958 proposed (as any conceivable Democratic President except possibly Kerr would have proposed) further reciprocal trade extension, no one could have been sure that either Martin or Halleck would then support such legislation. On the other hand, there was *no* particular reason to suppose that Martin or Halleck had any *strong* personal commitment against reciprocal trade.

But on the House Committee on Ways and Means, the three senior Republicans, Daniel Reed (chairman), Thomas Jenkins, and Richard Simpson, were all quite strongly opposed to reciprocal trade. Reed, a man of considerable ability and some influence, had reluctantly gone a quarter-way with the Eisenhower administration in 1954, but in 1955 his influence was felt against reciprocal trade. Jenkins, a very attractive man, was nevertheless a lightweight; during my interview with him (see Appendix B) I felt he observed rather than participated in Congress. Simpson was probably one of the three or four most influential Republicans in the House; his position as chairman of the Republican Congressional Campaign Committee helped, but, aside from that, he had all the manner and attributes of a real leader. Next to Richard Bolling, he impressed me more than any other Congressman on first meeting. And next perhaps to Cleveland Bailey (see below), he was the most convinced opponent of reciprocal trade in the House. Since he was some years younger than Reed and Jenkins, it was to be expected he would become chairman if the Republicans took over the House (in fact he died unexpectedly).

Off the Committee: A Congressman with some push, ability, and skill, when he has had a little experience and knows what he has to deal with, *if he attaches great priority to one or two issues,* can make a difference even if he is not on a committee. Representative Cleveland Bailey, Democrat of West Virginia, was a very strong opponent of reciprocal trade (see the Bailey interview in Appendix B), and he devoted a good deal of his time to trying to defeat reciprocal trade measures. Several informed people estimated to me that Cleveland Bailey singlehanded was worth fifteen votes in the House against reciprocal trade. This may have been true. At any rate, some Appalachian Congressmen who wanted, on the one hand, to follow Rayburn, Martin, and Eisenhower in support of reciprocal trade were, on the other hand, fearful for the dying industries in their mountain towns. Bailey let them know, emphatically, that they would be more uncomfortable, then and there, as a result of his pushing and pressure, if they did not oppose reciprocal trade; whereas future unpleasantness from the leadership and the administration, if they opposed it, was contingent and more distant. And Bailey had one great advantage, of course, over the leadership and the administration: this was his *one* major issue, whereas the leaders and the White House would be asking for many other votes in the session and in future sessions. He could go bullheaded, therefore, in a way the leadership could not.

I ran across only one member off committee, serving in the House during the period, whose personal commitment to reciprocal trade was regarded as being in any way really analogous to Bailey's opposition (and not anywhere near as strong or as single-minded): Frank Smith of Mississippi.

While I was actually engaged in field research, we were concentrating on political communications, rather than political effectiveness. Accordingly, we made the mistake most people make and assumed the way to study reciprocal trade was to study reciprocal trade. That gave us the advantage of a definite bill to follow; but had our focus of attention been Congress and its effect on foreign economic policy, as it should have been, we would have addressed ourselves to all relevant measures. It was not enough just to follow reciprocal trade. (See pages 35–37 above.)

Our mistake was a double one. *From the standpoint of theory,* we let the data define the problem—which is always a mistake. *From the standpoint of practicality,* we did not learn what would have been very important for anybody really concerned with the way elections affect legislative outcomes. All of which is to say that we did not study, for instance, the Merchant Marine and Fisheries Committee at all. I do not know whether there was some member there who was very important, one way or the other, from the standpoint of trade policy, and whose election or defeat might have been very important to reciprocal traders or protectionists. We did not study the Agriculture Committee either, where the same thing might have been true. And so on.

Anyone trying to figure out what to do about elections—anyone trying to evaluate his own Congressman—would need information about the *effect* of legislative action, *taken as a whole,* and should not concentrate on just one bill or one committee.

II

The Senate: The situation in the Senate was considerably more complex than in the House from the reciprocal trade–protection standpoint. Harry Byrd, Sr. (Virginia), and Walter George (Georgia) were the two senior Democrats on Senate Finance. Neither of them was known to hold at all the same intense commitment to reciprocal trade that Cooper and Mills were believed to hold in the House. Indeed, Byrd was reportedly rather affected by the problems of the Appalachian coal-mining fringe of Virginia with foreign imports, and by his own brand of conservatism; he would not, probably, make any substantial effort to support reciprocal trade, and might well demand certain modifications in it. In any case, Byrd apparently continued active involvement in his business as an apple-grower, and, much more important, he was the working leader of a very busy political organization in his own state. All these things must have taken a good deal of his time. George was deeply involved on the Foreign Relations Committee.

Robert S. Kerr, the third-ranking member of the Senate Finance Committee, was called at this time or a little later "the uncrowned king of the Senate." He was the archetype of the wheeler-dealer. But the variety of his interests, political and business, meant that he did not have a great deal of time to devote to an issue like reciprocal trade except when it really involved him or his state or business interests. Almost certainly, other issues before Senate Finance—such as tax policy—mattered more to him than trade. Also, the general impression one received from his statements and his office staff was that he tended to be mildly protectionist in sympathy; Oklahoma, from which he came, is one of the states where there is considerable apprehension about foreign competition. Nevertheless, the attention his staff paid to foreign competition seemed to me to be highly disproportionate except in terms of a general tendency to suspect reciprocal trade.

In 1955 Kerr seriously conceived of himself as a potential presidential or vice-presidential candidate, an ambition that might have modified the protectionist sympathies he may have tended to have. "The tariff is a local issue"; but would-be Presidents tend to think nationally.

Eugene D. Millikin (Colorado), the senior Republican on Senate Finance, was widely regarded as the brainiest protectionist around. He knew when he had to deal and just how far he could go with the strengths and weaknesses of his side. Furthermore, and importantly, he had on his staff in the Senate an adviser who was said to be the intellectual generator of many anti–reciprocal trade plans, Serge Benson. Millikin was credited with having led the President's foreign economic policy adviser, Clarence Randall, into great concessions without giving anything away himself. In hearings, he could make an ill-prepared opponent look and seem ridiculous; for instance, he completely rattled Acting Secretary Butz (Agriculture), the administration's lead-off witness for reciprocal trade. He was widely regarded on Capitol Hill as knowing as much economics as any man in the Senate.

The second Republican on Senate Finance, who would serve on conference committees and, if anything happened to Millikin, take his place as ranking member and potential chairman, was the seventy-six-year-old Edward Martin (Pennsylvania). He too was a protectionist, but no one credited him with the astuteness of Millikin. The next two Republicans on Senate Finance, John J. Williams (Delaware) and Ralph E. Flanders (Vermont), probably tended to sympathize with reciprocal trade, although it is not by any means Williams' major interest. (Williams is chiefly involved in tax matters and honesty in government.)

III

Party Votes: So in 1956, from the standpoint of the House of Representatives, any citizen who regarded reciprocal trade or protection as the major issue, the matter that would determine his vote and activity, had a simple choice. He could and should have voted for the Republican candidate for the House, were he a protectionist. This would be true even if the candidate in his district were some "Eisenhower type" like John Lindsay or Jacob Javits, and even though Eisenhower had proposed reciprocal trade extension. It would be true because the seniority system determines who is influential on committees; and the senior Republicans on House

Ways and Means were much more protectionist than the senior Democrats. Vice versa, a person in favor of more liberal trade policies should have voted Democratic, because so many of the senior Democrats in the House genuinely believed in reciprocal trade and would go a long way to expand it. Elect a Lindsay or a Javits to the House and he would have next to no influence on foreign trade policy—at least not for many years, until senior men retired, and then only if he could get a personal following in the House (which Javits did not do at all and Lindsay only to a limited degree) or if he were appointed to a relevant committee and worked at it (and the national attention and New York base of both Lindsay and Javits meant that much of their time was spent outside matters of House concern). So no protectionist had any occasion to worry about an occasional Republican Lindsay or Javits. He could be very sure that the leaders of the big state delegations (who in fact appoint new members to committees on the Republican side) would never appoint such men to committees like Ways and Means.

The exceptions—occasions when a protectionist should rationally support a Democrat—are two:

1. A protectionist or quasi-protectionist Democrat like Aime Forand (Ways and Means) on a key committee may be worthwhile from the protectionist standpoint if he is sincere and effective. And, of course, a really dedicated, experienced protectionist Democrat who works at it, like Cleveland Bailey, is very much worthwhile, whether on or off committees.

2. There were some supporters of reciprocal trade among the Republicans on the House Ways and Means Committee who, if anything happened to Reed, Jenkins, and Simpson (and both Reed and Jenkins were elderly men), might become senior members or even chairman. The top-ranking among these men were Robert W. Kean (New Jersey) and Hal Holmes (Washington). Most, although not all, of the men following them on the seniority ladder were again protectionist—so from the standpoint of a protectionist, knocking off Kean and Holmes was particularly important. (In fact, both of them were knocked off before they got to the top.) In such cases, protectionists should have supported even the most radical, fanatic free-trading Democrat—assuming again that protection was the key issue—because such a Democrat would be unlikely to be appointed to Ways and Means, and the House Republican leader in 1957 would be unlikely to appoint people as committed to liberal trade as Kean and Holmes to Ways and Means. Even if they did,

such men would start at the bottom of the seniority list, whereas Kean was fourth and Holmes sixth.

Such efforts to defeat Kean and Holmes would be particularly important from the protectionist standpoint, because both came from close districts; Kean won in 1954 with only 53.1 percent of the two-party vote, and Truman carried Holmes's district in 1948 with 56.5 percent of the two-party vote.

Of course, if it could be foreseen that after the 1956 elections the House would be divided by only two or three votes, and Holmes and Kean might make the difference between Republican and Democratic control, then protectionists, swallow as they might, might even find it worth supporting Holmes and Kean, in order to make Reed, Jenkins, or Simpson chairman of Ways and Means. But such close calculations are really impossible in regard to 435 congressional seats.

Reciprocal Traders' Choices in the House: Vice versa, reciprocal traders should, generally speaking, have supported any Democrat for the House, even a Democrat who himself spoke and voted for protection. The major exceptions, again, would be men like Kean and Holmes. To keep such reciprocal traders on the Republican side of Ways and Means would be very much worthwhile, for one could be almost sure, the Republican leaders of the big state delegations who select new committee members being what they were, that their successors would be much less favorable to reciprocal trade.

And, of course, reciprocal traders would want to defeat Aime Forand and Cleveland Bailey, for the same reasons that protectionists would support them, even though they were Democrats.

IV

For Senators: The situation in the Senate was by no means so clear. As we have seen, the difference between Democrats and Republicans on Senate Finance was far less sharp than between Republicans and Democrats on House Ways and Means. There was no reason at all to believe that Lyndon Johnson, then the Democratic leader in the Senate, had at all the same intense commitment to reciprocal trade as Speaker Rayburn in the House. In any case, only one-third of the seats in the Senate change hands at any given election; and it rather looked in 1955 as though the Democrats would, in any case, retain control of the Senate in 1956.

Finally, because the Senate is a smaller body, and for other procedural reasons, the individual Senator off a committee can make more of a difference than the individual House member off a committee. Senator Wayne Morse, at that time a Democrat from Oregon, did succeed, for instance, in getting the Senate to adopt an amendment to the Reciprocal Trade Extension Act of 1955 designed to protect Oregon cherries (although the amendment was cut out by the conference committee).

Of the three top-ranking Democrats on Senate Finance, it was generally believed that Byrd and Kerr could be reelected as long as they wished. Senator George, on the other hand, was in grave danger of being defeated in the Democratic primary of 1956, if he chose to run again, by Herman Talmadge. One of the issues that Talmadge, or at any rate Talmadge's adherents, were using against George was that the latter was too internationalist, too unresponsive to the interests of Georgia textiles, which were allegedly being threatened by foreign imports. It would probably not have made a great deal of difference to the way the Senate handled the 1958 extension of the Reciprocal Trade Act whether George still served on Senate Finance or not. But a victory for Talmadge, after a campaign stressing such issues, would have frightened some other southern Senators and Congressmen toward protection, away from reciprocal trade. In fact, my impression is that one of the momentous events of the 1955 reciprocal trade fight was partly a byproduct of Talmadge's projected fight against George: a number of southeastern Congressmen who had always previously supported reciprocal trade opposed it in 1955 because Talmadge scared them. Had Talmadge made a fight on this issue, that tendency might have been accelerated; furthermore, had Talmadge made a public fight on this issue, he might himself have come to pay more attention to opposing reciprocal trade than he did.

In the event, George decided not to make a contest of it. From the standpoint of reciprocal trade, this was probably lucky; protectionists probably should have urged George to run! For, as the situation seems to have been, George had little chance of beating Talmadge and would have been badly whipped. (One of the numerous things I wish we had done in our trade study as to study a district in Georgia and another similar district in South Carolina, instead of two of the six districts we did choose to study. For it was in these southeastern districts that the great bulk of communications about reciprocal trade seems to have been exchanged in 1955, and we missed them.)

On the Republican side, Senator Martin, ranking second to Millikin, was a man who might well retire or be beaten anyway. As chairman he would not have been particularly effective. Millikin, however, as pointed out above, would have been a very effective chairman. Colorado, his state, is given to greater swings between elections than most states. Although, as far as I know, reasonably popular, he did not have the kind of hold on his state that Byrd or Kerr or Kennedy had. He could, in other words, have been beaten. And if he were beaten, Williams would move up to be second man on Senate Finance. So from the standpoint of people to whom reciprocal trade was the issue, and who were not concerned with Millikin's general value to the Senate as a conservative willing to "satisfice" and who worked hard, the thing to look into would have been the prospect of beating Millikin. Wheat areas in Colorado and big business interests in Denver might have been responsive to opposing him on trade grounds—though most locally oriented businessmen would have had many other reasons to be for him!

V

Malone: The fifth-ranking Republican on Senate Finance was, in 1955, Senator George Malone of Nevada. Martin, who would step into first place if Millikin were retired, was seventy-six; Flanders, fourth in line, was seventy-five. If anything happened to them, Malone would then have become second-ranking Republican on Senate Finance (and, of course, if some accident had also befallen Williams, then third in line, Malone might even have become chairman; actually Williams has remained in the Senate for fifteen further years).

Malone proclaimed himself—and he was probably correct—to be the greatest enemy of reciprocal trade in the United States; he regarded it as worse than communism. He told me that he came to the Senate in large measure to fight reciprocal trade. He kept the Senate Finance Committee sitting night after night in 1955 to "make a record" against reciprocal trade, filling ten volumes of hearings.

As conference committee member, and even more as chairman, he would have done anything and everything to defeat reciprocal trade. He had no notion of tactical adroitness at all; he sometimes so infuriated reasonable people (such as Millikin) on his side that he did himself more harm than good. But he was single-minded and utterly impervious to the atmosphere of gentlemanly reasonableness that directs the Senate. To be sure, he might have provoked his colleagues so much that they would have informally stripped him of seniority rights; but the tradition of seniority being what it is, there was a chance that as second-ranking member or chairman he could have single-handledly stymied any serious reciprocal trade extension in 1958.

Now, Malone's term did not expire until 1958; accordingly, supporters of reciprocal trade, opposed as they might be to Martin or Millikin, should rationally have said to themselves: Is beating them worth the risk of moving Malone up? My own feeling, had I been a strong supporter of reciprocal trade, would have been never, never Malone. Millikin in particular fitted the model of a Senator, procedurally and tactically speaking; Malone was the kind of man who could wreck the system.

VI

How Feasible Is Activity for People on Your Side or Against You, Emphasizing Your Issue? Richard Simpson, who as chairman of the Republican Congressional Campaign Committee ought to have known, told me in the spring of 1954 that protection would be an issue in at least ten House contests that fall. Although I did not follow all contests, I did not hear of any where it was really seriously emphasized. In a few cases, two candidates, each promising to protect the district's interests, argued that the other was insincere or incompetent. For instance, Walter S. Baring, Democrat,

maintained that he could protect Nevada minerals better than
Cliff Young, Republican. (From the standpoint of the House party
structure, the claim was absurd.)

The only congressional contest of which I heard where the issue
of reciprocal trade versus protection was stressed in 1954 was in
Iowa, for the Senate. Guy M. Gillette, incumbent Democratic
Senator, was being challenged by Thomas Martin, who had several
years of service on House Ways and Means. Gillette attacked Martin for being a protectionist—which was correct. Gillette emphasized, by citing various economic surveys, that protection hurt the
interests of Iowa farmers. But Martin, more than any other man
in Congress, had always supported protection on theoretical *national defense* grounds. The issue was not, of course, joined; it
rarely is in campaigns. Gillette was beaten, the only Democratic
incumbent who had served six full years in 1954 to be beaten. But
I heard no reference in 1955 to his defeat as demonstrating anything of moment the following year (had I been on my toes, I
would have interviewed specifically about the matter).

VII

*Difficulties of Organizing Supporters of Reciprocal Trade; Ironies
of Multiple Priorities in Elections:* Strong support for reciprocal
trade was found, as far as I know, among (a) university social scientists, (b) members of the League of Women Voters, and (c) some
bright young suburban lawyers and businessmen, the type who
in 1968 would be called Rockefeller Republicans and contribute
to the Ripon Society. Members of the former group would probably
vote Democratic anyway for Congress—thus, in terms of the analysis
given above, tending on the whole to support reciprocal trade. If
such Democrats as Forand and Bailey were opposed by Republicans with more middle-class style, university Democrats would
have been willing enough to oppose such incumbents, if they
lived in their districts. It is not entirely accidental that most of the
Democrats who were committed against reciprocal trade did not
have a university style. (To be sure, West Virginia Democrats like
M. G. Burnside and, more recently, the present Congressman, Ken

Hechler, who were and seem like university professors, have testified and made formal statements against reciprocal trade and foreign imports. But, with all deference to what these gentlemen may think they are thinking—and I suspect both of them would claim that they really are serious, earnest, and committed against unfair extension of reciprocal trade—they used chiefly the formal channels, which signal to their colleagues, "Men, this is for the record," rather than the informal ones, which say, "Fellows, this is something I really want and need.")

It would be more difficult to get university social scientists to see the importance, from the standpoint of supporting reciprocal trade, of retaining Kean and Holmes in Congress (see III above). Naturally, the voting record of these men involved votes on other issues where most social scientists supported the Democratic position.

But the other two groups are much more seriously handicapped in supporting reciprocal trade Democrats. Members of the League of Women Voters, by tradition and regulation, are not, *as such,* supposed to take part in partisan campaigns. But the really difficult situation, in terms of any effectiveness, was that of the group of bright young men who really were committed to expanded international trade, and whose associations were Republican. Could they be expected to oppose men of their own sort who were thinking of running for Congress in 1956? Could they, indeed, be expected to oppose *any* Republican candidates for Congress in their area?

The most they could reasonably be expected to do would be to try to lend special support to Congressman Kean and possibly to raise money for Congressman Holmes. As a practical matter, of course, most of them did support Jacob Javits for the U.S. Senatorial post in New York State in 1956; Javits as a Congressman (he was out of Congress for the two years 1955–57) had certainly expressed great concern with foreign trade. But, as a Congressman, he had not been particularly effective; it was not necessarily the case that he would be effective as a Senator. In fact, therefore, Kean and Holmes were far more important from the reciprocal trade standpoint.

But Javits stirred the enthusiasm of these liberal young Republicans in a way that Kean and Holmes did not. Javits was running for Senator, which most people regard as a more important office. Javits was going to be engaged in what looked like a tight race.

And, of course, as far as Holmes went, out in the state of Washington, few of them could manage any personal involvement in his campaign; they had jobs and contacts in places like metropolitan New York, and not in Washington State.

So, despite their concern with reciprocal trade, these people would have found it quite difficult to exert any great amount of influence on the congressional elections of 1956 *in a way that would strengthen reciprocal trade.* As a practical matter, even the seemingly simple decision to work for the undramatic Kean in New Jersey as compared with the dramatic Javits in New York was a hard one to make. It was hard because, even if one supposes that they regarded reciprocal trade as the most important issue, it still was not the only issue. And, taking most of the important issues put together, it was quite arguable that the election of a liberal Republican (and, incidentally, a Jew) *to the Senate* in New York State would do more for the things they were concerned with, *taken as a whole,* than the reelection of a somewhat less liberal old-stock Anglo-American in New Jersey. Add to this that Javits had more inspirational qualities than Kean; and add, too, that working for Javits would probably have helped more of these men in their own business and political careers.

I have discussed working for Javits versus working for Kean because working for Kean would have been easier than anything else of moment that such people could have done to strengthen reciprocal trade in Congress. In most of the other contests, a New York—based group such as this one would have been able to contribute little more than money, if that. And again, there were many other ways to spend the very small amount of money that can be raised for political campaigns—for Eisenhower himself, and for Javits, for example.

VIII

The Problem of Priorities Is a Tough One: Priorities for the Interests: So, in essence, these people who believed in reciprocal trade could have had some influence on the matter in Congress if they had been able to give it a very high priority—a priority high enough to warrant sacrificing other issues of importance and sacrificing some of the fun and personal advantage of taking part in politics.

What about the "interests?" There is a picture of businesses and other wealthy groups spending millions of dollars on political campaigns in order to get people elected who uphold their own views. Actually, business firms or trade associations ordinarily have a problem of priorities, also. It is a positive risk for them to take part in politics, because, if they are unfortunate enough to support the losing side, they run the risk of continuing ill will—or they are afraid they will do so. Much that they want from government and from Congressmen—probably most—is something the majority of Congressmen and Senators will try to do as a service to a constituent. For example, business firms are concerned with this or that application of the tax laws, or this or that clause in a revision of the tax laws. Members of the Ways and Means Committee may be in a position to do favors on such matters. But a business that has incurred actual ill will by opposing some member of the Ways and Means Committee *or opposing someone he is friendly to* may not get such service. Du Pont, for instance, may in 1953, 1954, and 1955 have had some reason to wish that reciprocal trade extension would be limited and protective. But Du Pont in those years was probably more concerned with legislation to permit a particular sort of tax treatment to its General Motors holdings as divested. Either of Delaware's Senators, J. Allen Frear, Jr. (who was a member of Senate Finance), or John J. Williams (who was also a member of Senate Finance), might have helped Du Pont on such a matter, because, essentially, from the standpoint of members of Congress, such an effort would be simply a matter of doing a favor for a constituent. But, quite aside from anything else, it would have been absurd for Du Pont to jeopardize the possibility of support on this issue by pushing hard on reciprocal trade. Actually, in the case of Du Pont, there were many other reasons why it feared to throw its weight around, reasons I have discussed elsewhere.[1]

The general point, however, is that it quite rarely happens that any one issue is important enough to a firm of any size to warrant the risk of getting into electoral politics on any significant scale. There are too many potential costs to make it worthwhile. Aside

---

[1] "Delaware: Where the Elephant Fears to Dance Among the Chickens. Business in Politics. The Case of Du Pont," published as chap. 16, pp. 265–76, of Raymond Bauer, Ithiel de Sola Pool, and Lewis A. Dexter, *American Business and Public Policy: The Politics of Foreign Trade* (New York: Atherton, 1963); several times reprinted.

from corrupt-practices legislation and the possibility of trouble with stockholders (after all, some members of the Du Pont family who held stock were believed to be stalwart supporters of free trade and others of protection), it is not generally worth the while of a big corporation to try to elect or defeat candidates. For corporations, after years of business legislation, have discovered that, usually, they can live with whatever legislation is imposed. (Defense contractors, like General Dynamics, might be an exception!)

To be sure, there may be occasions when a threatened measure is one of life or death to a big corporation. This would rarely—in fact, in 1955–58, not conceivably—be true of any aspect of reciprocal trade legislation (for a big corporation; small corporations are a different matter). For reciprocal trade legislation is essentially an authorization to the Executive Department to sign certain agreements that have yet to be negotiated. And during the process of negotiation there are many opportunities for affected parties to protest, to suggest modifications, etc. And, in any case, although we made some effort to find out, we could not detect many instances in which big companies could pinpoint the effect of reciprocal trade legislation upon them, pro or con; they are apt to gain in the swings what they lose in the roundabouts—that is to say, they may lose some portion of their U.S. sales to a foreign competitor, but they gain some foreign markets, and also the cost of some raw materials or services they use is reduced.

There are, certainly, cases of big industries and interests that *over a period of years* have been severely penalized by government policy, and of others that might have received benefits they did not in fact get. But the operational phrase here is "over a period of years." It seems to be widely characteristic of human nature and of administration to concentrate on the immediate and scheduled event, about which something must be done, rather than on the long-term situation, which is perhaps more basic, but which does not matter so much immediately.

The railroad industry seems to me to represent such a case. Had the railroads organized in the 1940s or even the early 1950s to push for government subsidy on a large scale, equivalent to what the highways were getting, they might have avoided the economic blows they have suffered. In order to organize in this fashion, they would have had to have friends in Congress who would favor such subsidies (but be adamantly opposed to government ownership). They might have found it worthwhile to create a situation where some of the Congressmen most eager to spend federal funds on highway building would recognize that it would be electorally wise to give railroads as much support as highways.

But, in fact, this would have meant that top railroad management would have to devote a good deal of its planning to long-range political analysis and investment. But throughout the 1940s and 1950s railroads were faced, of course, with numerous operational emergencies. Some of them were faced with immediate problems of potential bankruptcy; all of them had to deal with very serious issues in labor relations. Most of them had immediate politico-business issues involving the various regulatory commissions and, potentially or actually, the Congress—matters involving the shipping of goods, safety regulations, the discontinuance of passenger trains and the abandonment of terminals, etc. Most of them also were involved in merger proposals, which, for historic reasons particularly, tracing back to the days when railroads were monopolies, involved numerous political matters. Some of them were beginning to study diversification—which, for a heavily regulated industry like railroads, also means many political problems.

All these matters had some immediacy about them. Action had to be undertaken soon,[2] or some risk incurred or advantage sacrificed. All these matters involved also the extension and development of contacts that had already been established, skills already developed, methods already familiar. It would have been something quite different if the railroads had entered into a large-scale program of the sort indicated above. The payoff would, necessarily, have been long delayed; the risks would have been considerable; and above all, the development of such a campaign would have taken considerable creativity and adaptability. There were perhaps a few railroad managements in the 1940s and 1950s which might be described as creative and adaptable; but, if so, they were the exception, not the norm.

These considerations get us to the heart of our problem. In the American political and economic system, an established firm or industry of any size will need a good deal of adaptability, creativity,

---

[2]In some instances, even, diversification had to be considered immediately; for one advantage of diversification, if and when feasible, was that it helped use up a tax loss, which after a given number of years might expire. Further, insofar as diversification was specific, rather than general—insofar, that is, as the proposal was to merge with a particular firm—that firm would not wait indefinitely for a wedding; the railroad would have to explore the matter fairly soon.

and willingness to take risks in order to get into electoral politics. If it is a regulated industry, it has already established—as the airlines and the railroads and the public utilities have—a way of getting along; even its worst enemies in Congress or a state legislature will generally cause it only marginal losses (again possibly excepting defense contractors), and it can be—simply because it is established and serves a business or community need—sure of consideration and help from some members of Congress or a state legislature, unless it is unlucky in a most extraordinary way. If it is an essentially unregulated industry (of course every industry is regulated in some respects), it will have found that it can live with most governmental and political changes, even some that appear fairly unpleasant. It knows that, on the whole, tending to its business pays off better than spending a great deal of time in electoral politics.

And it knows too that very few members of Congress or the state legislatures will want to tolerate any possibility of immediate, considerable harm to any constituent—whether a business firm or a private individual—if that possibility is called to their attention. Any business firm of any size is likely to have had experience with modifying legislation or regulations to avoid some danger to it unanticipated by the original drafters of the statute or regulation. If it has not itself had such experience, it will surely have legal counsel who have. Now, this is not to say that in the long run, gradually, over a period of years, governmental programs may not be adopted which hurt a particular firm or industry badly—as the railroads were in fact hurt by federal subsidies for highways and airports. But the key word here is "gradually." And, for reasons of the sort just given in the case of the railroads, very few firms or industries are foresighted enough to try to resist through electoral politics a government-stimulated gradual deterioration of their position.

Our emphasis upon creativity, adaptability, flexibility suggests that it is perfectly possible that some business firms do get into electoral politics effectively. On the whole, however, they will not, for the reasons mentioned, be established firms of any size. It would not be surprising, however, to find that some of the space industries in California and Texas, especially, have in fact concerned themselves actively with electoral politics; although it is perfectly possible that they have not had to do so. But these industries are new, high-risk industries, with management that is adaptable and flexible, which are not in the ordinary sense regulated, but which are dependent upon the government entirely. It has probably been unnecessary for the weapons producers to intervene in politics in the same fashion; until 1968, there was not enough threat to them as a group, and their major problems were intra-industry, not from public opposition. From now on, this may be different. It is difficult to call to mind any other industries that *on a Washington basis* would be likely to feel often that resort to electoral politics would be a reasonable priority.

Industries most likely to be really outraged by government action and to want to take part in election campaigns are those that are not yet regulated but are threatened with regulation. The pharmaceutical industry[3] is now in this position. The automobile industry, in regard to air pollution and safety, may also be in this position. But when there is any strong threat of regulation, this is because there is widespread public feeling that the industry has indeed let the public down. Under such circumstances, an industry will find it hard to get allies in any campaign of resistance to regulation. And in these cases, though not generally, the public is indeed sovereign. Schattschneider, in his review quoted in Chapter 1, says, "There is a long way around to explain why buinessmen are timid; but there is also a short explanation; in a political system so geared to elections as our is, *businessmen do not have the votes.*"[4] Generally, this is, of course, true; generally, however, nobody else has the votes either—in the sense that it is unlikely that whatever the Congressman or Senator does will actually influence his reelection. But when people get excited about the cost of drugs, or the threat of deformed children, then most Congressmen feel that the votes indeed are against the industry. And, under such circumstances, it is hard for an industry to recruit allies and supporters.

It was precisely this sort of experience that Du Pont went through in the "merchants of death" investigation. And, in the early part of the century, the railroads were very active in politics, supposedly buying and selling state legislators on a rather large scale, and certainly resisting safety devices at traffic crossings. Public indigna-

---

[3]In *How Organizations Are Represented in Washington* (Indianapolis: Bobbs-Merrill, 1969), I have several times discussed the current problems of the pharmaceutical industry.

[4]E. E. Schattschneider, review of Bauer, Pool, and Dexter, *American Business and Public Policy*, in *Public Opinion Quarterly*, 29 (1965): 343–44.

tion did, after a time, hurt Du Pont in the one instance, the railroads in the other, so that since then they have been extremely reluctant to stick their necks out.

IX

Congressmen and Senators must very often assume that the bitterest complaints are more or less well founded, but at the same time, as a senior member of the Ways and Means Committee told me, "In regard to these small segments of business or agriculture which get upset, you find there is a sort of fashion in what they blame. At present [1955] they are blaming foreign imports. The coal people, for instance, tried to hide the effects of dieselization and natural gas behind Venezuelan fuel oil, exaggerating the role of that one factor, and never mentioning the others" (in testimony before the committee).

Another small industry, the cherry industry of Oregon, Washington, and Michigan, spent a good deal of time and probably money waiting upon members of Congress to present their case against foreign imports. (The foreign imports about which they were worried were not of fresh fruit, but of maraschino cherries, used extensively in alcoholic beverages.) "They can," said one knowledgeable person, "show (like other small industries) that in a given year foreign imports do hurt . . . because they do not have complex problems of joint costs, alternate uses, etc." (which make such proof difficult for larger industries).

In fact, however, even here it was believed that a change in the method of cherry production in New York State had meant a shift from selling fresh fruit to processing more of it as maraschino cherries in that area, and that this also had hurt the West Coast and Michigan producers. Nevertheless, in the sixty-odd very carefully written, intelligent, and individually phrased letters from Michigan producers to Senator Patrick V. McNamara in the spring of 1955, not one of them mentioned this New York factor. Nor had the West Coast Congressman most likely to hear about such matters heard it mentioned. One Republican member of Congress, commenting upon similar small interests such as the tuna-fish people (who in both Washington and California kept up a running campaign against foreign imports; see the description of Congressman Cecil King in Appendix C), said, *"The State Department often overlooks the basic political fact that these small groups never look beyond the ends of their own noses;* in other words, the State Department needs to remember that these specialty products (such as tuna fish, chicory, toy marbles, cherries) are usually interpreted in terms of the picture of home folks, and when home folks 'don't get their due,' that means there is a lot of screaming." (I should except the cherry people—almost uniquely—from his general indictment!)

Nevertheless, the small industries in his district, vociferous as they might have been about legislation, had not, as far as the Congressman could recall, ever made it an issue in his campaigns. "You haven't spent any time, have you," he said, "on the plains? You don't know coyotes, do you? Oftentimes, you can't tell whether it's one coyote or a dozen screaming." (Which is a comment on a good deal of so-called pressure, much of it seriously reported in the newspapers and sometimes in books. Of course, some people respond to one distant coyote!)

Still, it might be a dozen coyotes, and they might someday shift their votes (or campaign activity, if any—see again the King sketch in Appendix C) because of something the Congressman or Senator has done or not done in regard to their interest. But, in fact, it is very hard for any industry to determine whether a Congressman or Senator is only going through the motions or is really trying to accomplish a result; indeed, it is sometimes hard for a politician himself to determine what his objectives are. If I may cite my own somewhat parallel experiences when I have been in a political position, I have sometimes not realized I was not serious in trying to accomplish something for some constituent until I found myself disappointed rather than pleased—or at any rate ambivalent—when my requests were in fact acceded to by the agency I was trying to pressure. I have seen similar cases in Congress, I believe.

This is not necessarily hypocrisy; it is rather a kind of unconscious Hegelianism, an awareness that, if one presents a case, perhaps those to whom he is presenting it will come forth with a compromise solution that achieves both the objectives he is putting forward and those that led to the initial decision or act he is criticizing. Although it is not my present major task—it would better fit a book on the political philosophy of the legislative process—such a process of synthesis does sometimes take place as a result of making requests that on the face of them are probably not taken seriously by the legislators who present them.

From the practical standpoint of tuna fishermen or cherry growers or toy-marble manufacturers, however, they can only judge if a Congressman or Senator has been polite, sympathetic, considerate, and informed about some method of getting a hearing for them. They cannot, usually, tell whether the method he suggests is likely to achieve the desired result, whether there are alternate methods that might be more effective, whether another Congressman in the same district might have done much more for them. For example: Senator Morse of Oregon succeeded in 1955 in getting an amendment tacked onto the Reciprocal Trade Extension Act of that year which would, supposedly, have helped cherry growers against foreign competition. The amendment was, *almost inevitably,* struck out by the conference committee. Did Senator Morse know and expect this when he introduced the amendment? Even if he did not articulate the matter to himself in this fashion, did he subconsciously realize it? Would the amendment in fact have had the effect it was supposedly intended to have if it had been enacted? (A great many measures are more or less innocuous or ineffective because the agency that administers them is unwilling or technically unable to accomplish the goals that the measure was presumably intended to serve; a classic example of this was provided in the mid-fifties by the superfumbling fashion in which the bureaus concerned with implementing the Kennedy-Saltonstall measure to aid the Massachusetts fishing industry, etc., went about their task.)

Even if Senator Morse himself was completely serious, and the amendment was completely workable, would not the temptation for Senators from Michigan and Washington to support the measure on the floor, regardless of their own commitments to more liberal trade, have been great, since they would know that the amendment would be unlikely to survive the conference committee? Consider: Conference committees, as we have seen, usually consist of the senior members of the relevant committees, in this case Senate Finance and House Ways and Means. The Morse amendment was tacked on on the floor. Senior members of committees are likely in principle to oppose amendments that are added on the floor, without having been carefully considered in committee, and in this case Morse himself was very unpopular with the senior members of Senate Finance, so it was reasonably certain that the Senate conferees would make no stand in favor of the amendment if, as was likely, the House conferees preferred their own bill. And cherries simply were not important enough to any member of Congress, in any case, to delay passage of the entire bill. These Michigan and Washington Senators could then claim, in reasonably good faith, to have struck a blow for the cherry industry; they would have suggested to State Department negotiators that the United States Senate looked very much askance at putting Italian maraschino cherries in American cocktails while there were Oregon and Washington and Michigan cherries available, so perhaps the State Department would be a bit more cautious in dealings with Italy or other foreign producers of cherries!

A neat example of a parallel case was supplied by Senator Irving M. Ives of New York during the Truman administration. Under the offshore procurement policy then in effect, designed to build up western European industry and/or reduce defense costs, negotiations were started with a north Italian manufacturer to supply optical goods that otherwise could have been made in Rochester, New York. Ives, in support of the Rochester interest, protested rather strenuously the prospect of finalizing such contracts, and presumably made this stand well known to Rochester manufacturers. Ultimately, a split (I believe 50 percent to Rochester and 50 percent to Italy) was agreed to; whereupon Senator Ives's office issued a release to the Italian-language papers in New York State about the Senator's part in getting this contract for an Italian firm!

In this case, of course, anybody putting the whole story together might have had some doubts. But ordinarily no such basis for suspicion is provided; and come election time, specialty interests will feel closer to a Congressman who knows their case and their concerns and has apparently tried to do something for them than they will to an unknown opponent, who ordinarily is unaware of their particular industry and its problems. *In other words, in general, Congressmen are much better equipped to use efforts at pressure from specialty interests as a means of winning publicity and support for themselves than specialty interests are actually to persuade or direct Congressmen to do anything effective for them, if the latter do not really want to.* The Congressman can go through the motions of helping, and the industry or firm cannot tell how hard he tried, whether he could have done more, whether he was defeated by his colleagues, or whether he used parliamentary procedure to disguise the fact that he really did not try.

The other way around, the Congressman, if he is wise, knows that people in dying industries are likely to be resentful, and hostile anyway. If they do not stay in business, they may blame it on the incumbent, regardless of how much he did to help them. As a matter of fact, if he did a good deal to try to help them, but failed, they are perhaps more likely to blame him than if he did not do anything in particular. And, in most cases, these dying industries have a multiplicity of problems anyway.

X

Specialty Unions: The only place I heard people talk in old-fashioned pressure terms, with a real spirit of vengefulness against the politicans who did not or would not help them, was in some of the unions representing dying industries. Cleveland Bailey's influence in the Congress was created, in part, by the fact that he also talked in these terms—a very rare thing in the Congress of 1953–55—and that the Appalachian Congressmen whom he especially influenced were exposed to these unions. Most of these labor people were elderly.

I had been warned of this possibility by an economist who did a good deal of consulting for labor unions when I started our study. "It seems to me," he said, "that if you want to study communications, you chose absolutely the worst subject for a study that you possibly could [reciprocal trade]. It's a subject on which people feel so very strongly that—"

I interrupted him to say that I'd not noticed a great deal of strong feeling among the businessmen with whom I talked.

"Businessmen!" he said. "I'm not talking about businessmen. I guess businessmen in general don't know or care too much about the tariff or reciprocal trade. But if there ever were an issue on which labor-union leaders were willing to *kill,* and I mean that, it's the tariff. We see three or four of them every week going into the headquarters of the federation, or into an international union headquarters sometimes, complaining and screaming about the stand of the federation [in favor of reciprocal trade]. Mostly little small specialty unions or trades." (Although this particular man had no contact, that I know of, with the United Mine Workers and District 50, its catch-all for all sorts of trades, I may add that in the U.M.W. in the mid-fifties, one found more hostility toward reciprocal trade than I ever encountered anywhere else.) "Why, except possibly for minimum wage, there is no other issue, absolutely none, on which they feel as strongly— except, of course, for jurisdictional problems in the unions and things like that. So I don't see that you could learn much about how people feel about other more low-key issues from studying this one!"

The significance of this statement is, in part, that our study showed relatively little *felt* pressure—threats and intensity of demand—on reciprocal trade in the Congress. If this was an intense issue, from the standpoint of certain unions—and I think the economist was right, it was—nevertheless relatively little of that pressure got communicated to the Congress. I would, however, say that what pressure there was, was from the dying specialty unions in the Appalachian area and from Cleveland Bailey, one of their representatives in the Congress; but I encountered only one representative who I think was actually coerced by such pressure into taking a position in which he *profoundly* disbelieved. There was one other who perhaps would have felt more comfortable if he had been able to support reciprocal trade; but, in fact, if the leadership had ever asked him to do so, he would have gone along on it. In these two cases, the men in question may have believed that they would actually lose strength in the next election if they supported reciprocal trade.

I doubt, since they had generally voted with the United Mine Workers and the other unions and industries in their districts, that they would have lost any votes by supporting reciprocal trade. It is, however, probable that one of them, who was not, I judge, personally well liked by the union leaderships, might have forfeited campaign funds if he had not gone through all the motions of bitterly opposing reciprocal trade. (His manner of doing so was, I infer, quite ineffective, but his constituents did not know that; and perhaps he did not know it either.) The other might have needed rather larger campaign funds than most candidates for reelection in the area because in 1955 it looked as though his opponent in 1956 would be a particularly formidable one.

XI

Corrupt Practices and Campaign Funds: I have not placed any emphasis on corrupt practices acts as limiting the participation of businesses and other interests in elections. This is because they are so phrased and worded that any business firm with a competent counsel can often figure out reasonably safe ways of contributing to campaigns. In fact, these acts are so little known that one of the middle-level executives of a very up-to-date and intelligently advised business firm told me in 1960 how that firm had made contributions in kind to certain candidates (as it happens for state office), which violated the state corrupt practices act—and he was, if anything, merely proud of the company's civic spirit, quite unaware of the legal problem.

But although there are a good many ways around and through corrupt practices acts, if anybody desires to find them, the fact is that most business firms do not desire to do so, in regard to electoral politics on the national level (though some feel themselves obligated to contribute on state or local levels), and the corrupt practices acts operate like the community chest in many towns and cities: they give business firms a good excuse to refuse to do what they do not wish to do anyway.

It is also pretty widely recognized by candidates—and still more by incumbent Congressmen—that it is unsafe and impractical to make clear promises in return for campaign gifts. The contributor may hope a man will follow a certain line and that he will be effective in so doing; but he has no way of assuring himself on this point.

And the proposition mentioned above within one context applies here within another: very often, if a politician makes enemies in one direction, he makes friends in another. He may cut off the possibility of funds from a union that opposes reciprocal trade, but he may increase the prospect of funds from somewhere else if he votes for it. And vice versa.

However, if one were looking for the most likely source of "pressure" at the present time, it probably would lie in the area of campaign funds (and means of repaying campaign debts). This is a far more important matter today than it was in the 1950s because, owing to the cost of television and other public relations techniques, campaigning generally costs much more now than it did fifteen or twenty years ago.

In the House, however, the risks involved here are not as great as they may seem, because the significant decisions in the House are made by senior Congressmen who have established themselves safely in their districts, and do not face, in most cases, any serious threat of defeat. I was somewhat fearful that the series of reapportionment decisions would jeopardize many established Congressmen and therefore increase the cost of their reelection campaigns; I do not know of any evidence that this has as yet been proved to be the case, although, in general, this possibility is a serious argument against the one-man–one-vote principle. Once a Congressman has established himself safely in a district, he should be permitted to keep that district as long as he stays in Congress![5]

XII

Other Possibilities: Primary Contests?   Of course, this discussion by no means exhausts the possible ways of exerting electoral pressure on a candidate for Congress. No doubt, in some cases, devices to exert some pressure have been tried successfully which are not now recorded or widely remembered. Certainly, I can think of half a dozen ways that *might* threaten a Congressman electorally, but which have not, as far as I know, been tried out.

One way that has sometimes been tried is to run a candidate in a primary against an incumbent. For example, John Elder, a dean of the Harvard Divinity School, ran against seven-term Congressman Torbert Macdonald (Massachusetts) in 1968, as much as anything else on the Viet Nam issue. Actually, during the course of the year, Macdonald himself came to oppose the Johnson policy on Viet Nam. Did Elder have anything to do with this? It seems likely. On the other hand, Macdonald was close to the Kennedys, and they changed their views during the year, too; and, of course, public opinion shifted greatly. Certainly, by the fall of 1968, when the primary took place, Elder had not gained the widespread enthusiastic support that, on the basis of the McCarthy primaries in the spring, he might have hoped for. Perhaps one reason he did not get this support was that Macdonald had, in fact, made public doubts and criticisms of the Viet Nam War.

Running a candidate in a primary—or threatening to do so—can presumably be effective even if the primary opponent has no chance

---

[5]See my "Standards for Representative Selection and Apportionment," in *Representation, Nomos X*, ed. J. Roland Pennock and John W. Chapman (New York: Atherton, 1968), pp. 155–66.

of winning. It can be effective for two reasons: Very few Congressmen and Senators would be self-confident enough simply to disregard such a primary opponent. The incumbent would have to spend some money in opposing him, if he were at all serious. And that means more difficulty in raising money for the general election. Furthermore, if the potential challenger turns out to have any strength, the incumbent will have to spend a minimum of some weeks campaigning in the primary while Congress is in session. Hence, he cannot exert nearly as much influence on developments in committee.

I spoke earlier of the way in which Senator Malone of Nevada held up the proceedings in Senate Finance on 1955 on the Reciprocal Trade Extension Act. Supporters of reciprocal trade would have been well advised to see if there were any possibility, under the Nevada laws of that time, of getting a strong challenger to run against him for the nomination in 1958. Then the hearings on reciprocal trade could have been scheduled during the period he was most likely to have to be back home for the contest. Since he was not popular with his colleagues, it would have been easy to arrange such scheduling. A popular Senator or Congressman might have bent the scheduling of hearings to his own convenience. But Malone was not popular with his colleagues.

XIII

Another Irony of the Electoral System: A Candidate Just as Bad or Worse Is Usually Better if the Incumbent is "Bad" and Senior: One of the ironies of the American congressional system, with its emphasis upon seniority, is that, if a given cause is opposed by an incumbent Senator or Congressman, the supporters of that cause are well advised to support a candidate even worse from their standpoint than the incumbent. For the incumbent has seniority—sometimes a great deal of seniority. If he has a great deal of seniority, and is reasonably competent and feared, he has influence. The new man—almost universally in the House, often in the Senate—will start at the bottom. In the House he is very unlikely to be placed on a major committee in his first or second term, and obviously he cannot become a committee chairman during that time. So if one is convinced that the incumbent is bad, and the people next to him on a relevant committee are better, it is worth voting for, and even financing and working for, a worse man.

This is particularly true because a great many new members of the House do not stay the course; they quit Congress or quit politics. A man who has beaten an incumbent in a primary probably starts off, anyway, with a slight disadvantage. It will be a little harder for him to get good committee assignments (the incumbent's friends will be somewhat resentful), and he in turn may be opposed the next couple of times around (the incumbent's friends back home will be looking for revenge).

So supporters of reciprocal trade might rationally have found themselves in the position of supporting a House candidate even more systematically committed to protection than, say, Jenkins, second-ranking Republican on Ways and Means, against him in 1954—because if Jenkins were defeated, then Kean and Holmes, supporters of reciprocal trade, would move up on committee.

Vice versa, if the situation in the district of Chairman Cooper of Ways and Means was such that a primary contest could be mounted against him with any chance of success in 1956, it might possibly have benefited protectionists, for it would move Forand, a quasi-protectionist, up on Ways and Means. It happened, however, that as the cards were stacked in 1955–56, liberal traders had much more to gain from the electoral process and mounting primary or general election fights than had protectionists. I had not been aware of this until I started to analyze the situation. But it was one additional reason I heartily agreed that this analysis should not be published in 1955—I did not want to appear to be in the position of counseling liberal traders against protectionists.[6] It just happened that the cards fell that way. I would therefore like to add that if there are any people who wish to apply this analysis to the reciprocal trade–protection fight in regard to the 1970 elections, the situation on Senate Finance now appears quite different. Albert Gore of Tennessee, third-ranking Democrat on Senate Finance, is probably more committed to freer trade than anyone else on that committee; he is likely to have a hard fight in 1970 and may possibly have a primary contest. The man who

---

[6]See my "Role Relationships and Conceptions of Neutrality in Interviewing," *American Journal of Sociology*, 62 (1956): 153–57, for a discussion of the correct feeling of most relatively protectionist people that most academics are biased in favor of reciprocal trade extension and of my consequent efforts to lean over backward to avoid any identification with freer trade views.

would become third-ranking Democrat on the committee if Gore were beaten is Herman Talmadge, whose commitment to reciprocal trade is not very strong, for reasons partly indicated earlier in the discussion of the projected George-Talmadge contest. Since Eugene McCarthy, now fifth-ranking Democrat, probably will not run for reelection, this moves up Vance Hartke of Indiana to the fourth-ranking Democratic spot on Senate Finance—and Hartke on many matters has great sympathy with forces concerned with protecting American industry. In fact, if Gore were beaten, this might leave Senate Finance, as far as I know, without any Democratic member strongly committed to reciprocal trade and likely to be able to spend a great deal of time on it; Fulbright, now fifth-ranking member, is, of course, chairman of Foreign Relations; Abe Ribicoff, sixth-ranking member, has much more involvement in some of the issues for which he has become widely known, primarily public safety and health; Fred Harris has many other irons in the fire and comes from Oklahoma; and I would know of no reason to suppose the younger Byrd is concerned, and anyway he may well be beaten in 1970!

XIV

Election and Primary Contests Can Also Be Taken as Clues to Public Sentiment: Their Effect from This Point of View: There is another way in which election and primary contests can have a quite disproportionate influence on legislative actions.

Experienced politicans have, naturally, learned that general public sentiment does not necessarily mean too much to their reelection prospects. The sentiments that count are those that lead people actually to shift their votes or give their money or time. For instance, for many years public-opinion polls showed that most people favored the admission of Alaska and Hawaii as states; but it is highly improbable that Senators and Congressmen who opposed the admission of these territories to the union lost a dozen votes apiece by so doing. Vice versa, there have been various occasions when an election or a primary contest has made politicians feel it is safe to take a particular stand, even though previously the fashion or hunch among politicians was that such a stand would be risky. It is probable that when

Endicott Peabody, who could hardly clear from the record the fact that he had once favored liberalization of birth control laws, was elected governor of Massachusetts in 1962, it made a difference.

More nationally significant was the election of three Republican newcomers to the Senate in 1966—Edward Brooke, Mark Hatfield, and Charles Percy. All of them had indicated grave doubts about the Viet Nam War; one of them (Percy) had been beaten for governor two years previously and another (Brooke) had the seeming disadvantage of being a Negro in a state without a large Negro population. Yet they constituted three out of the five newly elected Republicans in 1966. At a minimum, their election tended to make Republicans feel it was safe to be against the Viet Nam War; and, had they all been badly beaten, it is conceivable that the Republican Senate leadership would have pressed strongly for an all-out war. In fact, of course, as always, there were accidental factors in these victories, but Hatfield and Percy nevertheless defeated Democratic opponents who took a hard line on Viet Nam.

The significance of these victories was not that they made any particular policy decision inevitable or even highly probable. What they did do was to show Senators and Congressmen, *many of whom already had doubts about Viet Nam,* that it was safe enough to oppose the President on that matter. Since there had been a feeling among politicians that anyone who did take such a stand might be permanently damned as unpatriotic, these elections thus made a difference.

Now, is there anything that could have been accomplished on the reciprocal trade issue in 1956 which would have had a similar effect on the Reciprocal Trade Extension Act of 1958? There is one very clear possibility. Folk wisdom among politicians generally asserted that in the Appalachian mountain area, with its dying industries, politicians could *not* support reciprocal trade. Much of Cleveland Bailey's ability to influence his colleagues in the House (see section I above) arose from this feeling. I do not believe the feeling was well founded; it seems to me there was a very large head of protectionist mail, etc., but very little beer. I base this statement upon a set of interviews in Cumberland, Maryland, called "Appalachian City" in *American Business and Public Policy,* and upon study of the mail and interviews with several Congressmen, labor leaders, and businessmen elsewhere in the area.

Of the fifteen or so Congressmen from this Appalachian area, some of them certainly would have been vulnerable. Of course, reciprocal traders should have looked first at Cleveland Bailey himself, Richard Simpson, also from the fringe of this area, and Thomas Jenkins, second-ranking Republican on Ways and Means. In Jenkins' case, for reasons indicated above, anyone who could beat him would have been desirable, because of his committee position; this would in some ways also have been true of Simpson, but Simpson, as chairman of the Republican Congressional Campaign Committee, otherwise a genuinely effective Congressman, and a man of great ability, was probably quite safe. Bailey impressed me as a man who by temperament and attitude would make a good many enemies; he did not even live in his own district; and he might well have been studied carefully. If a strong candidate could have been found who could have beaten him—a candidate who during the campaign announced that he favored reciprocal trade—it would have been far harder to rally the Appalachian Congressmen against it in 1958. The United Mine Workers and their allies would no longer have been able to convince these men that, as a matter of electoral safety, they had to oppose it. (My impression is that, whether a Congressman was Republican or Democrat, it was not business firms but the United Mine Workers *leadership* that coerced them; but as people have since become aware, the leadership of that union in the 1950s was progressively losing its own influence with the rank and file of workers.)

If Bailey was invulnerable, there were other protectionist Congressmen up and down the Appalachian range who could have been beaten.

The other group of Congressmen about whom reciprocal traders should have inquired in 1955 with a view to challenging one or more of them in 1956 were the southerners who voted against reciprocal trade. For the first time—chiefly, apparently, as a result of concern about the textile industry—a number of southern Congressmen, at one stage or another in the proceedings, opposed reciprocal trade. Unfortunately, we conducted no studies or interviews in the South; but it would seem highly probable that in some of these districts, a man appealing to the farmers (who benefited from increased reciprocal trade) and the old southern tradition of supporting freer trade could have beaten a southern "renegade" on this issue. For example, Hugh Alexander had succeeded "Muley" Doughton in a North Carolina district. Doughton, who retired at the age of ninety, was an able, aggressive chairman of Ways and Means for many years—much more like Mills than like Cooper. Doughton had always supported reciprocal trade; but Alexander "deserted" what Doughton had always stood for. I met a man who had come to Washington some years before as a protégé of Doughton's and was himself a strong believer in reciprocal trade; he had kept up contacts in the old district and thought, at least, of going back home to challenge Alexander (he could have quit his lobbying job, he thought). Had I been in the business of influencing legislation in favor of reciprocal trade instead of studying the issue, I would have looked into his situation, seen if he could be persuaded, and explored ways of financing the campaign.

Here, again, the prospects were not quite as inviting for the protectionists, in terms of the congressional setup. Gore, who had committed himself more firmly to reciprocal trade than any other Senator, did not come up until 1958. From their standpoint, as I pointed out earlier, the most hopeful thing would be to persuade George to run again and then let Talmadge attack him on the issue of "softness" to foreigners on trade and aid. But Talmadge was too strong and George decided not to make the race.

In the House, if Smith of Mississippi, who was as strongly committed to reciprocal trade as anyone in that body, were beaten, it would merely have been interpreted as an expected defeat for a man too liberal *in many ways* for his district. Probably the best thing for protectionists to look into would have been the possibility of defeating any of the senior *southern* democrats in a primary campaign discussing recriprocal trade—Cooper himself, for instance, might have been vulnerable. But the trouble with this possibility is that any reasonably competent senior member of Ways and Means does so many favors and acquires so many supporters that it is hard to get a campaign against him financed on an issue; this is, of course, particularly true of a chairman. (I do not believe Jenkins on the other side had this kind of competence, so he might have been beaten.)

The other possibility might have been to look at the Detroit Congressmen. In the business world, and to some extent, possibly, in Congress, Detroit was regarded as the center of "liberal trade" sentiment—although here again it was a matter of a great deal of head with relatively little beer. If any of the Detroit Congressmen were, for some factional or personal reason, vulnerable to a primary contest, and if any of them had said or done something that could nail him as an all-out supporter of reciprocal trade, no doubt primary opposition could have been encouraged and financed. My impression is that there was no such situation; but, again, had I been in the business of trying to influence legislation on the protectionist side, instead of studying it, it is something I would have looked into.

Unfortunately, from the standpoint of the protectionists, any candidate in Detroit, at least after he won, would have wanted to make his peace with the United Automobile Workers. And just as the leadership of the United Mine Workers, for what were basically traditional and ideological reasons, opposed reciprocal trade strenuously, some of the leaders of the United Automobile Workers supported it strenuously. *In neither case did their sentiments strongly represent or influence the rank and file;* but, in terms of future financing and future elections, any victorious candidate in Detroit would need to be on good terms with the U.A.W. *leadership.* And, too, he would find it easier to be on good terms with the various chamber-of-commerce-type groups in Detroit which strongly backed reciprocal trade. So, even if a man won in a primary on such an issue, he might not stick after his victory!

XV

And Finally: Is Legislation the Best Way to Affect Policy Anyway?
The assumption upon which this and the following chapter is based is: legislation actually affects policy. People who attach priorities to an issue and have skill and competence can sometimes have some effect on legislation.

But an important question is: Is legislation the best way to affect policy? In my book *How Organizations Are Represented in Washington* I describe at some length the following situation: A particular firm tried to get its Congressman to help it get protection against certain foreign imports. Apparently, although the president and the legal counsel of the firm were not clear on the point, they would have welcomed legislation. But I point out how, in fact, in their particular situation, a public relations campaign directed against the importing firm and the country from which the imports came would have been more useful—because certain aspects of the manufacture of the competing imports would offend the institutional buyers who chiefly used the product. There are a number of other instances in which aid by legislative action is harder to get than aid in some other way. For instance, the U.S. textile industry was composed of many small producers in 1955 and did very little in the way of market research.

Market research studies would, in a good many cases, have been possible, could have been financed, and, if acted upon, would have had more lasting value in keeping out foreign competition than government protection.

The other way around: several of our interviews with medium-sized manufacturers and retailers showed that tariff barriers, one way or another, are not the major factor to all of them. Many of them do not want to buy or sell abroad, because they do well enough in the domestic market, and buying or selling abroad is a nuisance. They don't have interpreters on their staffs, they don't know the procedures, foreign exchange is complicated, measurements are metric, etc. So they ignore or overlook opportunities to make profits by selling abroad or to reduce costs by buying abroad. For instance, in 1950 a friend of mine who was a small manufacturer of butchers' supplies was annoyed rather than pleased by an inquiry from a Venezuelan firm about his products; he had no Spanish-speaking person on his staff, and, although there were plenty of Spanish-speaking people in the city, he finally asked me to translate the letter. Of course, I did not know the technical terms of the butchers' supply industry, either in English or in Spanish. Any group, any foundation, any government agency could provide help on such tertiary matters as translation and foreign exchange. Such help would, almost certainly, interest a lot more medium-sized businesses in foreign trade than any change in tariffs, "Buy American" acts, etc.

Put another way, the obstacles to foreign trade for many such firms are matters of information cost. The immediate economic gain is not worth the immediate bother in short-range terms. Anybody who could help them reduce the information cost might create a situation where they would be interested in the immediate economic gain as a basis for making a really worthwhile long-term economic gain.

And, of course, from the standpoint of supporters of increased foreign trade, not only would such help considerably increase the *volume* of foreign trade. It would mean that many medium-sized businessmen who do not care, one way or the other, whether there is or is not foreign trade would begin to have a stake in it.

CHAPTER THREE

Suppose You Want to Influence the Congress on Legislation?

CONGRESS AND ENVIRONMENTAL DEFENSE

I

The previous chapter, dealing with reciprocal trade and tariff legislation in the 1950s, pointed out ways in which the citizen could—and could not—have influenced Congress on that matter. The conclusion suggested is that citizens are, generally speaking, semisovereign.[1] They can make a considerable difference; but this does not mean— even if they are a powerful majority to which there is no strong, manifest opposition—that the Congress is sure to do what they want.

The reciprocal trade and tariff issue was in the 1950s, on the whole, a rather low-priority, low-key one. Sensible and experienced Congressmen realized that few votes were likely to be won or lost from it. They knew, too, that, although their stands and actions on it might affect campaign funds and organized support, they had many other ways of obtaining campaign funds and organized support. So, on the whole, they had on this issue a considerable amount of freedom, so far as constituency and public influences were concerned.[2]

---

[1]E. E. Schattschneider, *The Semi-Sovereign People: A Realist's View of Democracy in America* (New York: Holt, Rinehart, & Winston, 1960), has well expressed the conception here.

[2]Of course, some Congressmen had ties and affiliations, both within Congress and in the constituency, which would have made it difficult or impossible for them personally to imagine

This matter of freedom is worth a moment's attention. Probably a Congressman or Senator who voted against all, or most, of the significant interests and concerns in his constituency would find it difficult to be reelected. If it became very clear that he was voting against all of them, reelection would probably be unlikely. But there are a great many interests and concerns in every constituency; a man would have to be really perverse to vote against all of them. And, indeed, he would have to be lazy or politically indifferent not to work for some of them or at least to hire assistants who would work for them—or at the very least go through the motions of working on them.

For instance: a Congressman may be close to and indebted to various trade-union groups. They may be in favor of protecting some industries against "unfair" foreign competition. But these same groups are in favor of minimum-wage laws; they want federal school funds for their children; they are concerned with some public-works matters in the area, highways or ferries or post offices, or something of the sort. They are interested in safety regulations for workers; their wives are concerned with consumer protection and clean food. And so, if the Congressman picks and chooses among these other issues, and gets some publicity on several of them, he is free enough on the specific matter of foreign imports—free enough in the sense that if, in general, he seems likable and trustworthy, he will not lose any significant number of votes by opposing his labor constituents on reciprocal trade. In fact, such balancing of appeals and issues has made it possible for Senators like John Sparkman and Lister Hill to be reelected repeatedly in Alabama even though they did not really stand with Alabama sentiment on race—plus their willingness to con-

---

taking another stand than that which they actually took in 1953, 1954, and 1955. For instance, some Congressmen would not have been willing to vote against Speaker Sam Rayburn on reciprocal trade; others felt close to and obligated to particular unions or industries in their districts, and perhaps to helpful groups outside their own districts. But such attitudes represent individual orientations. Often another Congressman elected from the same district could have made a different decision on reciprocal trade without any great risk, provided that in general he carried out his role with moderate skill—that is, did not amass too many enemies and create too many disappointments simultaneously. Put abstractly, a Congressman has to have a balance sheet of favorable impressions in order to be reelected; but there are a great many different ways open to him of building such favorable impressions. He can and does *choose* among the possible ways open to him, bearing in mind that on *controversial* legislative matters, creating a favorable impression in some group will create an unfavorable impression in some other group, and that it is usually difficult to determine how lasting or intense such impressions are. As a practical matter, an incumbent, by the mere fact of receiving more publicity and with the opportunity to do personal favors (case service), starts out with assets that challengers nowadays can rarely equal. (Of course, if hostility to the establishment became sufficiently great in some constituency, then being the incumbent might be a disadvantage there.)

form to constituency demands on symbolic issues like the Southern Manifesto. A Congressman of the sort described above might at most have to declare his rhetorical opposition to unfair foreign competition and to try to help specific industries to get anti-dumping or escape-clause protection; but on the major legislative issue, he could be as free as he chose to be.[3] He might, on the other hand, decide to go along with his labor constituents on reciprocal trade, because he considered it more important to break with them on something else. So his freedom is real, but limited.

I do not mean to say that most Congressmen make *calculations* of this sort; but, unarticulated or unconscious, this is the kind of *response* they make to demands and claims upon them. The most frequent response, without any doubt, and the greatest claim for freedom, is of the Congressman or Senator who says: "I have done all these personal service and constituency service matters for you. I have done them competently and well. Now, let me be free on the big legislative issues." A good many Congressmen and Senators do, in fact, say *in effect* just that. One famous example was Edmund Burke, who proclaimed to the electors of Bristol how extremely busy and competent he had been in doing their errands before government departments, and therefore claimed freedom to represent "your interests, not your desires" on the big legislative matters. What Burke failed to realize—because he was a bit of an academic—was that he should also have said, "On the big symbolic issues, I'll often *talk* your language; provided that, when it comes to legislative action, you let me go against you." He failed to realize this, but, wiser in their generation, the Sparkmans and the Hills make this additional concession to constituency demands.

II

Reciprocal trade and the tariff have been issues for a long time. They happen to be matters on which the parties divide a good deal. Recently, they have been rather low-priority and low-key. But what

---

[3]In earlier years, there were Senators who were particularly active in pushing for and enacting restrictive immigration legislation, but who, in individual cases, went to considerable pains to get exemptions. They probably won more support and conceivably even more campaign funds by their helpfulness in specific cases than they lost, owing to the fact that they had after all played a part in setting up the barriers to which exceptions had to be made.

about an issue that is relatively new? What about an issue that is likely to excite a great deal of feeling, pro and con?

Ecology: An issue that may emerge as *the* issue of the 1970s is ecology and the control of technology.[4] The human species is making its own life, perhaps even its own survival, difficult. I have already mentioned the laughing response of the governor to whom I suggested that he incorporate in his inaugural message a paragraph about water pollution and cleaning up rivers: "That's of interest only to those women." That was in 1956. Whatever may have been the case then, water pollution, air pollution, oil spillage, and so on are worrying thousands of people now. The present governor of the same state, in his first week in office in 1969, declared it his intention to make conservation a major political issue! An experienced observer of the situation has predicted that there may shortly be the same kind of concern about ecology—keeping the environment livable—as there is now about civil rights.[5] Certainly Secretary Hickel found himself walking into a buzz saw when, in his confirmation hearings, he appeared ignorant of the importance of ecology. The oil slick off Santa Barbara and air pollution in all big cities have been major news.

So let us suppose that one or another of the groups concerned with environmental defense and ecology wants to influence the Congress in support of its cause. How does it go about it? What is it necessary to know?

First: What Are the Central Policy Issues? Where Are They Determined? The first thing to do, naturally, is to determine the central policy issues. This sounds easy enough for any one person, sitting by himself; but when it comes to a group trying to work out issues, it is often very difficult. For example, some advocates of civil rights regard housing as more important than employment; others have regarded accommodations as more important; some have stressed

---

[4]Not only is the U.N. considering an international year, focusing on international collaboration to preserve the environment, but, while these pages were being typed, President Nixon appointed a national commission on the quality of the environment. I have the distinct impression, indeed, that in the first eight months of 1969 the biggest manifest change in American public policy, at least as reported in the New York and Boston newspapers that I read, was the concern expressed for protection of the environment against further deterioration.

[5]Frank Graham, Jr., in *The Audubon Magazine*, July–August 1967, pp. 77–78, in a review partly of Robert and Lena Rienow, *Moment in the Sun* (New York: Dial, 1967). See also my review of the Rienow book in *American Political Science Review*, 43 (1969): 582–84.

education. Establishing agreement on priority has not been easy. So, in regard to ecology, are we concerned with the health of those now adult? With the survival of the human species? With the survival of modern civilization? Beauty? Convenience? Many people, all terribly alarmed about the threat of technology to our world, may well differ sharply on such matters.

Assume, however, that an order of priorities has been established. The next question is: Where are the basic policies affecting the matters of greatest priority set? How are they determined?

Some very important matters are not chiefly determined, under present circumstances, by the Congress. It might well be, for example, that one of the high-priority issues in this field would be birth control. Although there are marginal respects in which Congress might affect birth-control practices, it does not seem that legislative action is the most important thing here, at present. *Discussion* of *future* legislative action, when the climate of public opinion has changed, may of course be very much worthwhile; payment, for instance, to people who refrain from having children may, in ten years or so, become a useful aspect of the War Against Poverty as well as of ecological campaigns. For the purpose of *publicizing* such ideas, it may be worth introducing a bill; but few familiar with the climate of opinion in the United States today, no matter how much they believe in the principle of such payment, would seriously try to get such a law enacted in the near future, because it would not become widely effective.

Clearly, publicity, action through voluntary organizations, and so on are necessary before legislative action on birth control becomes a major, central concern.

On a good many ecologically relevant matters, at present, more can perhaps be accomplished through the states than in Washington. Land use is largely controlled by state and local governments. Any state—or even any metropolitan area—could develop a demonstration plan for land use, taking account of ecology. Once such a demonstration had occurred, and once it showed, as it probably would, that general health and welfare were much improved by the ecologically based plan, then there would be a basis for going further. Perhaps such ecologically based plans could be financed now through the Model Cities programs; but that does not take further federal legislation. It takes the cooperative understanding and support of some bureaus in, for instance, the Department of Housing and Urban Development. So the place to start here is with a specific city or cities and with the Department of Housing and Urban Development. Congress is not the key here—although its appropriation power and power to disapprove make it of some importance.

There are other matters on which the executive branch already has considerable opportunity to set policy. For example, it might turn out that the adoption of some code of ecological consequences by several of the departments would be of greater importance than any legislation Congress could pass. Or, if one studied the automobile and its ecologically lethal consequences very carefully, it might turn out that more could be accomplished through the Department of Transportation and the Interstate Commerce Commission than through the Congress.

Now, the point here is not that efforts through the states or the bureaucracy are necessarily preferable. It is simply that in thinking about what to do and where to do it—how to set policy on ecology— it should never be *assumed* without study that Congress is the place to start.

It is also important to determine what a particular individual or group in its own specific, personal situation can best accomplish. People located at a state capital should give some weight to the fact that they are there and not in Washington; it is usually easier for them to deal with state officials than with Congressmen. People in some occupations are more or less debarred from formal lobbying; by tradition, such lobbying tends to mean trying to influence Congress. Trying to exert equally great influence on the executive branch is not regarded somehow as quite as reprehensible—it may not be as public, for one thing.

III

But Suppose that Congress Is Indeed the Target?   However, it may turn out that Congress is indeed the prime target for some groups concerned with environmental defense. They might, for instance, decide that a federal constitutional amendment, guaranteeing the unalterable right of people in soil and air, is desirable, and that such an amendment should be first passed by the Congress (rather than through alternative methods of amending the Constitution). Or,

more probably, they might decide that the two big issues are (*a*)
air pollution and (*b*) deforestation and stripping the land, and that
these matters can be best controlled through federal legislation and
appropriations.

What follows? *First* of all, of course, there have to be practical,
enforceable, acceptable legislative proposals—proposals that can in
fact be effectuated, and which will not permit so much individual
evasion as to become ridiculous. Some proposals that one can think
of as desirable for preventing destruction of the environment might
be widely evaded by individual farmers and householders. The situation, in fact, might be somewhat similar to civil rights accommodation legislation, where it was well to start with laws affecting builders
and developers big enough to be controllable. *Second,* and equally
important, there must be proposals that members of Congress themselves regard as enforceable and effective. Members of Congress do
not like to appear silly, so proposals would have to be worked out
and discussed with some of them. *Third,* the proposals must be
widely acceptable to a range of interests in the ecology and conservation field.

On this third point, many members of Congress have learned
through bitter experience that one recurrent difficulty confronts them
when they try to legislate about a problem on which a lot of people
feel strongly. Each group interested in the problem has its own priority; what is desirable or acceptable to one group is anathema to another. I am writing this precisely when, according to newspaper
reports, such differences of view are leading to a knock-down, drag-
out fight within the Sierra Club, hitherto perhaps the most effective
organization in the conservation field. One of the issues, to an outsider, seems to be: Should the club concentrate on preserving the
wilderness within California and North America especially, or should
it broaden its scope to the whole problem of human ecology, as discussed, for example, in Robert and Lena Rienow's book *Moment in
the Sun?* The kind of legislation that is particularly important for
preserving the U.S. wilderness is not identical with priorities for
ecology in general. Then too, some people may be more concerned
with beauty (keeping junk off the highways), while others will care
more about health (regulating air pollution).[6] Since you cannot do
everything all at once, there must be choices on these matters.

[6]Although I admired, in a way, Mrs. Johnson's concern with beauty, it seems to me, as one
who thinks ecology is a significant problem, a tragedy that she focused on what were really
cosmetic matters, rather than on basic problems like air pollution.

So, to get reasonable legislation, acceptable legislation, there must be some kind of consensus among the supporters of a cause. Such a consensus may be hammered out in a congressional committee; but Congressmen are more apt to be receptive to a consensus already arrived at. And sometimes they even insist that the various advocates of a cause agree among themselves; for Congressmen do not like to be caught in the position of saying, "Yes, I tried to solve a problem," and then be attacked by some of the very people most concerned about the problem.

What About the Structure of Congress? The Appropriations Committees: People interested in ecology will need to know what committees of the Congress are likely to consider the things they care about. There is one great and obvious difference between their situation and that of advocates or opponents of reciprocal trade. The cost of administering reciprocal trade programs or "Buy American" acts is not, at most, very great. But the cost of preserving the environment is, in dollars and cents, very heavy.

So the Appropriations Committees, especially the relevant subcommittees of the House Appropriations Committee, will be of major importance. Statutes may be enacted for air-pollution-control grants or for purifying dirty rivers or for establishing national parks; but unless the Appropriations Committees approve the money for such purposes, little will happen. In general, Appropriations Committee members, as Fenno[7] points out, are not easy to convince on matters that appear to them aesthetic, rather than central. They believe other committees give in too much too often to social or personal interests.

One of the first things for any advocate of environmental defense to know would be: What House Appropriations subcommittees handle matters in which they are most interested? In general, these subcommittees decide, and the full committee and the House accept their decisions. It would be probable that some matters of interest to defenders of the environment would go to one House subcommittee, some to another. So it would be important to know which subcommittee would take which budget—for example, one subcommittee may consider matters of health (air-pollution control, for instance) and another public works (water-pollution control, or dams). Of course, over the years, the subcommittee assignments and structures

[7]Richard F. Fenno, *The Power of the Purse: Appropriations Politics in Congress* (Boston: Little, Brown, 1966).

may change, so any account as of some specific date might be out of date fairly soon. But the nature of the Congress and of the appropriations process is such that it is almost certain that for some years the subcommittee procedure and process will continue.

So environmental defenders, having decided on their priorities, at least tentatively, will need to know: Who are the effective members of the subcommittee(s) with which they are concerned? What are their attitudes toward the issue in question? For instance, the late Congressman John E. Fogarty (Democrat, Rhode Island) was very much concerned with health and such diseases as cancer; had any air-pollution measures gone, as conceivably they might have, to the subcommittee of which he was chairman, it would have been important to get people with this sort of interest to talk with him and perhaps to testify before his subcommittee.

One would want to know of committee members: Who in their district do they pay attention to? Are there interests in their district to which they are responsive which might oppose appropriations for air pollution? For example, there may still be some remnants of opposition by some public utilities to air-pollution measures. Who in their district, preferably, or in organizations in which they are active, would impress them and is favorable to what is desired? Members of the Appropriations Committee tend to be responsive to a dollars-and-cents approach and not much interested in vaguer, more general issues. So they would probably be more responsive to engineers than to, say, members of an organization advocating beautification.

There is, however, often a sharp difference between the approaches to be made to the Senate Committee on Appropriations and the House subcommittees on appropriations—the difference between these committees in the House and the Senate is probably greater[8] than the difference between most other pairs of House and Senate committees. For the Senate committee, almost formally, acts as a court of appeal from House cuts. The Senate, the joke goes, is the "upper" chamber because it raises appropriations over what the House has allocated. House subcommittee members usually sit only on House Appropriations, whereas Senate committee members sit on a subject-matter committee or committees also. And whereas there has been some tendency, especially on the Republican side, to appoint House subcommittee members who have no involvement in a subject-matter issue (who just want to save money, or to get the

---

[8] *Ibid.*

taxpayer his money's worth), on the Senate side it seems that members of relevant subject-matter committees may be listened to a bit more than other members of the Senate committee.

For these reasons, it is likely that the supporters of ecological programs will get a better hearing from the Senate than from the House Appropriations Committee. So it will be particularly important for them to establish contacts on that committee.

Why Start with the Appropriations Committees? To repeat for the purpose of emphasis: Although some programs do not involve any substantial amount of *new* appropriations, in fact, if the legislation of the last several years is to be made effective in regard to ecological matters, there will probably need to be substantial new appropriations. In the field of air pollution, for instance, considerable sums of money may have to be appropriated for research in pollution, controlling automobile exhaust, grants to the states, financing of enforcement, and so on. Unless such appropriations are made, it may be rather futile to go ahead and try to enact further legislation. So that, right now, the most important congressional committee for advocates of a livable environment is Appropriations. This was not necessarily true a few years ago; it is not true so far as long-run aspects of protecting the environment go; but it is the immediate legislative situation.

Of Course, It Is Hard to Get Appropriations Committees to Appropriate More Money than the Executive Branch Wants; It Has Been Done, but It Is Desirable to Be Sure the Executive Branch Asks for Enough. In general, the House Appropriations Committee regards itself as protecting the taxpayer against excessive requests from the executive branch. In view of the obvious fact that many departments do in fact ask for large sums, which do not seem to most outsiders to be exactly necessary, this attitude of House Appropriations is quite understandable (and indeed desirable). However, the easiest way to try to keep down waste is to scrutinize very cautiously *new* proposals, *new* programs, *new* personnel authorizations; established patterns of waste are harder to deal with. So programs like those for environmental defense at present are handicapped.

Accordingly, it is necessary that the administrators of such programs—or someone on their behalf—be prepared to present the case for greater funding very vigorously. Frequently, when the new program goes through departmental analysis, it is cut some, and then when it goes through the Budget Bureau itself it can be cut more, before it ever gets to House Appropriations. This arises partly out of the practical, institutional fact that it is a lot easier to refuse funds for new job slots than to cut out jobs that are already filled by real people. It is also due to the fact that a senior budget officer in a department is apt to know and be familiar with the established programs, whereas he has had less chance to know the new ones and feels less comfortable with them.

So in fact—and especially when the case for funding for new programs is argued by somebody at the bureau or departmental level who does not know much about it—House Appropriations does not really get a very good presentation of the case for funds for new programs such as those we are discussing. (If the case for such funds is presented by the people who are actually managing the new program, they may be enthusiastic, and sound so to the men on House Appropriations, which does not help—or they may simply be unfamiliar with the established ways of talking over matters with that committee.) It could be, at times, very important to have outside supporters, without a personal ax to grind, prepared to demonstrate the need for adequate funding to House and Senate Appropriations. It could be crucial to have such outside support if the Budget Bureau has, as it allegedly tries to do, effectively prevented the heads of the new program from asking for funds they really need and can use. It could also be crucial if the department in which the new program is housed has refused to go to bat for it with the Budget Bureau or House Appropriations. (Even a losing case along this line in any given year may be helpful, because the Appropriations Committees may be softened up a bit for the next year; and if they look at all sympathetic, maybe the department or the Budget Bureau will risk asking for somewhat more next year.)

It is not enough to argue the cause as such to House Appropriations. Enthusiasm by itself will not cut much ice. One must be prepared to show that the requested *amount* is prudent *for the purpose*. The witness must have "done his homework," in a favorite congressional phrase, on the money angle, or he is wasting time. The best way—and sometimes the only way—to do homework is to consult with the bureau or agency early in the budgetary process. This means, however, a serious effort.

IV

Can the Citizen Do It? Yes,[9] occasionally. For our purposes here —showing the amount of influence citizens can have and the degree to which they are semisovereign and to which this sovereignty is limited but exists—it is worth going ahead with consideration of the times and circumstances when the citizen might have such influence.

Of course, efforts of the sort just described demand a good deal of continuing attention. The person who darts in and darts out is of no use here. It is much easier for the professional—the· professional lobbyist or Washington representative—to deal with such matters than it is for the outsider or amateur.

But if he confines himself to one or two areas, a person who is the master of his own time—a university researcher, perhaps a college teacher, a well-to-do housewife, an attorney, a businessman, a minister, even a mature-appearing graduate student—can have a greater impact than a professional lobbyist; because the professional lobbyist has, inevitably and necessarily, to pull his punches or overlook very important matters, for two reasons: (*a*) Like the Congressman, he has a great many matters to be concerned with. He is likely to have to confront the same House subcommittee on both industrial air pollution and control of air pollution by automobiles (and there may be different fundings involved—the items will almost surely be separate in the budget). So he has to calculate: Can he press on both these issues and on several others like them? Which ones must he go easy on? Of course, he can push on everything—but then the House subcommittee is likely to discount a good deal of what he says as cranky, unless he has established a very unusual relationship of trust with it. (*b*) The second handicap the professional lobbyist faces is that he has his own constituents—usually a number of them. He thus must spend a great deal of his time playing to the grandstand. He will not, for instance, be able to concentrate on any really vital aspect of appropriations because his constituency will be more impressed by testimony on some hopeless legislative proposal—or because to keep in contact with his constituency, just when he should be following up

---

[9] It is true, of course, that a really "ordinary" citizen cannot. A person must have unusual resources of determination and intelligence or of time or possibly of money to accomplish anything along these lines. But among readers of a book like this, a good many could accomplish the sort of thing described here.

some appropriations matter, he has to spend a month winning friends and raising money by giving speeches in the hinterland.

So a citizen who becomes semiprofessional as to knowledge, but retains his amateur status otherwise, may be more effective—provided he has friends in the House or Senate or on their staffs, or knows lobbyists who will advise him about the scheduling of hearings, and is willing to spend a certain amount of money on phone calls and trips to Washington. Such a person would have to endure some frustration waiting around to be heard—Congressional schedules change quite abruptly when there is a momentary crisis—and he would have to resolve to talk and advise only about that issue which he has studied, *nothing else,* or he will get a reputation as a do-gooder crank.

Under these circumstances, an amateur citizen could perhaps affect, for instance, a House subcommittee on appropriations a good deal. Here one faces the real difficulty of participation in American politics; all this is perfectly possible at the national level for those with some resources and very unusual qualities of patience and skill. But few people have the dedication and self-discipline that are required. So in fact many such decisions are made without outside participation.

Does It Happen? Is This a Speculative Discussion or a Realistic One? I do not know of any citizen who has deliberately tried to develop continuing influence of this type in the ecological appropriations area. There have been a few people who have cultivated such influence, successfully and effectively, in some subject-matter areas with subject-matter committees. There is no reason that I know of why the same sort of thing could not be done in the appropriations field—except that the appropriations subcommittees of the House are tougher to deal with than many of the subject-matter committees.

But the mere fact that it has not been done is irrelevant to the major concerns here. First, any such discussion as this should focus upon the best possible situation and show how it could be developed; qualifications can be introduced later. In a sense, there is a parallel with economic man in economic theory; few businessmen in fact operate like pure economic men, but the better they understand how pure economic men would behave, the more rationally they can analyze some of their problems.

Second, the more we see what might be done, the more likely that somebody will invent a way actually to do it. Political science should be what it very rarely is—an effort to suggest ways of inventing procedures not yet developed, as well as description and generalization about existent processes. The more we deal with the best possible hypothetical cases *that actually could be put into effect,* the more likely such invention is.[10]

Third, and for the immediate present, practically the most important point: The more aware citizens are of the kind of thing that ought to be done, the wiser the support they can give their associations and lobbyists. As pointed out above, many lobbyists are much less effective than they might be because of tangential demands by their clients and constituents. Indeed, many associations do not have adequate lobbying because their members do not understand what kind of lobbying would be effective.[11] If people who are or might become interested in a cause understand the situation, there is a better chance of their letting their lobbyists do a good job; and a much better prospect of their finding and hiring the kind of lobbyists who will do a competent job.

V

Subject-Matter Committees: Because of its particular relevance to problems of ecology right now, I started out this chapter with problems of appropriations. But, of course, there will be many *legislative* issues of great moment to advocates of a better environment. Clean-air legislation will have to be modified; so will water-quality legislation. It may be that at some time in the future, those concerned about consumer protection will join hands with ecologists in insisting on numerous changes in regard to food production, foodstuffs, etc. Housing and land use will become national issues, rather than local ones, and so forth.

What can supporters of ecological balance do to promote their cause?

---

[10]See Harold D. Lasswell, *The Future of Political Science* (New York: Atherton, 1963), for a discussion of systematic inventiveness in political studies; see also Lewis A. Dexter, "Sociology of Innovating Leadership," in *Studies in Leadership: Leadership and Democratic Action,* ed. Alvin Ward Gouldner (New York: Harper, 1950).

[11]See my *How Organizations Are Represented in Washington* (Indianapolis: Bobbs-Merrill, 1969).

The majority of the committees of the Congress might be concerned with one or another of these matters. The *Agriculture* Committee, for instance, is obviously involved in matters of soil conservation, soil wastage, intensive farming versus balanced use of
the land, etc. *Armed Services* constantly touches on atmospheric
matters. *Banking and Currency* is concerned with housing; it is
likely that measures to discourage building on flood plains, for
example, could best be considered by that committee. *Education
and Labor* might initiate highly pertinent legislation; education,
after all, is pertinent to planning for ecological balance, and among
the conditions of labor are those that affect contamination of the
atmosphere. *Foreign Affairs* might get involved in terms of response
to the U.N. project (see footnote 4 above) for a worldwide concern with atmospheric degradation. *Interior* may be concerned with
national parks and minerals. *Interstate Commerce* handles air pollution. *Judiciary* is involved in constitutional issues and immigration. *Merchant Marine and Fisheries* would probably consider
matters relating to destruction of fishing grounds or care in ship-
building. *Public Works* handles waterways and water pollution.
Science and Astronautics cuts across every issue of technology. *Ways
and Means* handles taxes, and tax policy can become vital in any
of these areas; for instance, in 1966 Ways and Means approved
what amounted to a special tax concession to manufacturers who
spent money on air-pollution-control devices. I have listed here
major subject-matter committees of the House; Senate committees
differ somewhat in jurisdiction and title, but the point—that almost
any one of the subject-matter committees might get involved in
ecological issues—applies equally to them.

The supporters of ecological programs, having decided what their
priorities are, will then have to find out what committees *and subcommittees* of the Congress are likely to handle the issues to which
they attach greatest importance. But, vice versa, one factor in deciding which issue to give first priority and how to present it will
be what committees and subcommittees of the Congress are likely to
consider it. Some committees are busier than others; some committees are more sympathetic than others. Among several almost
equally important matters, the choice might be given to the issue
most likely to go to a sympathetic committee, one not currently
burdened with some emergency legislation. More important even
than general sympathy from a committee is a specific member of
the relevant committee who will really himself personally attach

priority to an issue. There are, always, many worthy causes. Many Senators and Congressmen will express sympathy with them. But such sympathy is a long way from the kind of hard, pushing work that turns an idea into a statute. Many Congressmen introduce bills; far fewer are those who can turn bills into laws on the statute books.

It is desirable to have both a Senator and a Congressman with push. Lacking such a Senator or Congressman, perhaps one can find a Senator who is generally sympathetic and has a legislative assistant who will provide the push. It has happened that a good deal of the steam behind certain measures has come from the legislative assistant, rather than from the Senator himself.

In any discussion or dealings on these matters, it is well to be clear at all times: Is a statute really wanted? Or is a bill enough? A bill may help get an investigation, which is important. Sometimes it helps get publicity. But the temptation for members of Congress and lobbyists alike is to do something that gets publicity rather than to concentrate on the harder work that may get a statute, when, if the purpose is to be accomplished, a statute is needed. After all, Senators, Congressmen, and lobbyists, from a selfish standpoint, often benefit as much in electoral terms by publicity as by a statute; few of their constituents will know that they took the easy way out.

If it is just a matter of a bill, a senatorial or congressional staff will not worry too much about committee reference, whether a particular Senator or Congressman is the right person to introduce the measure, etc. But if a member of Congress really wants a statute, then such issues become vital. It is, for instance, much more likely that a bill will go through if it has on it the name of a member of the sponsoring committee. And if the matter is to be referred to a subcommittee, it is desirable, of course, to have a stalwart supporter on the subcommittee. All these matters require much information about individual members of the Congress.

VI

Investigations: Citizens have done more, probably, to stimulate committee investigations and thus indirectly to influence legislation and appropriations than they have in directly influencing appropriations and legislation. This is probably because investigations often focus on the exposure of an admitted or seeming evil. A citizen with some special contacts or knowledge is likely to know more about some such evil than most members of the House or Senate. Consequently, the citizen can sometimes bring to the Congressman or Senator ideas and information about something to be exposed into which the latter can inquire. Although committee chairmen or a committee majority often can quash an investigation (or for that matter the House or Senate as a body or through appropriate instrumentalities can deny adequate funds to an investigative group), it is easier to get a rewarding investigation under way than to get a significant statute enacted—perhaps because fewer interests have to be reconciled or conciliated in initiating an investigation than in getting a workable statute enacted.

And, of course, an investigation, by exposing a problem and dramatizing it—hunger, for example, or dirty meat—can lead to appropriations or legislation. But some investigations, such as the Kefauver investigation of organized crime in 1950–51, although they have received a great deal of publicity, do not seem to have led to much significant legislation and appropriations. In the organized crime case, two reasons may be suggested: (a) Given the state of influential American public opinion as it was then, it would have been impossible to get such legislation enacted and enforced —too many agencies and organizations would not care for the kind of action necessary—and/or (b) the Kefauver investigation was conducted in such a way as to influence members of Congress *negatively:* the investigation often showed up connections between local party politicians and organized crime. In big cities, local party politicians are usually Democrats. At that time, TV was mostly a big-city affair, so the Kefauver hearings were held in big cities. The investigations were timed and staged in such a way that a number of Democratic members of Congress, not themselves in any way connected with organized crime, felt that they had to conduct harder reelection fights because of them; for in the public mind, they thought, the stigma attached to the local Democratic organization that backed them hurt their chances of reelection. (This circumstance also explains why Kefauver would always have found it extremely difficult to get the Presidential nomination.)

The experience of this Kefauver investigation and of other investigations suggests two requirements for effective publicizing investigations: (1) Somebody should have a fairly clear idea of the kind of remedy desired. For instance, the McGovern investigation of hunger is directed toward appropriate and clear remedies; the Kefauver investigation of crime was not so directed. (2) The investigation should naturally be conducted in such a way as to please as many and displease as few Congressmen as possible.

Information-Seeking Investigations: Select and Special Committees: The preceding section refers essentially to investigations of the sort that seek publicity. However, the majority of congressional investigations do not get onto the front pages, and some of them may never get into the press at all. They are genuinely *investigations*, trying to find out something of relevance to the job of the legislator. In regard to these, too, the interested citizen can be of some importance. He may, occasionally, interest a serious member of Congress in studying some issue that has not been adequately documented or some area where it would be worth putting information together. Quite aside from their value to legislators, scholars know that many congressional investigations gather enormous and valuable amounts of data. In the ecological field, investigations might well be undertaken, not necessarily to attract vast amounts of national publicity, but to help provide information and ammunition for special groups. For instance, a congressional committee might be persuaded to investigate building in areas susceptible to flooding: How could it be discouraged? What are the circumstances? Perhaps such an investigation might lead to valuable publicity—there probably are lots of readers who wish they did not live on flood plains— but even if it did not, it could nevertheless get together in convenient form viewpoints, complaints, experiences, and scientific information on flood-plain building. Or a congressional investigation of the problems of noise in our society might similarly put together a great deal of information that is not now available in any one place, and which is the subject only of speculation.

Clearly, a citizen or scholar who knows something about such issues and is able to describe how they could be handled might present the notion of such investigations to Congressmen and perhaps get one or another of them interested in carrying them out. In this way, again, a citizen can have a certain amount of influence.

There are and have been special committees of the Congress which continuously study specific problems. The Joint Economic Committee is one of the better known examples. These committees generally do not have formal legislative responsibility but represent various legislative committees or congressional groups in order to get unified treatment and analysis of some set of problems.

Senator Edmund Muskie suggested, in the winter of 1969, the establishment of a special committee to be concerned with the impact of technology on society—that is, with the ecological problems we have been discussing. Were such a committee to be set up, it would give the citizen who is an amateur a considerable advantage he does not now have; he would at least know with what staff to start inquiries about how to present a proposal! From this standpoint, the special-committee idea has great advantages. The fact that it has these advantages serves to illustrate one of the reasons why, in general, Congressmen are free. The sheer difficulty in mastering procedure and techniques means that few outsiders have the resources to influence Congress on legislative matters against its collective will. If a Special or Joint Committee on Technology and the Environment is set up, it will be because Congress as a whole is willing, among other things, to make it a bit easier for people who have something to say about ecology to be heard. This may not be the main reason for setting up such a committee; perhaps some people will support it because Senator Muskie asked for it and they would like to strengthen his Presidential bid in 1972 (either because they genuinely favor him, or because they think strengthening him is a good way to weaken Senator Kennedy's potential Presidential drive). But if there is any clear feeling in Congress that members do not want to hear from the public on ecological issues, then no such special committee will be set up. Or, if it were set up, it would be in a completely innocuous way. Since Congress, I judge, is not really resistant to hearing about such matters, a committee may be established such as Senator Muskie asks for—although there are real jurisdictional obstacles to be overcome.

CHAPTER FOUR

More on Elections, Constituencies, and Pressures:

HOW CONGRESSMEN ARE INFLUENCED ON ISSUES BY CITIZENS

I

The discussion of ecology as an issue in congressional politics has differed so far from the preceding discussion of reciprocal trade in Congress. The reciprocal trade chapter considered the impact of elections rather extensively, whereas there has not been up to this point any serious consideration of the way in which elections might affect legislation and policy on ecology.

There are several reasons for postponing such consideration.

First, I myself personally know far less about how individual Congressmen stand on ecological matters today than I knew about how individual Congressmen stood on reciprocal trade in 1955. There is an important difference, relevant generally as an example, in my relationship to the two situations. In 1955, I had spent the preceding two years studying reciprocal trade legislation and the Congress. I have not made any such detailed study of Congressmen in relation to ecological issues. But this illustrates a significant point in considering how elections do in fact influence congressional decision-making. My situation in 1955 was rare, almost unique. Not only had I been studying the situation for two years, but I did not have obligations of the sort that the professional lobbyist or even the Washington newspaperman has, obligations that make it necessary to refrain from criticizing embarrassingly or appearing to threaten some incumbents. Even so, it is obvious that, like professional lobbyists, I was unable to publish what I knew, until after it had ceased to have any practical value for interested citizens!

Although there is a great deal of journalistic reporting on Congress—some of it of extremely high quality, notably the weekly reports and Almanac of the *Congressional Quarterly*—such journalistic reporting does not generally tell the interested citizen which Congressmen are ineffective, which Congressmen are "going through the motions" but not really trying to accomplish anything legislatively, which Congressmen are passionately committed, or even which undramatic, hard-working Congressmen are particularly effective with their colleagues. Where and how, for example, could an interested citizen learn which members of the House subcommittees on appropriations have what effects on ecological matters? I have heard, for instance, several constituents (professional men) of former Representative Errett P. Scrivner of Kansas City, Kansas, speak of him rather scathingly as "a man who never gets anything done." Now, in fact, Representative Scrivner was, so far as I could infer, a hard-working and serious member of the vital House subcommittee concerned with defense appropriations. There might be differences of view about how to evaluate what he accomplished; but it is likely that as a member of that subcommittee, he exerted a definite effect. However, because much of what that subcommittee does is unglamorous, and because he added to this unglamorousness by his insistence on discretion and caution, and because, in general, newspaper reports focus on chairmen or on some particularly "newsworthy" figure, even his own constituents were almost totally unaware of his place in the congressional system.

This is not particularly to criticize or blame journalists; men like Scrivner or former Representative R. Walter Riehlman (Republican, New York), who was senior Republican and for a time chairman of the Military Operations Subcommittee of Government Operations, do not make particularly good copy. If stories about them were filed, they probably would not be picked up by many newspapers or radio stations. And the other way around: journalists who really know who is effective and who is ineffective, who is getting things done and who is not, are debarred—just as I was in 1955—from publishing what they know. They have, in essence, to protect their relationships with their sources or potential sources. Congress, after all, is a set of working groups; and men in a working group develop affection and concern for each other, to some extent independent of competence. Some of the effective Congressmen, that is, are quite fond of some of the ineffective ones, and they will resent any newsman who attempts to portray these latter as ineffective. And, for that matter, although effective ones are usually better news sources, some of the ineffective ones are quite good observers or make good copy in some other way—so they cannot be criticized by newspapermen who want to preserve their goodwill.

So who now is going to issue a document saying that such-and-such Congressmen are committed to policies that in fact will be harmful to ecological balance? No one to speak of (it should be noted) is likely to be opposed, *in principle*, to cleaning up the air and the water and making the quality of the environment better. But some Congressmen will be sympathetic with businesses that plead for all sorts of exemptions, and will support delaying tactics, and others will not. Some of those who support delaying tactics will, however, only be "going through the motions" to win friends and influence votes, whereas others will really be, in all likelihood, making a serious effort. Can any journalist or lobbyist report distinctions of this sort? Is it fair to the man who is just going through the motions to report what he does? Will he not be entitled to resent it if he is identified as a man who is really merely pretending?[1]

There are other practical reasons why any listing of enemies, effective or ineffective, of environmental defense would be risky for the lister. In the first place, as someone said, nothing is so powerful as an idea whose time has come. Put in less magniloquent form, it does seem as though environmental defense and ecological balance may become big issues to a great many people in the next few years; that Congressmen, like others, will be influenced by the changing climate of opinion and awareness of deterioration in the

---

[1]That is to say: Should John Sparkman's purely symbolic support of some southern racist views have been publicized prior to 1952, when (because he ran for Vice-President) it became somewhat public knowledge? Should a Congressman who makes a big play of supporting some lumbering interest or some oil firm that wants to protect its right to destroy the ecological balance be exposed if in fact he is just going through the motions? Maybe this will hurt his chances of reelection; maybe it will alert the lumber or oil interests really to try to put the screws on him, and maybe they will succeed (though often Congressmen are cleverer at wiggling out of undesired demands harmlessly than businessmen are in making them).

environment; and that a good many members of the Congress who are now indifferent to environmental defense will change their minds. Similar changes have, of course, happened before: Congressmen who in 1938 were hostile to involvement in resisting nazism had changed by 1940; Congressmen who in 1955 were lukewarm or indifferent about civil rights had shifted by 1960 and still more by 1965; Congressmen who in 1906 were hostile or would have been hostile to government regulation of consumer products were influenced by Upton Sinclair's novel *The Jungle,* and all the publicity surrounding it, and changed their minds on aspects of this matter.

Second, it is, practically speaking, difficult to make any target list of friends and enemies in the Congress, because, as has already been pointed out, so many committees are concerned with part of the ecological situation. Although other committees were surely concerned, some of them vitally concerned, with foreign economic policy in 1955, I assumed at that time that Ways and Means and Finance were the key committees. The assumption was probably correct, although now, on further reflection, I would want to reexamine it. But there is not any key committee on ecology or environmental defense as a whole. Possibly, taking everything into account, the Appropriations Committees are in a better position to exert favorable influence than any other pair of committees— but this is a debatable point; if it is true, in the long run they are only a bit more influential than several other committees. And it is far harder, in the nature of the case, to find out what kind of influence is exerted by whom in appropriations hearings and decisions than in many legislative committees. But, going beyond this, should one choose a committee concerned with air pollution as the key committee? Or one concerned with oceanography, which might help prevent ravaging the sea as the land already has been ravaged? Or . . . or . . . or . . .

About all that I can see that can be done through elections in influencing ecological matters, at best, would be the following:

1. If some member of the Congress who really has played an important part in favor of ecological matters is threatened with defeat, then, of course, supporters of ecology should help him. In most cases—and perhaps I have not emphasized this enough hitherto —this may mean raising money more than any other one thing. For unless they live in his state or district, or unless they have some qualifications as campaign professionals and are quite mobile, most advocates of environmental defense may not be able to do too much

for him personally in a campaign. But nowadays, in the age of television, most candidates need money.

Of course, willingness to support a candidate because of his stand on ecology may involve hard choices. But it is where hard choices have been made that other politicians see that an issue has political mileage, that it is worth getting tied up with and stressing. Politicians, perhaps even more than other people, like to be praised; but they have very mixed feelings when somebody praises them for their stand on such an issue as ecology, but contributes to or votes for their opponents. But if a group of *conservative* Republicans should raise money for Senator Edmund Muskie of Maine in 1970, because he has been so involved in matters of air and water pollution and the impact of technology on society, then other politicians would be impressed. Now, of course, for conservative Republicans, such an effort might be hard, for Senator Muskie, in addition to his concern with the effects of technology, is also one of the leading liberal Democratic possibilities for President in 1972.

At the present time it is hard to think of cases from an internal legislative standpoint where an incumbent member of the Congress will be so demonstrably hostile to environmental defense that his removal from the Congress would be something on which defenders of the environment should focus. For one thing, the currently flexible and overlapping character of legislation in this field makes something possible which is more difficult in regard to reciprocal trade. Measures in the environmental defense field can, as of now, perhaps be reformulated and replanned, so that they go to some friendly committee, even if the initial formulation would send them to an unfriendly one. Let us assume, for instance, purely for the sake of illustration, that the committee that would deal with *some* air-pollution measures might be unfriendly or lukewarm; perhaps the measures might be replanned so that they would go to Labor in the Senate, which is concerned with some health matters. But reciprocal trade legislation is quite certain to go to the Ways and Means and Finance Committees, unless there is a real revolution in congressional committee structure or those committees themselves decide they are overburdened.

2. If some campaign strategy can be planned in which one candidate—incumbent or not—is able to maneuver himself to support environmental defense, and to place his opponent on the other side, of course support in and outside the constituency would be desirable. Also in the case of some candidates who have held state or

local office, it might be possible to organize the campaign against them on environmental defense issues—if they have let forests be destroyed, or failed to exercise due diligence in regard to air and water pollution. Or, of course again, if a candidate makes some aspect of environmental defense a main issue and gets *surprising* support, that will help prove to other politicians that it is an issue with mileage. The best example I can conceive of would be this: In the 1968 senatorial campaign in New York State, James Buckley, the third-party Conservative candidate for the Senate, made seemingly sensible and enlightened statements about conservation and ecological defense. No similar statements were publicized (or at any rate came to my attention) from the Republican-Liberal candidate (Jacob Javits) or the Democrat (Paul O'Dwyer). Further investigation might have shown that Buckley really knew and understood these matters, and that, although Javits or O'Dwyer might provide a perfunctory endorsement, both of them cared so much more about other things that, in the Senate, they would not be of any great help to environmental defense. Suppose Buckley's superiority from this standpoint had been verified; if relatively liberal, humanitarian, somewhat New Dealish citizens of New York State had endorsed Buckley *on this basis*, it could have had an impact in several directions. As a practical matter, such citizens were free enough to support Buckley if they wished. They would not have needed to scrutinize his views on other matters closely, for his prospects of election were slight, and, in terms of liberal, humanitarian positions, both Javits and O'Dwyer were excellent prospects—and in fact Javits had the election sewed up anyway, long before Election Day. (A Senate with several score Buckleys in it might be quite inoperable; but one Buckley in a Senate might be, in terms of intellectual challenge, an asset, even from the standpoint of those who do not share his views on many issues.)

II

The examples just given probably appear unrealistic. And so they are—in one respect, but not in another.

Most conservative Republicans, no matter how wedded to the cause of conservation, are *not* going to contribute to Edmund Muskie's campaign fund in 1970. And *most* liberal, humanitarian New Yorkers, no matter how concerned about deterioration of the environment, would *not* have supported James Buckley's Conservative campaign in 1968 under any circumstances.

However, elections in the United States are usually decided by shifts of a relatively small proportion of the total population. Although few Senators or Congressmen have endured something as close as "Landslide Lyndon's" 87-vote margin in the Texas senatorial primary of 1948, many of them at some stage in their careers have been involved in campaigns where a shift of 3 percent or less would have affected the outcome. (And, too, every member of the present Senate and Congress knows about the Presidential elections of 1968 and 1960!) They therefore may pay attention to any cause or concern that seems likely to affect any substantial number of voters. That is not to say that they are going to adopt any such cause. But they are going to try to see if there is some respect in which they can, without getting into trouble otherwise, and without violating their own convictions, win the support of those who believe in this cause.

Of course, such a demonstration of strength is particularly important in cases like that of ecology, with which a good many Senators and Congressmen have a general sympathy but have been preoccupied with other matters. If James Buckley had *on the conservation issue* got extra votes or *support from quite unexpected sources,* it is quite possible that Javits, who won, would have rearranged priorities somewhat, studied some ecological issues, and tried to become identified with them, so as to prevent an ecology-oriented candidate from hurting him the next time around.

In the political situation as it is, the ability of a financially hard-pressed candidate to raise sums of money from unexpected sources may be even more impressive. For, again, it is becoming increasingly a strain on many candidates to raise adequate campaign funds. If any issue—such as ecology—helps a primary candidate running against an established incumbent raise sufficient money to give the incumbent a real challenge, it will be impressive. For primary candidates running against incumbents are often unable to raise any significant amount of money. There are, of course, incumbents who, in one way or another, have acted to resist legislation generally favored by people worried about environmental deterioration. From the standpoint under discussion now, a primary challenge to one or two of them, *provided the issue is formulated in conservationist terms,* might be very much worthwhile. This does not contradict the point made in the first section—that it is hard to see how, from an internal *legislative* standpoint, it would be worth the bother of trying to oppose any incumbent member for conservationist reasons. I am here talking about electoral impact on the legislative system.

The difficulty with such an effort is, of course, that it is hard to be sure the issue is mounted and stressed as one of conservation and ecology. An incumbent may be vulnerable on other matters, and so his difficulties may be attributed to them. As a practical matter, this tendency is the biggest argument against trying to mount issue-oriented campaigns. Sometimes they have the desired impact; Senator Eugene McCarthy's victory in the 1968 New Hampshire primary certainly did. (Although a case could have been made that much of his vote came from people who just did not like Lyndon Johnson, the victory was widely seen as a protest against the Viet Nam War.) But in some cases, the desire to be intellectually comfortable will lead people to interpret the results to conform to what they hope for. Since few Congressmen or Senators are obstinately opposed to the ecological movement, that is not a great danger in this case. But in a good many cases, some "issue," personality clash, etc., develops in the campaign which overshadows the issues announced by the candidates and their speech writers.

Money in campaigns has, from the standpoint of influencing the professional politician's reactions, one great advantage over votes. It would be relatively easy to demonstrate with considerable credibility that if out-of-state ecologists and conservationists were to give money to Senator Muskie's campaign in 1970, they would be doing so precisely because of what he has done on air pollution, water pollution, etc. But if there is a shift of 3 percent or 5 percent in the vote in some campaign or other, how do you demonstrate that ecology or conservation was the reason? Such shifts in voting are usually complex to explain and due to many factors. Logically speaking, what really happens when a candidate takes a stand on a politically unfamiliar issue and does better than is expected is this: He shows that the issue does no great harm. It takes a refined analysis to demonstrate that the issue actually was the reason for his relative success. It may be, for instance, that the fact that he sounded concerned, involved, sincere, was what was really important, and it did not matter what he sounded concerned, involved, sincere about. Now, on some issues—notably the Viet Nam War in

1966 and to a degree in 1968—this negative demonstration is all that is necessary. Once several candidates—Brooke, Hatfield, and Percy—had shown that opposition to the war was politically safe, other Senators and Congressmen (among them, of course, Robert Kennedy) who were basically opposed to the war proceeded to make an issue of it. On some aspects of the conservation-ecology issue, all that is needed is such a negative demonstration. If a candidate should campaign, for instance, on the issue of paying people for *not* having children (a negative income tax for the childless), and do well at the polls, a point would have been made. And an election campaign would be the best way to make the point, if it is indeed true that such a proposal is now politically safe. (I do not have any judgment on the matter at this time. A few years ago I would have been sure it was unsafe; now, from the standpoint of its proponents, it might be worth investigating in districts like those in Westchester, Greater Miami, and Delaware.)

Again, the point to underline is that the citizen who spends some time on an issue and who has some resources may, with reasonable luck, have an impact on the legislative process. Most of the time, however, he is only semisovereign; for *the ultimate effect of what he says or does depends upon legislators' interpretation of its meaning, weight, and significance.* For example, in the 1930s the Massachusetts League of Nations Association organized a whole series of public policy referenda, possible under Massachusetts law, in state senatorial districts. In all these referenda, supporters of the League of Nations won, usually by considerable majorities. But they had no slightest effect on the opposition of Senator David I. Walsh to the League of Nations, or on the complete lack of interest in the League by the members of the Massachusetts delegation in the House of Representatives. These legislators were quite safe in calculating—whether the voters knew the meaning of the referendum or not—that there was little likelihood that views on the League would affect their prospects of reelection in those years. Yet it would have been perfectly possible for members of Congress and the Senate to interpret such referenda as showing wide-based public support, had they been motivated to do so.

There have, of course, been issues and groups that could make very clear precisely what they wanted. But these were groups well organized around a passionately felt cause. Prohibition was certainly such a case. But the prohibition movement was organized through various Protestant churches in such a way that it was clear that people who did not shift their votes on much else, or pay much attention to politics, might change. In those occasions and circumstances where the trade-union movement in the United States has had a similar electoral effect, it was because there was an organized group of union members who very likely might shift their votes in response to advice from their leaders. And both the successes and the failures of the trade-union movement are instructive. The trade-union movement could succeed in electoral pressure when there was a simple issue, easily explicable to the rank-and-file membership, about which some of the latter felt strongly. When trade-union issues became more complex and general, it was harder for labor leaders to have electoral impact.

And prohibition and, in its earlier days especially, the trade-union movement rested upon groups whose members were in continuous daily or weekly contact. Such closeness is not characteristic of most interest groups. And, of course, still more important, in the early part of the twentieth century, when they were most effective, these groups had two other unusual characteristics. First, most of their core members did not belong to any other group with competing interests. The evangelical ministers and the really devout laymen who constituted the nucleus of the prohibition movement were not, in any way, shape, or manner, identified with the demon rum, nor were they for the most part sufficiently active on other political issues so that they had to compromise the priority they gave to prohibition and "temperance." (In this respect, the hard-core prohibitionists were more fortunate than their predecessors, the hard-core abolitionists: individual ministers and antislavery crusaders were, naturally enough, free of any connection with "the monster slavery," but most people who had any connection whatsoever with business or politics in the 1840s and 1850s were eager to preserve the federal union, and many of them had commercial or social relationships with southerners who felt themselves dependent on slavery.) Similarly, in the early part of the twentieth century, the dedicated nucleus of many of the trade unions was utterly unconcerned with anything outside the labor movement; the trade-union leadership of the 1900s would not have had to balance a whole agenda of demands against each other, as their successors of the 1970s must. Such matters as recognition, the right to strike, and the minimum wage were obviously far more important in their view than general matters of the sort about which labor now expresses itself. And in those early days, one did not find, as one does now, a substantial group of labor-union members more concerned about property taxes and income taxes than about specifically labor matters.

The dramatic and presumably effective agitation organized by a few groups, such as labor and the prohibitionists, has probably played a part in slanting the general notion of what pressure can accomplish in politics. In British history, the notable activity of the antitariff reformers under Cobden and Bright may have had similar consequences in leading people to think pressure in general will be effective. I suggest that *dramatic pressure on general issues can be effective only on a few issues at most in any one political generation.* And my guess would be that the widespread knowledge and adoption by many people of some of the techniques originally devised by the Anti-Corn Law League, the prohibitionist movement, etc. means that no group is likely to be anywhere near as effective with such pressures in the 1970s as these groups were in their time.

Analogically, it seems to me that the early pressure groups resemble some of the great innovators in military history. In general, the first two or three or four commanders to make *effective* use of a new technology or to adopt a surprise maneuver are likely to upset the enemy, and, given reasonable luck, to win. But in the history of the military art through the nineteenth century, at least, their later imitators were often less successful, because the defenses had been planned and counteraction prepared—and because, in any case, the new weapons and new movements, become familiar, were no longer so frightening. In much the same way, politicians can be and are frightened by some unfamiliar manifestation of public opinion and public demand. For instance, Father Charles Coughlin in the 1930s succeeded in getting thousands of voters to send telegrams to the Senate, urging Senators to vote against U.S. membership or participation in the iniquitous (from his standpoint) World Court. These telegrams do seem to have had an effect upon some Senators. But the subsequent lack of much electoral effect or carry-over from Father Coughlin's concern on this matter, and the shrinking of his movement within a few years, meant that this particular stunt—this way of making an impression—was harder to work the next time it was tried. Senators were vaccinated against such a telegraphic blitz. In regard to the Reciprocal Trade Extension Act of 1955, I believe I saw an example of the effects of vaccination of this type. Some southern Congressmen received literally thousands of communications, chiefly from textile workers or people living in textile towns, protesting reciprocal trade extension as a threat to the textile industry. Many of these southern Congressmen received, even at that time, very little mail from the constituency in the normal course of events. So this outpouring of mail, stimulated though it obviously was, impressed some of them, and it played a part *no doubt* in switching some Democratic votes against reciprocal trade extension in 1955. But there was no electoral carry-over from this outpouring of mail. It is an absolutely safe statement that when these Congressmen went back home, most people, including most of the people who wrote them, had no idea how they had voted on reciprocal trade extension.

Now, northern Congressmen, receiving similar amounts of mail, were less impressed, simply because they were accustomed to receiving such large amounts of mail. Senator Theodore F. Green was unaffected by the mail from Rhode Island, I would say; in Senator Thomas C. Hennings' office, which received enormous quantities of mail against reciprocal trade extension, as we saw earlier, the Senator's legislative assistant and his administrative assistant (and almost certainly the Senator himself) were hardly aware of it. Of course, people who get mail that supports their view tend to cite it, if they know about it, but the mail does not really have a dominant influence in such cases.

It was also my impression that, allowing for region and type of district, younger Congressmen were more impressed by the volume of mail than older ones. Older ones had had more experience with demands that had no carry-over or follow-up, the difference is much like that between an inexperienced teacher or social worker who takes a hard-luck story at face value and an experienced one who discounts it. And, perhaps more important, older ones were much busier; under the congressional seniority system, congressional mail is one of the few things a Congressman can handle by himself, and so some young Congressmen, disappointed that they initially amount to nothing in Congress as compared with their hopes, sometimes pay a lot of attention to it. Older ones have other things to do. But I did see another example of vaccination here: A Congressman received a good deal of mail in his first term on protecting a firm in his district against competing toys from Japan. He made an effort to go part way to meet these demands, rather hesitantly. He was somewhat annoyed later on, when he visited the toy plant and talked with the leadership of its local, to find that nobody seemed to have any idea how he had voted. But the national leadership of the

AFL-CIO (and also the League of Women Voters) reported his vote on reciprocal trade, which he had cast to please these toy workers, as a *wrong* vote when they tabulated votes in 1956 for the session.

This sort of experience is more or less typical; that is, Congressmen and Senators learn that a good deal of "pressure" is synthetic, in the sense that it has no follow-up. Since, once in a while, pressure may have a genuine follow-up, some new, credible form of making demands may have same effect—until once again it is shown that it has little follow-up; or that, even if acceding to the demands wins some support *here*, it loses some support *there*. Suppose the toy workers' local had really publicized the Congressman's vote on reciprocal trade and been able to get the membership positively excited about it—how many votes could he actually have gained? For ethnic, personal, and traditional reasons, in the local and in the district, he would have been likely to do well with the toy workers' local anyway, unless faced by an exceptional opponent. On the other hand, the League of Women Voters contained some independent voters who might actually switch sides on the reciprocal trade issue. This is to say that pressure very often begets counterpressure; and that Congressmen and Senators, in thinking about pressure, can and rationally should think about the possibility or probability of counterpressure. And once they start doing this, then they may decide that, under all the circumstances, since they cannot judge which is stronger, pressure or potential counterpressure, they might as well vote on some ground other than public demands, such as the public interest.

III

Demands can be most effectively made and most readily responded to when they are limited in character—that is, marginal to the way politics and government is carried out—and unlikely to provoke any substantial amount of counterpressure. Under the pre-1934 system of making tariff schedules, it was often possible for demands for the protection of some industry or other to be effective, because (a) the basic decision had been made to protect American industry against low-cost foreign competition and (*b*) most buyers would not be aware of the increased costs due to tariff duties on most goods. It was my experience, in talking with executives and buyers for various firms in 1954, that none of them ever knew whether they had to pay more for supplies because of duties on foreign goods. They purchased supplies and raw materials from wholesalers, and the wholesalers did not bother to separate out the cost of the duty. (There are, certainly, exceptions to this—where the tariff duty is a very high proportion of the total cost, or where duties in some way lead to or can be blamed for a sharp sudden increase in price.)

Schattschneider, in his *Politics, Pressures, and the Tariff*, which describes the great Smoot-Hawley tariff and schedule construction, suggests how demands were effective in that situation. If, for example, the cherry producers in 1955 had been operating under the old tariff system, no doubt they would have been warmly received by House and Senate committees. For what imbiber of a Manhattan or Tom Collins would have known or cared that a tariff duty raised slightly the cost of the cherry in the glass, and forced the bar owner to omit the second goody from the Shirley Temple? But when the Reciprocal Trade Act was passed, early in the F. D. Roosevelt administration, *the system changed.* Congressional action to protect a particular industry became thereupon somewhat of a threat to the reciprocal trade system, and whereas in 1929 the odds were in favor of the demander, in 1955 they were against him. So, although the impressive campaign from the cherry industry did get the Morse amendment to the Senate version of the Reciprocal Trade Act accepted on the Senate floor, that amendment was later dropped in conference—and the industry did not get the protection it sought.

Even had the old system continued, a demand that evoked a counterpressure would have been considered more carefully. For example, when any substantial number of people are worried about the price of foods or clothing, it is somewhat dangerous to raise duties on widely used foods or clothes. If babies' diapers, say, were imported from some low-wage country in large quantity, and their price was raised or might have been raised because of a tariff change, counterpressures might have been organized.

It should be emphasized, therefore, that there is no unchanging, objective standard that shows whether a demand is limited in effect or not. And there is certainly no certainty as to whether a demand will evoke a counterpressure. A few years ago, the demands from various industrial interests for lumbering concessions in national parks might not have provoked resistance; now, in line with the fight about the redwoods and the general concern with conservation, these demands are interpreted as having general consequences and evoke counterpressures. It may well have seemed to the Armed Services Committees of the House and the Senate a year or two ago that the ABM program, or at any rate the installation of ABMs in Greater Boston and other metropolitan areas, would pass without any serious reaction; but anyone who read the newspapers in January or February 1969 found reports of strong counterpressures. This is to say that the arenas of political conflict shift, and the nature and direction of the shifting is often extremely difficult to predict.

The Congressman or Senator, eager to make friends and influence voters, would like to be able to discover unsatisfied demands that he could satisfy, or at any rate appear to help to satisfy, in such a way as to associate him with the satisfaction in a long-remembered way. Preferably, the makers of such demands should include people who will contribute money or other resources to the Congressman's future campaigns. And, of course, satisfying the demands, or trying to satisfy them, should not lead to trouble, either with the Congressman's colleagues in the Congress and elsewhere in politics, or from the voters in his constituency.

The fact that it is quite difficult to locate such ideal demands means (a) that some Congressmen are constantly alert for an "issue," something that comes closer to the ideal than anything they are now identified with, and (b) that a good many Congressmen devote most, and most Congressmen devote some, of their time to what is essentially "case service," doing something for somebody that does not demonstrably deprive somebody else of something—helping a person get into a veterans' hospital or straighten out a social security claim or break the red tape in getting a relative from abroad admitted to this country. Even here—for instance, on tax matters—there is the danger of being criticized for showing favoritism or somehow getting associated with something later regarded as scandalous.

Interestingly enough, getting jobs for people is not usually as rewarding as any of the three services mentioned in the last paragraph. Essentially the same thing would apply at the congressional level, but the experience of my colleagues in the Massachusetts state government (and to a limited degree of myself, insofar as I was concerned with patronage) is that jobs are likely to create more resentment than gratitude. It is not only that, as the old political saying goes, every appointment means ten disappointed people who hoped for that job; it is that many appointees are resentful because they expected a better job than they got. But if one can get somebody ahead on the list for an old people's home or an institution for mental defectives, or have such a person shifted farther from or nearer to the family residence, whichever the family wants, the families of those who are held up on the waiting list longer than in strict equity they should have been do not know about it.

But, of course, case service of this sort is generally a retail matter. It is only rarely that it can be dramatized or publicized so that a large group of voters appreciates the Congressman who provides it. And although many of the recipients may be grateful enough, on the whole, people who want this sort of case service are not the kind of people who organize voters *en masse,* bring them to the polls, etc.

So the third kind of demand that almost all Congressmen necessarily try to serve comes from local businesses, local hospitals, local governments, local trade unions, for the heads of these organizations can and do influence groups of voters.

In these terms, it is easy to see why the kind of campaign described by Kenneth Kerle in the following chapter was successful. It met most of the preconditions. Here were businessmen, locally based, indeed at the center of a communications network, who needed or thought they needed something rather badly. The counterpressure would come largely from the Treasury and a few tax-analyzing agencies and groups, not likely to organize any great numbers of voters. The fact that movie theaters actually were suffering hard times in the early 1950s because of the growth of TV just then made them a hardship case a bit different from other groups subject to tax at that time. The fact that the big movie exhibitors and companies were interested gave the Congressman a prospect, at least, of campaign funds and even publicity. It was a "natural."

CHAPTER FIVE

The Motion-Picture Theater Lobby in Action

A CASE REPORT

by Kenneth Kerle

[The following report shows a situation where, under the American legislative system, demands were made of a sort that Congressmen would almost certainly heed. Here was an industry suffering considerable hardship; television was hurting theater owners. Here was an industry scattered throughout all districts—every Congressman had a number of motion-picture theaters in his district. Here was an industry asking something that was not very likely to hurt anybody very specifically or very much—an additional tax burden would, presumably, fall on everybody else if the motion-picture tax was removed, but one so small that nobody would care. There was nothing in the request of the motion-picture theater lobby which would lead

This material is derived from a master's thesis offered in the Department of Government and Public Administration at American University, Washington, D.C., in 1955. The thesis itself offers a much more detailed account of the episode and is recommended to those interested in lobbying practices. At the time, Professor Kerle was employed by Howard S. Miller, then Congressman, First District, Kansas, on a part-time basis; he later acted as Congressman Miller's campaign manager in two unsuccessful efforts at reelection, in 1954 and 1956. He is now associate professor of government, Hagerstown Junior College, Hagerstown, Maryland. His article "The Kansas Local Government Research Corporation," taken from his Ph.D. dissertation (also at American University), "The League of Kansas Municipalities," was published in the December 1967 issue of *American County Government*.

to counteraction by any competing industry or interest. In the early 1950s, it seemed hard to believe anybody would be upset by a small favor to motion-picture interests; they were not widely regarded as bad or evil (to be sure, intellectuals regarded them as vulgar, but most intellectuals would not care about this tax aspect). Because the motion-picture theater owners had pinpointed their campaign so specifically to individual Congressmen, individual Congressmen might reasonably hope that their help to the industry would be remembered by the individual owners in their district specifically and personally.

Yet, with all these pluses in their favor, the Treasury and apparently to some extent the White House were able effectively to resist for some time the demands of the motion-picture people for any tax change. It seems fairly clear that neither the Treasury nor the White House cared about the particular tax; they had no wish to impose any special burden on motion pictures, and probably, if the tax had not already been in existence, they would never have thought of imposing it for the first time in 1952 under the hardship conditions that the industry then faced. It was simply that the Treasury and the White House did not want to let go of a tax that was then being collected, since they might then have to figure out a way to make up the difference; and it is always easier to keep a tax in being than to work out the administrative and political problems of imposing some other tax. Both the Treasury and the White House, probably, were afraid that if the motion-picture theater owners succeeded in getting their tax removed, other interests that were still subject to nuisance taxes imposed during the war would be able to push, in the name of fairness, to have these removed. In other words, the Treasury and the White House were simply upholding the status quo against changed conditions.

The final action of the Congress in the matter shows, contrary to the general impression that Congress is always more conservative than the administrative branch, one occasion when Congress actually was more responsive to changed conditions, because it was more open to demands from an interest group of citizens. (Of course, I am not saying that this is always the case. Some interest groups of citizens, in particular the poor and the southern Negro, have recently had better access to the executive branch—though to be sure not, so far as I know, to the Treasury!)

But the case is also interesting because, despite all the appeals to Congressmen—and according to Professor Kerle's account, prac-

tically every Congressman heard them—the theater owners were not completely successful at first. (Although Kerle does not document this, my suspicion is that the Ways and Means Committee shared some of the attitudes I have attributed to the Treasury and the White House.)

It is especially interesting to me for this reason: Reading Kerle's account, one would think that this must have been a big issue on Capitol Hill, an issue that would be remembered and discussed by Ways and Means Committee members and staff, an issue that many Congressmen would cite in discussing pressure from business. Yet the fact is that although my own interviewing around Capitol Hill (again concentrating on Ways and Means matters) overlapped the period when this matter was before the committee and the Congress, I never consciously heard of it. I have no recollection of ever hearing it discussed. I am quite certain no reference to it occurs in the 175 or so interviews we conducted with Congressmen, staff members, and lobbyists (and also some people in the executive branch), who might have been expected to notice any intensive campaign, and remember it when we asked about business pressure. It is particularly likely that I would have noticed any reference to this topic because both Ithiel Pool and I are especially interested in matters affecting mass communications and politics. Yet I never heard of the matter at all until, late in 1955, Lowell Hattery kindly told me about Kenneth Kerle's thesis.

Another reason I am including Dr. Kerle's report here is this: My own work, in this volume and in American Business and Public Policy *and in* How Organizations Are Represented in Washington, *and even in* Elite and Specialized Interviewing, *emphasizes the low-key approach to efforts at and interpretations of effective pressure. In so doing, I am reacting against what seems to be a common view that pressure is effective, and to a previous period when political science writers placed a good deal of emphasis on the conversion of demands into legislation, with Congressmen acting as transformers. Of course, I believe my general approach and interpretation, and the transactional model on which they are based, is more correct than earlier work. In Chapters 8, 9, and 10, I have tried to state the nature of that approach explicitly. But, as with any other approach or model, there is a danger that it will be overemphasized and carried too far. I find Dr. Kerle's statement to be a particularly clear and comprehensive account of an occasion—involving the same committee with which I was chiefly concerned in my work on* American

Business and Public Policy—*when a pressure group did make de-mands and was successful. I do not think that anything of any moment could be added to his story by trying to interpret it in trans-actional terms. The interactional model is completely successful, so far as I can see here; and except for general theoretical purposes, there would be no point in transactionalizing what he says. Taking the case as it stands, transactionalizing it would make complex what is now clear and lucid, and is ruled out by Occam's razor.*

Now, were I known as a writer who stresses pressure, interaction, and so on, in the manner of Bertram M. Gross (or even Drew Pearson), there would be less value in my inserting the Kerle report here. But since I am known, I believe, as just the opposite, there is some value in my indicating that I clearly recognize that there are occasions when interactionism is a sufficient and parsimonious means of describing legislative activity.

As was the case with my own Chapter 2, above, Dr. Kerle could not publish his report at the time it was written or for some years thereafter. Although Ithiel Pool and I arranged to have it published in a special edition of the Public Opinion Quarterly *in 1956, dealing with political communications, the COMPO official who acted as Kerle's major informant objected. That man is now dead, and after all these years we can now see no reason why anyone would protest the publication; in fact, many readers will wonder why there ever should have been any objection. Here, then, is Dr. Kerle's report.*]

During World War I, the federal government levied an admission tax on the amusement industries. Lower priced admissions were ex-empted shortly after hostilities ceased, but in 1932 such a tax was again imposed, owing to the depression. The moving-picture industry did not complain, probably because the transformation from silent to talking pictures was bringing it large profits. During World War II, in April 1944, this tax was increased to 1 percent on each five cents or major fraction thereof.[1]

This is a report on the methods used by the industry to try to get this tax repealed during the 83rd Congress (1953–54). The short time span of the campaign and the writer's position in a congressional of-fice placed him in a favorable position to collect the necessary data and to conduct strategic interviews with people involved.

---

[1]U.S. House of Representatives, Committee on Ways and Means, *Hearings on H.R. 157: A Bill to provide that the tax on admissions shall not apply to moving picture admissions,* 83rd Cong., 1st sess., April 20, 1953 (Washington: U.S. Government Printing Office, 1953), p. 4.

COMPO

The Council of Motion Picture Organizations (COMPO), a public relations group, was chosen to handle the amusement-tax repeal campaign for the motion-picture industry. By the summer of 1952, COMPO had disseminated a large amount of written advice and material to some fourteen thousand local theater managers who were dues-paying members. As a "grass-rooter," each manager was delegated the responsibility of arranging an initial meeting with the Congressman at that time running for reelection in his district, and another meeting with his opponent. Once these men expressed sympathy to the COMPO plea for tax repeal, they would then be asked to make a definite commitment, so as to prevent any reneging after Congress convened. Testimony before House Ways and Means by more than one hundred Congressmen, all of whom favored H.R. 157, the proposal to kill the amusement tax on motion-picture admissions, indicates that this method of lobbying produced the intended effect.

Procedures of the campaign were decided by the Tax Repeal Committee of COMPO. It decided that the campaign should be run strictly by motion-picture people, and that the exhibitors should show their own books to their respective Congressmen to make a good case. Each exhibitor was to organize his story so as to present it in the most convincing possible manner. As the instructional pamphlet distributed to exhibitors says: "In other words, *you* have to organize your own story, so that it will present your situation most impressively. This is a drive in which the facts need not to be colored, exaggerated, or twisted. The truth—the bare, unfortunate truth—tells our story."[2]

To coordinate the work with the National Tax Repeal Committee, leading exhibitors formed a state committee in each of the forty-eight states. These state committees then appointed committees for each congressional district, composed of managers of local theaters. Although the committees in the congressional districts received literature from the parent organization on how to approach the legislators, each committee was on its own as far as specific approaches went. It

---

[2]Council of Motion Picture Organizations, *Your Plan for Tax Repeal—What You Can Do!* (pamphlet), p. 8. It may be added that, as a result of the introduction of TV in the early fifties, motion-picture attendance was in fact universally declining, so most exhibitors could show books that indicated they were hard-pressed.

did not have to answer to either the national or the state committee for any method it might deem prudent to use to influence the Congressman.[3] The local tax-repeal committees, however, followed the same general procedure. First, the Congressman's name and address were verified, as well as the name and address of his opponent. Then a luncheon, breakfast, or some other affair was arranged for each gentleman, to give the committee the opportunity to meet him. As many exhibitors in the district as possible would attend the various functions held, bringing with them the facts and figures concerning their own theater or theaters. After these discussions, the exhibitor was confronted with the problem of getting a definite commitment. COMPO's advice was:

> A Congressman does not carry around with him his secretary and her typewriter so you can request that upon his return to his office or home he send you a letter confirming the understanding. If he neglects to do this after a short time, have a letter written to him, retaining a copy, stating your understanding of his commitment and asking that he confirm it.[4]

COMPO expected trouble with this phase of the campaign. To educate the theater owners about the ways of their political representatives, six possible responses were enumerated in the pamphlet to demonstrate how a legislator reacts to a request from a constituent.

(1) He will consider and give due attention to your request when the time comes. (*This is the kiss of death.*)

(2) He is favorable towards your request but cannot commit himself at this time. (*This, too, probably is the kiss of death.*)

(3) He thinks that he probably can do what you want. (*This is a little bit more encouraging, but only a little.*)

(4) He is for elimination or reduction in the admission tax. (*The guy needs a lot of working on.*)

(5) He is for the repeal. (*This is fine, but press him a little further.*)

(6) He will vote for the repeal and he will do his utmost to influence other Congressmen—and, especially, the members of the House Ways and Means Committee—to help put it through. (*Perfect!*)[5]

[3]Interview with a representative of COMPO, New York, May 26, 1954.
[4]*Your Plan for Tax Repeal*, p. 9.
[5]*Ibid.*

If the Congressman committed himself in writing or orally before witnesses, or if he merely sympathized with the aim of the campaign but did not declare himself definitely, the information was relayed to COMPO for its files. All the folders in the file initially contained red cards. A blue card indicated written or oral support. A yellow card was placed in the folder of the man who sympathized but did not declare himself definitely for repeal. During the campaign many changes from red to yellow or red to blue occurred. Each week the COMPO office in New York City sent out the card results to all the district committees in order that each committee could check its progress in relation to the other committees. By the time that the first session of the 83rd Congress convened in January 1953, a majority of members of Congress had committed themselves to repeal of the amusement tax on motion-picture theaters.[6]

COMPO did not directly solicit support from any other lobby, business, or union, but it encouraged the local grass-roots exhibitors to get local support from these sources. The businessmen, it felt, realized that the presence of a prosperous movie theater meant potential customers, and labor-union officials, it reasoned, would be eager to help after proof that unemployment increased when a theater had to close its doors.

An important aspect of the campaign was the fact that COMPO discouraged an appeal for support from the general public. In a previous year, the motion-picture industry had conducted a tax-repeal campaign in which the movie patrons were requested to sign petitions and write letters to Congress urging repeal of the tax. The reason for discouraging a public appeal in the 1952 campaign is stated in the pamphlet:

> This is very important! Unlike the industry's last tax-repeal campaign, this one does not and cannot contemplate at this stage of the drive an appeal for the support of the general public. The reason for this is that many theaters, if the tax is repealed, will have to keep the tax money to insure their continued existence. It also is the opinion of some exhibitors that emphasis on ticket taxes to the public makes our customers more price-conscious and could hurt business. Therefore, there will be no petitions to be signed by your patrons; no trailers; no public ballyhoo of any sort. If the tax-repeal

---

[6]Interview with COMPO representative, New York, May 26, 1954.

campaign is successful—and there is excellent reason to believe it will be—theaters can then decide what to do with the tax money— to keep it, or to pass all or part of it along to the public, as best fits their individual situations. Therefore, it is urged that no appeal be made direct to the general public.[7]

CONGRESSIONAL TESTIMONY

During the hearings on H.R. 157 in April of 1953, 114 members of Congress from thirty-three states testified before the Committee on Ways and Means concerning the motion-picture amusement tax. Fifty-one members gave oral accounts of the financial condition of motion-picture theaters in their districts and sixty-three members submitted written statements which altogether encompassed two-thirds of the printed hearings on the bill.

For example, in the fall of 1952 Representative Laurie C. Battle, Ninth District, Alabama, attended a meeting with Mr. R. M. Kennedy of the Alabama Theater Owners Association, Mr. N. H. Waters of the Waters Theater Company, Mr. F. E. Walker, president of the Moving Picture Machine Operators Union, and other representatives of the motion-picture industry, for the purpose of discussing the crisis facing it. Battle stated that representatives of the companies and the union had contacted him on various occasions urging repeal; in addition, he received letters from theater owners in his district, elaborating on statements they had made to him in many meetings concerning their theater troubles.[8]

Congressman John A. Blatnik, Eighth District, Minnesota, told the committee that he had conferred with the theater owners in his district several times during the past few years. The 20 percent admissions tax, television competition, and the increased costs of the three-dimensional films then in vogue had placed the theaters in a difficult economic plight, according to the Congressman. His sources of information were letters from the theater owners and studies showing that theater attendance had fallen off badly since 1946. Expressing the opinion that the Congress did not desire to contribute

---

[7]*Your Plan for Tax Repeal* p. 5.
[8]*Hearings on H.R. 157*, p. 45.

to forcing these theater men out of business, the Congressman gave his support to H.R. 157.[9]

Representative Clair Engle, Second District, California, informed the committee that the theater people had invited him to a meeting in Red Bluff, California, during the fall of 1952. Some twenty-five or thirty exhibitors traveled a distance of 150 to 200 miles to attend. After a round-table discussion about the theater situation, the Congressman was convinced that many theaters, particularly in the rural areas, were going broke. He felt that they had such a good case that he introduced a bill similar to H.R. 157 in the Congress.[10]

Representative J. Vaughan Gary, Third District, Virginia, testified that he had attended a meeting in Richmond, Virginia, with some of the local motion-picture theater owners in the autumn of 1952. The group, according to Mr. Gary, included gentlemen whom he knew personally to be of high integrity. Profit-and-loss statements of their businesses shown to him at this meeting convinced him that a great many theaters were operating at a loss. The operators, he said, admitted that television and other forms of amusement had hurt them, but they maintained that in many instances the admission tax paid to the federal government made the difference between profit and loss.[11]

Representative George H. Mahon, Nineteenth District, Texas, said that he talked with theater owners in his district in the autumn of 1952. He was shocked, he stated, to see that, although the theaters collected quite a bit of money for the federal government, their margin of profit was small in some cases, and in other instances they were actually losing money.[12]

Congressman H. S. Miller, First District, Kansas, said that the exhibitors presented to him an extremely convincing case for repeal—so convincing, in fact, that he agreed to go along with them. No mention of COMPO was made when they met, and he had not heard of it until Congress convened and his office began receiving correspondence from the organization.[13]

When Congress convened in January 1953, one might assume that, since a majority of both houses was already committed, the pressure might have ceased. But it continued. Congressman Miller received numerous letters and telegrams urging him to battle for repeal. Most

[9]*Ibid.*, pp. 46–47.
[10]*Ibid.*, p. 55.
[11]*Ibid.*, pp. 59–60.
[12]*Ibid.*, p. 70.
[13]Interview with Congressman H. S. Miller, May 27, 1954.

of these were from exhibitors in his district. The office received a letter from COMPO about once every two weeks, on the average, describing the worsened condition of the theaters, and monthly tabulations of the number of theaters that had closed in his state. A spot check revealed that Patrick J. Hillings, Twenty-fifth District, California; Peter Frelinghuysen, Jr., Fifth District, New Jersey; James A. Byrne, Third District, Pennsylvania; Joel T. Broyhill, Tenth District, Virginia; and Robert C. Byrd, Sixth District, West Virginia, received substantially the same type of correspondence from the theater owners in their respective districts, and monthly tabulations of theater closings in their states from COMPO.

VISITS TO WASHINGTON

According to one report, hardly a week passed during the first session of the 83rd Congress that delegations of motion-picture exhibitors did not call on their representatives and senators.[14] Theater owners traveled to Washington from the districts of members of the House Ways and Means and Rules Committees, and from the states of members of the Senate Finance Committee. The traveling expenses, hotel bills, and meal checks of these delegations were all paid for by COMPO. These delegations called on the Senators and Representatives to get them to reaffirm the commitments that most of them had made. Twenty-two or twenty-three of the twenty-five members of the Ways and Means Committee had previously committed themselves before the bill even came to a committee vote.[15]

THE PICTURE SHOW

A twenty-two-minute film at the hearing presented the theater situation in outline form. The movie consisted of picture sequences shot in front of closed theaters in the states of the members of the Ways and Means Committee. An actor walked in front of a certain

---

[14]*New York Times*, July 23, 1953, sec. L, p. 20.
[15]Interview with COMPO representative, New York, May 26, 1954.

closed theater, addressed the Congressman of that particular district by name, and then followed through with a short, vivid description of the deteriorated condition of the theater business in that Congressman's state. Total cost of this film was estimated to be between $24,000 and $50,000. Half of this amount was raised through dues collected from local theater owners by the COMPO Finance Committee. This amount in turn was matched dollar for dollar by the big film corporations. All twenty-five members of the committee were present for the showing of the film, along with many other Congressmen who were not on the committee. Everyone was reported as being extremely attentive.[16]

So convinced was Congress that it passed H.R. 157 by a voice vote during the last few days of the first session. The Senate Finance Committee held no hearings, and when the Senate passed the bill it made no changes, which eliminated the need for a conference committee.

PRESSURE ON THE EXECUTIVE SIDE

Mr. Robert Coyne, of COMPO, told the House Ways and Means Committee that COMPO's staff had been working for some weeks with the Treasury Department in an effort to aid Treasury officials in formulating their judgment concerning repeal of the tax on theater tickets, attempting to show them that, although the Treasury would lose money that year, it would lose more money in the long run if the tax were continued, since more theaters would be forced to close.[17] It is generally accepted that the President's position in 1953 was that the budget must be balanced. One may infer that the Treasury Department did not listen sympathetically to the lobby's case because of this position. But despite the apparent unwillingness of the executive branch to go along with the lobby's plan, pressure was still exerted. On July 30, 1953, Colonel H. A. Cole and Mr. Pat McGee, co-chairmen of the COMPO Tax Committee, Mr. Coyne, and other

---

[16]*Ibid.*
[17]*Hearings on H.R. 157*, p. 24.

movie industry people called on President Eisenhower and were introduced to him by Senator Frank Carlson, Republican of Kansas. Mr. Coyne had drawn up a rough memorandum for the event, which said in part:

> It is a tragic single choice that pushed us to Congressmen at home, to the Congress and the Treasury here, and finally to you. In desperation we've blundered and fought through this far. We've been heard by the Treasury. We've been helped by the Congress. The Treasury, in all honesty, feels it cannot accept conclusions on financial facts not in full view from Washington. The Congress, equally honest, acted overwhelmingly on facts that were plain and ugly at home. And the spectacle of the small-town theater and the big-town theater facing certain ruin *that is avoidable* is ugly waste in its worst form. We say, respectfully, that the Treasury is wrong! We feel with the deepest conviction that Congress is right! This is the tragedy! If the Treasury is right and we prevail, the government later, by reimposition of tax or other method, can correct its position. Money only is involved. If *we* are right and *lose,* no power, economic or governmental, can restore 5,000 theaters ready to close their doors—or save the industry the complete ruin to follow. Your decision is tough. *If you help us* you will be accused of many things from favoritism on down. If you *do not help us* you will be credited with guts and strength and firm consistency. We don't ask your decision, Mr. President, but we must tell you our story or we can't go home. We've timed it and I've got three minutes to go. There are three points . . .

The three points dealt with the effect of the revenue, public benefit, and discrimination. On the first point, Coyne argued that the Treasury would get $4 million more from all theaters in corporate and other taxes than it would from all taxes (including admissions) if these theaters were allowed to close. He believed that this would surely happen unless the President saved them. Coyne denied that the public would not benefit from this tax reduction. It would benefit, he felt, through reduced prices in places where theaters were showing a reasonable profit. However, where theaters were losing money, they would take advantage of the tax, totally or in part, in order to continue in business. In any event, the public would benefit through the keeping open of theaters, of which 8,000 were small, unincorporated, family businesses, theaters the small towns needed.

Although admitting it would be discrimination to give one industry a break, Coyne remarked that it would be the same discrimination one would use in throwing a life preserver to a drowning swimmer rather than to a person holding onto the dock. In closing, Coyne raised the question of whether the industry could stand the tax for another year. His answer was:

> The tragedy I have referred to is that if it cannot and we fail here, for us there is no second chance. I have not touched on the social values of theaters. You know them! Nor need we mention the movies as a tool of morale in war or peace. You, of all people, know that. We ask no artificial stimulant or subsidy. We ask only for the removal of a burden, imposed and borne cheerfully when we could bear it, and one we can no longer bear. We ask this only if you believe us; if you think we have been honest. We ask this only if you feel we have been diligent and fair in our own protection and if you feel that we and the industry to which our lives have been devoted are worth the saving.

The interview lasted from one-half to three-quarters of an hour, and the President was described as courteous but adamant in his approach to the tax-repeal bill. Tax relief, he felt, would be inconsistent with the administration's recent action requesting and receiving from Congress an extension of the excess-profits tax.[18]

With the gloomy prospect of a Presidential veto hanging over its head, COMPO made another attempt on August 6, 1955. This time the interview was with Secretary of the Treasury George M. Humphrey. After discussing the seriousness of the problem, the Secretary agreed to talk the matter over with the President. At that moment the telephone rang. It was a secretary from COMPO's New York City office calling to say that the President had vetoed the bill. It was a dramatic moment, for it looked as if Mr. Humphrey had been deliberately stalling because he knew all the time that the President was going to veto the bill.[19]

A memorandum of disapproval was issued by the White House on August 6, 1953, which said in part:

> I am withholding my approval of H.R. 157, entitled "To provide that the tax on admissions shall not apply to moving picture admissions." . . . Because of the need for revenue I recommended an ex-

---

[18]Interview with COMPO representative, New York, May 26, 1954.
[19]Pressure tactics used by COMPO in trying to influence the Treasury Department were discussed with a Treasury official, who requested that the discussion not be used.

tension of the excess-profits tax for six months and the extension has now been made. Tax relief for one industry now would be inconsistent with that action. It is estimated that the repeal of the admissions tax on motion picture performances, which has been on the books at the present rate since April 1, 1944, would result in a gross loss of revnue of $200 million. After alowing for a resulting increase in corporation income taxes, the net loss is estimated to be between $100 million and $120 million a year. It is not contended by the industry that the present scale of admission prices which reflects the 20 percent tax is responsible for the existing distress situation in the industry. Indeed, the industry apparently expects in many cases to maintain the present price to consumers even though the tax is repealed. There is distress in large but not all segments of the industry. The basic causes of the industry's distress, however, arise from new forms of competition.

THE SECOND SESSION

In the second session, as compared with the previous one, reduction in admission taxes came packaged in the form of a large excise-tax reduction bill, H.R. 8224, which contained 50 percent tax cuts for many industries, including the movies, since the administration had committed itself to do something about excise-tax cuts in general. Daniel A. Reed, Republican chairman of the Ways and Means Committee, brought to the floor of the House a bill tailored to meet administration specifications, after rejecting an attempt by committee Democrats (aided by a few Republicans) to provide extra relief for theaters by an amendment to the bill. Once the measure reached the floor of the House, it was moved to recommit the bill for the purpose of including extra theater relief, but this was defeated by a vote of 213 to 200 along party lines.[20] Administration pressure held the Republicans in line and kept them from bolting over to the Democratic proposal. Just as in the first session, theater delegations were brought in by COMPO to remind the Congressmen and Senators of their commitments on the theater exemption.

---

[20]*Congressional Record*, Proceedings of 83rd Cong., 2nd sess., vol. 190, no. 45 (March 10, 1954): 2865.

Members of the Senate Finance Committee met with exhibitors' delegations from their states, who persuaded them to support an amendment that would provide outright exemption of movie admissions of sixty cents or less. After the bill passed the Senate and went to the conference committee, Representative Richard Simpson of Pennsylvania offered a compromise. He proposed the fifty-cent exemption on movie admissions that the Democrats had originally offered in the House. This was accepted and the bill passed without any trouble. Simpson, who was chairman of the Republican Congressional Campaign Committee, is reputed to have commented, "We've got a campaign to win."[21]

COMPO's failure in the first session probably is explained by the procedural and political aspects of the situation. Congress passed H.R. 157 near the end of that session by a voice vote. A voice vote is often used when the legislative body wishes to conduct business quickly, or in order to prevent the votes of members from being made public. The latter instance seems to be a plausible answer here, because the administration had opposed H.R. 157 for fear it would nullify part of its program of trying to balance the budget, and because the general taxpayer and other industries were granted no relief. Had the vote been recorded, some members might have weighed the alternatives more carefully before approving a measure that was conceivably not in the national interest and might have put them on an administration blacklist. Whether deliberately or by accident, the vote was held near enough toward the close of the session to put the blame on the President after Congress had adjourned.

By the second session the administration was committed to excise-tax relief for many industries. Excise taxes were due to expire April 1, 1954, which made quick action on the excise-tax bill imperative. Pressure on the House Republicans by the administration in an election year kept them from giving the theater exhibitors more relief than anyone else. The compromise that followed in the Senate-House conference committee, exempting lower priced admissions, had to be quickly approved to meet the April 1 deadline. The administration had no alternative. It had to accept the bill as a whole; it could not run the risk to the revenue of a veto. Had the President possessed (as some state governors do) any form of item veto, the upshot for

---

[21]*New York Times*, April 5, 1954, sec. L, p. 16.

the moving-picture theater lobby might have been quite different; institutional procedure was an important determinant of success in this case.

Other Pressure Groups Testifying for Repeal of Amusement Tax[22]

Actors Equity Association and Chorus Equity Association
American Federation of Musicians
American Hotel Association
American Legion
American National Theater Association
American Recreation Society and District of Columbia Recreation
    Board
American Theater Society
Ballet Russe de Monte Carlo, Inc.
Circus Fans Association of America
Council of the Living Theater
Hotel and Restaurant Employees and Bartenders International, AFL
Kennywood Amusement Park, Pittsburgh
League of New York Theaters
Los Angeles Chamber of Commerce
National Association of Amusement Parks, Pools, and Beaches
National Association of the Legitimate Theater
National Ballroom Operators Association and Arena Managers
    Association
National Conference on State Parks, Inc.
National Park Service, Department of the Interior
Roller Skating Rink Operators Association of America

---

[22]U.S. House of Representatives, Committee on Ways and Means, *Forty topics pertaining to the general revision of the internal revenue code: Hearings on Part 4 (Topic 40)* . . . 83rd Cong., 1st sess., July 28–August 12, 1953 (Washington: U.S. Government Printing Office, 1953).

Part Two

THROUGH THE FOG
OF POLICY DEMANDS:
WHAT DO CONGRESSMEN
PAY ATTENTION TO?

CHAPTER SIX

The Multiplicity of Possible Subjects for Attention by Congressmen

I

Liddell Hart calls one of his great books *Through the Fog of War.* He is referring to a common expression among military writers, "the fog of battle." Almost nobody knows, at the time, what really is happening in a battle. Too many individual skirmishes and actions demand attention. Action is too confused. There are too many encounters. Orders are modified, distorted, or made impossible of realization because of unforeseen developments. The historian of a battle or of a war often tries to make sense out of the whole pattern by ruthless, and more or less misleading, oversimplification and rationalization.

Such oversimplification and rationalization are characteristic, too, of political writing. They are found often in the reports and recollections of participants as well as in the treatises of journalists and scholars. Even the participant who tries seriously to portray the inchoate, awkward, unplanned, complex way in which things actually happened often is compelled by his listeners to sharpen and dramatize the story. I myself, in talking about my own experiences in

Massachusetts politics and in national political campaigns, usually conceal my ignorance, and find that I oversimplify, sometimes to make a good story, sometimes to communicate with my hearers. There is not, as far as I know, an adequate vocabulary to picture briefly the chaotic nature of political relationships. It is possibly true that I am somewhat biased (either for reasons of temperament or because much of my political experience has been in Massachusetts) in favor of observing the fog of politics rather than its highlights. At any rate, in Maryland (especially Montgomery County) and to some extent in Missouri (Kansas City), where I have also had considerable political experience, things seem a bit sharper. There are no doubt differences of degree from state to state, time to time, issue to issue. But the prevailing tendency, I suspect, is to oversharpen.[1]

One of the big factors in making events seem sharper and clearer than they were is the cognitive tendency to fill in details and relationships that fit one's expectations. For many people, there is some degree of cognitive dissonance in reporting on the complexities of, for instance, attention and inattention. Outsiders—journalists on the one hand, trying to make a story comprehensible to their readers, and enemies on the other—find it very unrewarding to report on political action in the foggy way here suggested. Ithiel Pool has presented one important factor explaining oversimplification of the ways in which pressure groups operate in commenting on our observations about reciprocal trade lobbying:

> It is tempting to speculate on the extent to which the pressure groups have themselves generated their traditional image. They have certainly aided in the growth of a myth. They are inclined to exaggerate their own effectiveness and at the same time to overrate the resources of the opposition. In full good faith, each side depicts the other as well-heeled professionals, whereas "we are amateurs operating on a shoestring." . . . It would be interesting to know how much of the generally held notions about pressure groups comes actually from propaganda the pressure groups have put out about themselves *and the opposition.*[2]

I have had relevant experiences in shifting from Democratic campaigning to Republican campaigning; each side has a picture of the

---

[1]See my *Elite and Specialized Interviewing* (Evanston, Ill.: Northwestern University Press, 1970).

[2]Raymond Bauer, Ithiel de Sola Pool, and Lewis A. Dexter, *American Business and Public Policy: The Politics of Foreign Trade* (New York: Atherton, 1963), p. 399 (italics added).

other as well organized, purposive, intense, which is quite incompatible with what one sees and feels when one is actually over there.

It seems to me that one of the important contributions of *American Business and Public Policy* (following, of course, in the line of other works; for instance, Bernard Cohen's *The Influence of Non-Governmental Groups on Foreign Policy-Making*[3] and Stephen Bailey's *Congress Makes a Law*[4]) is that our interviewing showed how different the picture looks from different angles. Had we interviewed only Congressmen, we might have taken at their face value those statements that suggested that powerful groups were powerfully pressuring their colleagues; had we interviewed only lobbyists concerned with reciprocal trade, we might have credited what they told us about their opponents and about their own inputs to Congress; interviewing Congressmen and lobbyists—and interviewing some Congressmen concerned with the issue and others indifferent to it—we came to doubt such a picture of contrasts. More important, perhaps, were two somewhat accidental factors in our study of the situation:

1. I myself did the bulk of the elite interviewing *in Washington* and in two of the six congressional districts we selected for concentration. Since I was nervous about interviewing Congressmen, partly because, as I noted earlier, I knew there was hesitancy about the whole project by our sponsoring agencies, I started out doing a good deal of interviewing with businessmen and politicians in Delaware and western Maryland (the then Sixth District of Maryland) *before* I saw many Congressmen. In starting this way, I became vividly aware that most business and trade-union constituents—even those supposedly involved in trade and tariff matters—really did not know what was happening in that field and were paying precious little attention to what they heard.

2. As I have discussed at greater length elsewhere,[5] I was and am also nervous about asking people direct questions—more so than many interviewers, I am sure. I never said, if I could avoid it, "What about reciprocal trade?" but I said to Congressmen, "What do you hear from business?" or "What is worrying business in your district?" and to businessmen and trade-union leaders, "What are your problems in Congress?" or "with government?" But, by good luck, questions of this sort showed that reciprocal trade and foreign imports

---

[3]Boston: World Peace Foundation, 1959.
[4]New York: Columbia University Press, 1950.
[5]See Dexter, *Elite and Specialized Interviewing.*

had a very low priority in the *attention* of most of the people we interviewed.

So that I came to see more and more that what people hear—constituencies from Congress, Congressmen from constituencies—is a matter of what they are paying attention to, and I came to see, too, that there were far more issues they might rationally have paid attention to—taking each issue by itself as a discrete unit—than they could actually pay attention to, looking at all the issues together. Later, experience in Massachusetts state government and interviews with Congressmen and others on military and civil defense policy[6] led me to attach still more significance to the factor of attention, and to greater awareness that the importance of attention is due partly to shortage of time, partly to shortage of energy. (I have recently taught a seminar on the politics of attention.)

II

The two chapters immediately following—Chapters 7 and 8—are essentially concerned with this problem of attention. The general theme underlying them is indicated in the title of the present chapter. For any given "policy-maker" or set of "policy-makers" in any central "decision-making" body, such as Congress, there is an indefinite and very large number of significant demands to which he may or feels he must pay attention. These demands are not confined to those actually expressed by someone he regards as significant; Congressmen are also, to a greater or lesser degree, concerned with demands that are (*a*) *contingent,* (*b*) *potential,* and (*c*) *internally determined* by their own conceptions of obligation and situation. Contingent demands are those that are likely to be made if some expressed demands are granted. For instance, if Congress grants special treatment to some particular industry, this may suggest to other industries that they ask for something—and Congressmen may wish to take such possibilities into account in considering the expressed demands of

---

[6]Reported in my "Congressmen and the Making of Military Policy," in *New Perspectives on the House of Representatives,* ed. Robert L. Peabody and Nelson W. Polsby, 2nd ed. (Chicago: Rand McNally, 1969), pp. 175–94; republished in, among others, *Readings on the Politics of American Democracy,* ed. M. Irish, R. Lineberry, and J. Prothro (Englewood Cliffs, N. J.: Prentice-Hall, 1969), pp. 371–84.

the first industry. Similarly, the demand for equality of treatment for Negroes seems to have increased somewhat demands on behalf of the white poor, American Indians, and women.

Congressmen are concerned with potential demands, partly for the reasons we have just discussed (some of them are looking for a really promising issue to latch onto); but the more statesmanlike among them also have some concern with what may be national problems in a year or two, even if not now. It was probably the foreseeing of potential demands, as much as the presence of actual demands, that led to the activities of the Tolan Subcommittee on Migrant Labor and to the GI Bill.

And, in the nature of their professional responsibility, most Congressmen, as statesmen, become aware of things that it seems to them ought to be done, things that are needed. George Norris' concern with the lame-duck amendment to the Constitution was not, chiefly, a response, so far as the record goes, to external demands; it was chiefly a consequence of his own feeling about what was good for the country. A classic example of the same sort of thing is found in the measures put through the British Parliament by Henry Dundas, later Viscount Melville, in the latter part of the eighteenth century, to remove Scottish miners from a state of serfdom; he did this purely and simply in his capacity as chief Scottish minister, without, seemingly, having been pressured by any complaint or protest from anyone in public or political life.[7]

Of course, as a practical matter, it is hard to distinguish between actual, contingent, potential, and internally determined demands. The demands of conscience may have guided Norris; but he did receive some public support, obviously. Chet Holifield of California has done a great deal in recent years to support and develop civil defense programs, through the Military Operations Subcommittee of the House, of which he is chairman. No doubt he has been influenced and to a certain extent reinforced by support from the small group of people in the country actively concerned with civil defense. I have definite and specific reasons for believing that no one in his district who could materially alter Holifield's personal political status was, at least in 1956, particularly concerned with the issue. In the main, this is a matter with which Mr. Holifield is concerned for reasons of con-

---

[7]See Henry (Lord) Cockburn, *Memorials of His Time*, vol. 2 of his *Works* (Edinburgh: Adam and Charles Black, 1872),pp. 67–69. "These two statutes [manumitting the hereditary serfs] seem to have been neither the effect nor the cause of any public excitement." See also Cyril Matheson, *Life of Henry Dundas, 1st Viscount Melville* (London: Constable & Co., 1933), pp. 38, 264.

science; the issue should, he feels, be pushed. And, of course, he is also interested in it for reasons of contingency—if something like the Cuban missile crisis should develop on a larger scale, plenty of people would wish that more national leaders had shown his kind of foresight.

Nevertheless, it is worth pointing out these different sources of demands, for two reasons: (1) They indicate the multiplicity of pressures upon a Congressman or Senator. George Norris was, very likely, as strongly pressured by the demands of his own conscience to do something about the lame-duck amendment and the TVA as he was by Nebraska farmers to do something for agriculture; I am reasonably sure it was Senator George Malone's conscience, rather more than demands from his constituents, that led him to fight reciprocal trade bitterly. (2) Naming these different sources of demands indicates one important reason why some expressed demands go relatively unheeded. There are so very many demands altogether.

The number of expressed demands is, of course, by itself significant for those who try to interpret and observe what they hear and read. Of course, here again a man's apperceptive mass really determines what is a demand and what sort of demand it is; Congressman X may hear a textile worker complain about foreign imports and interpret it as at most a demand for sympathy, whereas Congressman Y may hear in the same remark a demand for more tariff protection, Congressman Z may read it as a request for a retraining program or increased social security benefits, and Congressman O may not even notice what was said.

Some method of sorting out demands, determining which ones to pay attention to and how much attention to pay to them, is imperative. Otherwise, any member of Congress could easily be overwhelmed by the number of matters demanding attention.

In this respect, a legislature operating under the check-and-balance system differs from many, probably most, parliaments. In the British and Canadian parliamentary system, at any rate, there is no point in making many demands upon the individual member; the party leadership, and particularly the cabinet, the leaders of the majority party, decide the greater part of the agenda. Even if uninformed people make demands upon British and Canadian M.P.'s, the members themselves know there is very little they can do about many such demands, except transmit them. When, as happened under the Third and Fourth Republics in France, members can constantly negotiate with the government to withdraw or accord their votes, the parliamentary system comes, in this regard, much closer to the American one. (I am speculating here; people far better versed in the field than I may disagree.)

American members of Congress can seemingly do something about most of the demands upon them. So, being unable to protect themselves behind the shield of cabinet responsibility for the agenda, the Congress has evolved a system of committee responsibility, so that the individual member in most cases can excuse himself from doing anything except transmitting the demand to the relevant committee. But, in the first place, very few citizens realize that it is the relevant committees that make most of the decisions on a given type of issue—whereas the greater simplicity of the cabinet type of government probably means that more citizens believe members of parliament who say they can do nothing.

In the second place, it is often in fact possible for a member who wishes to do something about a matter to exert influence on it. This arises out of the overlapping character of committee jurisdictions; an experienced committee clerk says, in regard to military matters, "Jurisdiction is nine-tenths assertion." This figure is considerably exaggerated if one takes the totality of issues that might come before the Congress; but it is true that on a great many issues, a number of committees can get a handle. I have pointed out in Chapter 3, for instance, how many committees can do something or other about ecology or conservation or the quality of the environment. Too, it is often possible for committees that could not currently hope to upset the prevailing tradition of reference on substantive legislative matters to initiate investigations or studies that might later provide a basis for challenging or overthrowing the legislative committee's position. Few voters—even few businessmen or trade-union leaders —will necessarily be astute enough to see, however, that some such investigations are "eyewash," whereas other superficially similar investigations may have considerable effect. One example of an investigation that was a response to demands was a study of unemployment and related matters by the Senate Committee on Labor and Public Welfare in the 1950s, at the same time that Senate Finance and House Ways and Means were considering reciprocal trade. This investigation created the impression of being designed to show, among other things, that the conventional argument of protectionists, "Reciprocal trade is a means of importing unemployment," was correct. It was directed largely by a Senator from West Virginia, who probably was responding to the demands of the United

Mine Workers, which had an experienced Washington staff. The odds that Senate Finance or House Ways and Means would be materially affected by such an investigation were extremely poor; yet the investigation, whether regarded seriously by the Senators who took part in it or not (and I think it was), did take up a good deal of their time, so that they had less opportunity to pay attention to something else.

There is another reason why some members not on a relevant committee can exert influence. There are members who are respected, looked up to, and consulted by colleagues. For example, Congressman Henderson Lanham of Georgia, despite his brief service in the House, was in 1955 clearly regarded by the Democratic Congressmen from Georgia and the Carolinas as their spokesman on trade and tariff matters. I have the impression that he was a man whom most of these men, at least, and also some Representatives from Alabama and Florida, would have followed on a great many issues. The communications he received from his constituents on the failure of escape-clause action, etc., to protect the textile industry did have a definite effect, not only on him, but probably on ten or a dozen other Congressmen. I am saying here, of course, that some members of Congress are in that body "natural leaders." (For a discussion of an "effective gadfly," Cleveland Bailey, see Chapter 2.)

It is, of course, also possible—frequently for Senators, sometimes for House members—to achieve results in the policy field by using their legislative position to influence decisions made somewhere else or simply by getting publicity for a cause or idea. Senator Ernest Hollings' recent statement apologizing, in effect, for the fact that in his previous post as governor of South Carolina he had overlooked and ignored the issue of quasi-starvation in that state was far more effective coming from a Senator than it would have been from just any ex-governor; and its impact was not dependent upon his committee positions. As a Senator, Edward Brooke of Massachusetts has a national platform that he did not possess when, although still a Negro, he was merely attorney general of Massachusetts.

And, because members of the House and Senate run on their own (see Appendix A)—unlike members of parliament in the majority of parliamentary countries—they must of necessity do their best to encourage the feeling that they can do something about issues, so as to encourage people to consult them, trust in them, and talk about them.

III

This leads to another obligation—a demand not of constituents but of the situation. Congressmen and Senators must advertise themselves. One form of advertising is making statements about issues.

IV

Now, of course, any Congressman or Senator who takes committee work and legislation seriously is likely to spend a great part of his time in working on a relatively few issues. For, obviously, it is easy to say, "Yes, I will do something about that," or "I will vote for that," or "I will vote against this"; but it is often extremely time-consuming to reach a formulation with which those involved can live. For instance, a *decision to do something* about applying civil rights principles to public accommodations may take relatively little time. But *working out*, in the appropriate committee, *the definitions and guidelines* as to what is exactly, for the purpose, a public accommodation involves reconciling several different interests. Let anybody who doubts this try to wrestle with the "Mrs. Murphy" problem: If Mrs. Murphy runs a boardinghouse two blocks off the main highway in a small town, sometimes but not very often renting rooms to transients, shall she or shall she not be required to rent to minority-group members? If so, or if not, how do you draw the line? If so, what penalties? What mechanism of enforcement? And this is an infinitely simpler problem than that of determining who is and who is not liable to specific taxes.

And of course any member of Congress, like any other professional man, has administrative and maintenance problems—proportionally somewhat greater in the case of Congressmen than in many professions. Members must spend part of their time on election campaigns and, unless they are quite fortunate, in raising money for reelections; they must spend some of their time in the sheer mechanics of the Congress and the Senate (such matters as roll-call voting, for instance); they must, if they are active and energetic and engaged in a controversial matter, devote a lot of energy and attention to trying to shift other members' votes one way or another. Of necessity, all of them have some concern with patronage, and some of them have a good deal of concern with it.

All of this means that attention to most of what one might think they would be concentrating on is marginal or limited. Ironically enough, the necessity for concern with many issues does in most instances relieve Congressmen from being pushed by pressures as much as the outsider might think they would be. There are so many matters to pay attention to, so many kinds of potential and actual pressures from so many sources, that a man acquires a thick skin, a considerable capacity for discounting pressures, a considerable ability to overlook or ignore inconvenient and uncomfortable demands. He feels that what is lost here may be made up there—and that luck is always a big element in elections anyway.

At the same time, members often have an eye cocked for possible electoral or other consequences. A Congressman who shall be known here as Widesight bemoaned to me the fifty or so letters he had received from workers in a particular industry, demanding protection—"I, whom they never used to bother at all!" Yet I suspect, as I recollect the day and the attendant circumstances, that he was in a mood to worry. Most of those letters were from people not resident in his district, anyway. At about the same time, the mail clerk to the Senator from Congressman Widesight's state showed me many hundreds of letters and postcards on the same issue; but the Senator's legislative and administrative assistants did not even know that there was any such mail, and I am sure that the Senator didn't either.

As a shrewd and observant administrative assistant to one of the most politically astute and self-conscious members of the Senate said to me at the same time about the same issue: "You know how it is. I've seen it again and again. The United Mine Workers [who worked with his Senator closely] understand the Senator's position perfectly. You know [chuckling], we get some letters from them attacking him on this reciprocal trade business [which the Senator supported against the UMW position], and if they were published they'd sound mean as hell. But the same day the Senator may be on the phone to the same guys, working out an amicable deal on something else, so it doesn't matter too much.

". . . And you ought to go into this. A Senator or Congressman may one day get a letter on residual fuel oil [asking for a quota on it] and say, 'What the hell! That's nonsense!' and the next day get another letter from an almost identical guy in another county, and he may blow up and scream the house down and say, 'I've got to do something!' I've seen that often. He may just feel different that day or somebody may have called in yesterday and said, 'Senator, you aren't doing so well down in such-and-such a county,' the county from which the letter comes, so he says to himself, the Senator does, 'Well, this guy told me to get worried about Xavier County; maybe that's why I'm not doing so well down there,' just on the strength of putting the remark and the letter together. Yes, that's it; it just depends how a particular letter strikes a particular guy, what the guy's been listening to, whether the letter is pressure or is not pressure, whether he puts it in the wastebasket or gets on the long-distance phone about it or, for that matter, calls up somebody on the relevant committee."

Now, of course, neither this assistant nor I mean to say that it is sheer caprice and chance that determines what is heeded as pressure and what is not. Some communications may frequently be heeded; and some may almost never be heeded. Some fit into the particular attention system and communications system of a given senatorial office, and others do not. For instance, in a state where county chairmen are strong and Senators actually depend upon them, it is far more likely that a Senator will receive a warning about local sentiment from a county chairman and take it seriously than in a state like Massachusetts, where there is only a very rudimentary party organization. But we are only at the beginning, as far as I can see, of thinking about attention systems in politics in relation to time budgets, institutional channels of selection, and communications patterns. The following chapters may help to throw a little light on these problems.

For colleagues interested in studying such matters, I would suggest that on the whole it may now be more useful to study state legislators, senatorial assistants, and officials of national lobbying organizations along the lines just indicated than to study Congressmen. During the fifteen years since I first made my study, Congressmen have, it seems to me, become overinterviewed. One of the things that now takes a good bit of time from some of them is being interviewed by political scientists. I have heard estimates that there are congressional offices where over one man-day a week is spent being interviewed by scholars and students![8] It also seems to me

---

[8] See Lewis A. Dexter, "The Good Will of Important People: More on the Jeopardy of the Interview," *Public Opinion Quarterly*, 28 (1964): 556–63.

that we are now at the stage where we need comparative data from other professionals in somewhat similar positions more than anything else, if we want to understand political attention and communication. Once we have such comparative data,[9] then we may be able to go back and undertake secondary analyses of a lot of the information we have about Congress and make sense out of it without the need for so many primary studies on Capitol Hill.

[9]On the general subject of the development of appropriate comparative studies, see Barney Glaser and Anselm Strauss, *The Discovery of Grounded Theory* (Chicago: Aldine, 1967), especially chap. 5, "The Constant Comparative Method of Qualitative Analysis," pp. 101–16. Throughout, as in their discussion of library research, they also show us the possibilities of secondary analysis.

CHAPTER SEVEN

Marginal Attention, "Pressure" Politics, Political Campaigning, and Political Realities

There is a common, almost constant distortion in the discussion of political affairs, arising from the unfortunate fact that it is clumsy to talk about what you are *not* talking about—and yet what you are talking about is generally only a small segment of the total area of attention of those whom you interview or on whose doings you report. This is to say, the attention of most people to most political communications—including the attention of most Congressmen or legislators to most pressure groups—is marginal or peripheral.

Unless there is clear evidence to the contrary, indeed, I would suggest that any statements about pressure politics or political campaigns be subjected to the qualifying phrase "subject to the probability that attention was only marginal." In many interpretations of what Congressmen hear and how they react, one finds a great deal of discussion of the "pressure" on them; and "good citizens" argue that pressure by lobbyists, etc., is a bad thing from which legislators suffer. But the job of a Congressman is such that he is exposed to *what the outsider would call* pressure on a number of issues at all times. All one needs to do is to read the list of matters before the Congress at any given time, with particular attention to those discussed in the public press, to get some idea of the number of issues about which Congressmen may hear from somebody; and there are quite a number of issues that are of interest only to specific localities or persons, and so do not generally get much attention in the press, about which they will also hear.

In a series of interviews with Congressmen and senatorial assistants, I frequently discovered mail that, according to not uncommon habits of interpretation, would be regarded as "pressure," and sometimes heard of visits that would also be regarded as "pressure" —but the Senator or Congressman or assistant was sometimes indifferent to or unaware of any pressure, and in some cases explicitly said, "No, there's not much pressure in this." In one instance, as reported earlier, a highly regarded, long-experienced, and obviously astute senatorial legislative assistant said his office heard practically nothing about reciprocal trade; but the mail clerk reported it was the second most frequent source of letters to the Senator from his state, and had been for some time; and the Senator's administrative assistant told me of several delegations from back home who had waited on him, some of whom may have seen the Senator, urging more protection. The point is that neither the Senator nor his legislative assistant had the time or energy to devote even peripheral attention to these demands. The replies were written by the mail clerks and signed on behalf of the Senator by them or the administrative assistant; and the legislative assistant knew that the Senator had already made up his mind to support extension of reciprocal trade, so he didn't want to bother with the issue. Basically, such delegation of attention was due to the simple fact that the Senator was a member of subcommittees concerned with other matters, was involved with them, and was at the time preoccupied with his reelection campaign, as to which he had made the prior judgment that reciprocal trade and protection were trivial issues.

Even members of relevant committees may be so concerned with other matters—taxes and special tax considerations, for example, concern members of Ways and Means and Finance—that an issue such as reciprocal trade does not get attention. At the time I saw the late Senator George (in early 1954), he strongly created the impression that he was relatively unaware of what his constituents said about reciprocal trade, and his answers to my questions about what they said or communicated to him were speculative, so far as I could tell: They might do so-and-so. . . .

The marginal and differential nature of attention is illustrated by the response of two Representatives from the same city to a question about how much they heard about a particular economic issue. One said he had heard a great deal, the other very little. The actual point, on analysis of the two interviews, appeared to be that Mr. A, who had heard a great deal, interpreted discussion about unemployment as bearing on this issue, whereas B thought of unemployment as a separate issue, explicable in terms of various federal policies (such as federal overfavoritism to the South in economic regulations); and A encouraged people to write to him about this issue and to talk to him about it, whereas B did not (See Chapter 8 below.)

The almost universal denial of pressure from constituents on such an issue as reciprocal trade may be explained by the fact that real pressure is likely to involve patronage, jobs, passports, immigration visas, etc. These are the things that constituents really press on, and a Congressman often spends a good deal of time on them. Senators, on the other hand, belong to so many subcommittees and receive so much communication on so many issues over a period of time that they will pay attention only to those issues that strike them as really tough. During the period I was studying foreign trade matters, 1953-55, there were several issues that did perhaps demand central attention from several Senators—how to handle the Joseph McCarthy matter, for instance—and for those really worried about McCarthy, or about the St. Lawrence Seaway, or about something else, reciprocal trade automatically became of lower priority. The human capacity for worry and concern being, fortunately, limited, the issues to which central attention can be given are few.

But study of an issue frequently, journalistic analysis almost always, and very often the analysis made by politicians themselves when they talk about an issue give the impression that what the legislators hear, read, or say about it becomes a matter of central attention; usually it does not. I was extremely fortunate in that one of my first interviews on communications about reciprocal trade was with the late Senator Theodore F. Green of Rhode Island, who told me that, in connection with what Finance Committee members heard about reciprocal trade, I should study such matters as fast tax write-offs. I did not immediately see the point;

but it was in fact quite crucial, not only from the standpoint of the Senator, but also from that of some constituents. Tax write-offs, in his mind, mattered more to his business constituents than foreign trade or tariffs because they were more *relevant* to the questions of profits and employment in Rhode Island.

To take another example, several members of the Congress, generally supported by trade unions, disregarded completely the protectionist emphasis of friendly unions or their lobbyists, because they knew very well that, whatever these unions wanted in regard to reciprocal trade and protection, for most union leaders that was secondary to other legislative demands. Conversely, the expressed desire of the big CIO unions and of the automobile industry for a stronger reciprocal trade measure at that time, so far as one could tell, had little political effect, because everyone concerned knew that these unions and that industry had many higher priorities, and reciprocal trade was only marginal; the automobile companies, for instance, were much more concerned in those years about the St. Lawrence Seaway, just as the coal-carrying railroads, on the whole, although somewhat opposed to reciprocal trade, were only very marginally opposed to it as compared with their opposition to the Seaway and to the receipt of government favors by the trucking industry. Anybody who reads an account of the fight between the railroads and truckers in those years, in Pennsylvania, for example, knows that the railroads must have paid far more attention to this than to reciprocal trade.

So we found that in general those Congressmen and Senators who reported interest or concern on a matter among their business constituents *exaggerated* that interest and concern. The Congressman from the district including Cumberland, Maryland, for example, thought some of its leaders felt real protectionist sentiment, and *a priori* I had anticipated this would be the case, but there was really no one in business or in the unions in the entire community who cared about the matter, except (because of orders from headquarters) a few officers of one dwindling union. Almost certainly few in Cumberland knew at the time and no one remembered a year later how the Congressman voted on reciprocal trade. The Congressman from another district, similarly, reported thousands of letters, a number of conversations, and real interest among his campaign workers on the matter; but it was his belief after it was all over that no one in the district knew how he had voted. He was then in his first term; as he got on in seniority, he certainly came to learn more and more that "inspired" mail and stimuli of the sort he received on reciprocal trade usually represent momentary, marginal attention.

This situation—marginal attention—in part explains the constant disappointment that people who really deeply believe in some kind of legislative change experience when they find it does not matter very much—that it is only marginally significant—to the politicians and civic leaders who have supported it. Many of them become more or less bitter or cynical about the way they are misled, but in fact it is their own enthusiasm, equating fleeting concern or courtesy with central attention, that misleads them. Even experienced politicians who happen to care about some particular matter fail to take into account the wide range of attention and emphasis, and complain about the opportunism, etc., of those who give in early or shunt that issue to one side—yet the latter may have always regarded the issue as marginal.

A good deal has been written purporting to explain how it happens that broad-gauged organizations have little political influence as compared with special-purpose organizations. Actually, if one added up all political influence put together on all issues, this might not be true, but representatives of broad-gauged organizations are faced with the same problem that politicians themselves face, central attention versus marginal attention; and they similarly have to pay special attention to nonpolitical issues of organizational survival, office politics, and the like, which can make the legislative program secondary. (Some special-purpose organizations, though by no means all, actually do get together people to whom their purpose is really central.)

In any event, multipurpose organizations cannot exert pressure on *many* issues at once. Either they have to focus attention on a few or they have to jump constantly from one to another. And in general it is only the organization that has both an interest and a purpose that is legislative or involves governmental action, *and which is reasonably narrow*, that can focus continuing attention upon its governmental purpose; the National Guard Association is a case in point. But in trade associations one often finds the same grumbling about indifference, unconcern, and opportunism that one finds in civic groups or in lay analyses of politics, because most trade association members have more interest in running their businesses and in local matters than in remote governmental programs.

Political campaigning and candidacy are, still more generally, efforts to capture the marginal attention of people whose major interests are elsewhere. This is obvious in campaigns for most offices, including congressional office, where the mere fact of incumbency or of a name that is known is a tremendous advantage. It is this marginal nature of political attention that makes the possession of a euphonious or striking or ethnically compatible name advantageous; literally, this may be all that some voters perceive about a candidate, and they make their choice on this basis. Handshaking, buttons, and the other paraphernalia of campaigns are efforts to capture marginal attention from people preoccupied with other matters. And the seeming incongruities of election results—a man for one office receiving the same votes as a man for another office who holds quite a different program (Ben Butler for Congress and Grant for President in the Essex congressional district of Massachusetts in 1868, for instance), or a "nice guy" who shakes hands very amiably winning because he is a nice guy, while for another office a dramatic s.o.b. who never even pretended to be a nice guy wins—are explained again by this same phenomenon, marginal attention. Of course, there are people who are consistently concerned with legislation; and there are more people who are consistently concerned with politics, patronage, contracts, etc.; and there are people who know and are personally devoted to individual candidates; the attention of these people is not marginal. And there may be issues on which substantial numbers of people have a direct central concern, although I can think of precious few issues so far in American history to which anywhere near a majority has paid central and accurate attention. *History is distorted very badly, just as journalism is, because of the implication that most people were continuously and centrally concerned with the political issues.* Except in cases of warfare, starvation, and epidemic, this seems unlikely. A painting of a French citizen, calmly fishing, his back turned to the guillotine where the royal family was awaiting execution, illustrates the nature of inattention in matters political.

Obviously, simply to point out the phenomenon of marginal attention is not enough; I was inhibited for some years from writing anything systematic about politics because I felt *but could not formulate* the point; and having formulated it is simply a beginning. It seems probable that the most promising line is to try to develop ways of stating the magnitude and nature of attention. How much greater (in what way?) was the attention of whom to Joseph Mc-Carthy's allegations in the mid-fifties than to reciprocal trade? How much greater is the attention (of whom in what way in what relationship to the Congressman) directed toward filling a vacant postmastership or routing a particular highway than to foreign aid appropriations?

It is perhaps worth adding that awareness of this point came to me when, as a member of the staff of the governor of Massachusetts, I was (*a*) engaged in obtaining and analyzing reports from about two hundred autonomous agencies for the governor and (*b*) preparing (with three others) and writing drafts of his program (what in most administrations would have been his inaugural message).We got together enormous masses of material, containing numbers of ideas; in general, no one subsequently did anything significant about 99 percent of them, including most of what was said in the inaugural message; I, like others on the governor's staff, was at times reminded that we had said we were going to try to do something valuable, important, and significant. I chose for myself two emphases, on which I accomplished nothing whatsoever; nor, with two exceptions, do I see any indications that anyone in that particular governor's office chose and carried into effect any priorities. Most attention in fact was marginal, so far as the central state administration went.

I may say that I was never aware of any pressure exerted at my level on legislative matters, except for a few that were in essence private, special bills, and to a very limited degree on the legislation requiring garbage to be cooked in accordance with statutory regulations. On the other hand, I was continuously, many hours in the day, aware of patronage pressures of one sort or another. This arose partly out of the immediate political situation, partly because I had chosen civil defense as a special interest (in several eastern states, and particularly in Massachusetts, the handling of civil defense then resembled an old-fashioned spoils system), partly perhaps because my office was on the same floor as those of the patronage secretaries, who in this administration were on the governor's staff (rather than, as under his predecessor, being attached to the state committee), and conceivably because of my own special awareness of patronage issues, since I had previously taken part in the election campaign. In any event, continuing central attention to any legislative issue at all under these circumstances took a deliberate (or a neurotic) perseveration that would not necessarily guide or afflict most persons in such a post. The contrast between this reality and the journalist's, the college professor's, and the interested citizen's discussion of our legislative concern (particularly the discussion of our governor's campaign for a sales tax in 1957) was startling.

CHAPTER EIGHT

The Representative and His District

I

We talk frequently of a Representative or Senator "representing" or "failing to represent" his constituents. This is shorthand. The fact is the Congressman represents his image of the district or of his constituents (or fails to represent his, or our, image of them). How does he get this image? Where does it come from?

On Numerous Important Policy Matters, He Hears Nothing from His Constituency: But whether he hears anything on an issue, what

---

Reprinted (modified) from *Human Organization,* vol. 16 (Spring 1957). Copyright 1957 by Lewis Anthony Dexter. The present analysis is based upon about 650 interviews conducted from 1953 through 1957 (420 of them by the author) with politicians, businessmen, trade-union leaders, and departmental officials, about the influences impinging upon the formulation of policy. More than one hundred of those interviewed were members of Congress and forty were executive assistants on Capitol Hill. Four hundred of the interviews utilized dealt with formation of policy or communication of preference on the Reciprocal Trade Extension Acts of 1953, 1954, and 1955, and it is around these that the analysis was chiefly organized. An article by Frank Bonilla, "When Is Petition Pressure?" in *Public Opinion Quarterly,* 1956, is based upon the same set of interviews. Considerable use has been made of my own participation in politics, in, for example, the state government of Massachusetts, from September 1956 to August 1957, in the Stevenson primary campaign of 1956, and in an effort to arouse public interest in a civil defense bill.

he hears, whom he hears from, and how he interprets what he hears all *vary* depending upon the kind of person he is, the kind of associations he has had and has now in the constituency and in Washington, the public image of his interests and concerns, and the background information or misinformation he possesses. An editorial summary of an earlier draft of this paper said: "Congressmen make choices about which people communicate with them." In large part this is also a manner of speaking. It would be more precise to say that the people, in electing a Congressman, have chosen one sort of recording instrument or another, and that while one instrument may be adjusted to catch and hear one sort of communication, another will hear a different sort, and so on. Although Congressmen do, to a small degree, consciously choose what they shall hear, it is probably more significant that in large measure their personalities, careers, and public images make them choose what they hear and how they interpret it.

A good many Congressmen believe that their districts feel very strongly on this, that, or the other issue, and that they are constrained therefore to vote a certain way. The more sophisticated realize, of course, that legislative procedures and processes are so complex that it is more often than not possible to go through the motions of conforming to such views without helping to enact them, when they believe the public preference to be wrong. On most issues, out of a desire to serve the district or from indifference, many Congressmen do go along with any view they believe "the district" holds strongly. When the chips are down, and they have to declare themselves, *some* will vote against their convictions and for their constituents' (presumed) preferences.

This situation has led to a series of classical utterances on the moral problem of the Representative: *Should he sacrifice his judgment to his constituents' inclinations as he conceives them or not?* It would be more accurate to emphasize the ways in which representatives' beliefs about constituent preference are functions of the channels of communication and the special processes of transaction between constituents and Representatives rather than of anything else.

If this is in fact so, more students of representation and Representatives would concur with Congressman Herman P. Eberharter's interpretation of the representative-constituent picture. He had for years been at the center of the legislative issues that have provoked the most comments by critics of "pressure," and he told me early in my study of reciprocal trade (1953):

"You know, I am sure you will find out a Congressman can do pretty much what he decides to do and he doesn't have to bother too much about criticism. I've seen plenty of cases since I've been up here where a guy will hold one economic or political position and get along all right; and then he'll die or resign and a guy comes in who holds quite a different economic or political position and he gets along all right too. That's the fact of the matter."

II

The First Difference Between Some Congressmen and Others Is How (Consciously or Unconsciously) They Define Their Responsibilities: Many of the Congressmen interviewed about both tariff and defense matters referred to a personal conception of what they owed their jobs, of what in some circles would be called "professional obligation." A few had explicit and many apparently held implicit theories of representation. These theories of representation were not, except in a few instances, so far as I could tell, *directly* derived from philosophical or academic sources. They resulted from the experiences of men facing the actual moral complexities of a job.

Some members spoke of their obligation to select the right course, regardless of the views of their constituents. For instance, Congressman Noah Mason for a good many years represented a district that (according to interviews with business interests in the district and from an economic analysis of its industrial situation) was inclined to favor the reciprocal trade program. Nevertheless, he said, "Oh, knowing my stubborn characteristics, no one ever thinks he can change me, you know. . . . Some of my people say, 'You may not agree with this man Mason, but you know where he stands.'" Mr. Mason agreed that if fate were to select as his successor a Clarence Randall–type "free trader," such a man would be able to vote for a reciprocal trade program without much difficulty, but Mason interrupted an effort to probe this point further by declaring: "That's because they [my constituents] do not really understand the matter.

During the twenty-one years reciprocal trade has been in effect, it has had . . . [and he named various alleged or actual consequences that he regarded as evil]. There isn't any use trying to change me!"

Another Congressman, whom I shall call Mr. Emphatic, on the other hand, voted the same way as Mr. Mason on the Reciprocal Trade Extension Act of 1955 partly because of a different definition of his responsibility. He said: "My first duty is to get reelected. I'm here to represent my district. . . . This is part of my actual belief as to the function of a Congressman. . . . What is good for the majority of districts is good for the country. What snarls up the system is these so-called statesmen—Congressmen who vote for what they think is the country's interest. . . . Let the Senators do that. . . . They're paid to be statesmen; we aren't." (This was said sarcastically, but without humorous intent.)

A Congressman we may call Mr. Leader, as strong a supporter of reciprocal trade as Mr. Mason is an opponent of it, comes fairly close to Mr. Mason in his attitude toward constituent opinion. Said Leader: "You're not identifying me on this, of course? It's strictly confidential? Always bear in mind there are those in Congress who lead their districts and those who are led by them. . . . It makes a lot of difference. . . . The ruanga growers of my district never opposed *me* on reciprocal trade. . . . I think I have convinced these men that a program of high tariffs would not assist them and I think my viewpoint has gained general acceptance from them."

Several times he spoke of himself as having "straightened out" people who had seen the matter "wrongly." In another interview (by Kenneth Kerle, as part of the study summarized in Chapter 5) during the same session, but dealing with an unrelated piece of legislation in which he had also played a prominent part, Mr. Leader showed his conception of his role on this matter to be very similar. The reciprocal trade issue is so well known, the origin of Mr. Leader's views so deeply based, and his technical knowledge of the field so considerable that he is almost certainly right in his contemptuous dismissal of the possibility that any lobbying or pressure could change his position. However, regarding the moving-picture tax, it is entirely probable that a public relations campaign did manipulate *the facts* that came to his attention and to the attention of some of his colleagues, much as Mr. Fourth, as I shall call him, was influenced on the reciprocal trade issue.

Mr. Fourth represents a district in which there is vociferous anti–reciprocal trade sentiment. This district also has strong economic reasons for supporting reciprocal trade and a particularly influential number of intellectuals predisposed toward reciprocal trade. Mr. Fourth showed how a portion of the district can influence a man when he said, "My impulses when I came down here were in favor of trade, not aid, until I started to hear all sorts of things from my district. . . . So, actually, when you stack all these things together, well, you're in favor of trade, not aid, but goodness, there comes a time . . . If trade means wholesale layoffs in your district . . . I've got any number of letters against it. Carpets, imported rugs . . . There's been around three hundred layoffs in a local bicycle plant. Textiles, chemicals, electrical equipment, glass salesmen . . . It's difficut to get figures. I assume the Randall Commission report has them. I haven't had time to read it. I don't know. . . . I assume that the people I hear from exaggerate the seriousness of the situation, but still that it is serious."

Mr. Fourth ultimately voted against reciprocal trade on the key votes; the decisive factor appears to have been his unwillingness to separate himself from several members from his state, also of junior status, who were more certain in their opposition to reciprocal trade. Mr. Fourth, according to his colleagues, was wavering as late as two hours before the vote. Had the chairman of his state delegation (who strongly supported the reciprocal trade bill for party reasons) personally requested his support, he might well have voted the other way. But he was obviously uncertain, *on the reciprocal trade issue,* whether to adopt the role of servant of his district (as he conceived its desires) or to think in terms of the ideology implied by the phrase "trade, not aid." How he would vote was therefore completely unpredictable. Had he stumbled into any one of three Congressmen with strong pro–reciprocal trade views in the lobby or the corridors just before the vote, he might have voted the other way.

Congressman Fourth's vote was unpredictable because on this particular issue he did not have a clear conception of what his obligations were. On some issues—flood control or taxes affecting the major agricultural product of the district—one could predict that he would see his responsibility as being almost exclusively to the district. On others—particularly those under consideration by the very important subcommittee of which he is a member—he would be strongly inclined to emphasize national interest in some form as against district concern; on that subcommittee, national defense often enters in.

III

Congressmen Tend to See Their Obligations as Being Either to the Nation or to Their Constituency: Other equally possible obligations are seemingly not considered.

Obligation seemed to be conceived as national interest versus district interest (district interest was often, as in the case of Mr. Emphatic, related to reelection, and therefore to self-interest). No Congressman interviewed indicated any feeling of moral obligation to our allies or to any other country, although our allies are regarded instrumentally as means. This is contrary to a theory sometimes expressed that Americans tend to adopt some favorite foreign country as "theirs." Also, reference to representing a region (the South, the West, New England) was very slight.

The Congressman's Definition of National Interest and Responsibility on a Particular Issue Depends in Large Measure upon his Understanding of the Facts of a Particular Issue: Both Congressman Leader and Congressman Mason were quite clear on what they believed were the facts of the reciprocal trade question, and they had no doubt about the effects of the legislation (although their facts were to a great extent contradictory and their conclusions opposite). Congressman Fourth, on the other hand, was susceptible to influence from either side because he lacked any clear idea of what reciprocal trade legislation means or entails. His sympathy for the phrase "trade, not aid" came from a diffuse and generalized acceptance of a *slogan* rather than from an understanding of facts or consequences. He was really uncertain what, if any, difference his vote on reciprocal trade would make to the national welfare. Thus he, much more easily than Mr. Leader or Mr. Mason, could see the matter as one of simply performing a service for discontented people in his district. It is far less likely that he would, in the absence of external stimuli, feel any strong need to learn the facts. On *service* matters—and much of a Congressman's job is service—most Congressmen are willing to go along with those constituents who seem to know what service they want performed, and how it is to be performed (provided, of course, nothing irregular is requested). But if, for instance, Mr. Fourth were a New Deal "intellectual"—and his district is one that in my judgment might easily elect such a person—he would have interpreted the same situation quite differently. And, if he were a *politically astute* New Deal "intellectual," he would have seen that the major agricultural crop of the district is exported, that several large industries in the area depend on foreign trade, and so forth.

A Congressman's Conception of His District Confirms Itself, to a Considerable Extent, and May Constitute a Sort of Self-Fulfilling Prophecy: Remember Congressman Eberharter's words: "You know, I am sure you will find out a Congressman can do pretty much what he decides to do and he doesn't have to bother too much about criticism." Within the limits of the morally and sociologically conceivable (no Congressman from Alabama in 1942 could have advocated integration, for instance), a Congressman has a very wide range of choices on any given issue, *so far as his constituency is concerned.* His relationships in the House or Senate and with his party leadership, of course, limit these choices severely. It is a fact, however, that there is no district viewpoint *as such* to be represented on the overwhelming majority of issues. A few will care one way and a few the other, but the issue will be insignificant or unknown to the great majority. Indeed, in many districts, only a fraction of the voters know the name of their Congressman, let alone how he voted on a particular issue.

A Congressman of my acquaintance took about a hundred letters that he received on a particular issue and checked the registration of the writers. He found that almost three-quarters of them were not registered in his district. What difference, then, would their views make with respect to his prospects for reelection? Mr. Emphatic, who insisted that he was representing his district's desires, was led nevertheless, by my questions, to admit that more than likely none of the workers presumably represented by him actually knew how he had voted. "Not a single one of them," he complained, "wrote in to thank me, though hundreds had written asking me to vote their way." He attributed this in large measure to the allegation that the largest newspaper in the district was anti-Emphatic. However, since newspapers published outside the district which gave front-page publicity to his stand had far greater circulation in the district than the anti-Emphatic local paper, this seems an unsound explanation.

Actually, most of the letters Mr. Emphatic received and most of the comments he heard originated in three large plants in the district, and they represented less than 7 percent of the voters of the district. These plants were organized by national unions, which, ironically enough, in chalking up Mr. Emphatic's score in 1956, were inclined to regard his vote against reciprocal trade as an antilabor vote. Fortunately for him, his stand on other matters and his personal contacts offset this factor. Of the groups in the district, only members of the League of Women Voters wrote to him in favor of reciprocal trade. "They aren't," he averred, "God knows, a potent political force; and all their letters are damn stilted, right out of the same handbook." Actually, however, it was likely that the League members would remember in 1956, and perhaps again in 1958, how he voted. And because of the ethnic and academic composition of the district, League members may have had some influence outside their own membership. It would have been perfectly possible for Mr. Emphatic to take the reverse position, favoring reciprocal trade, and still to regard himself as representing his district—particularly since the area also had a strong port interest.

A Congressman has great difficulty in deciding what the viewpoint of the district is even on such an issue as reciprocal trade. Most persons with an interest or belief in the tariff will have interests or beliefs in other issues as well. Thus the most effective representation of their overall interests may necessitate concessions on some matters, in order to get along with party leadership, colleagues, or prominent committee members in the Congress. "Joe Martin and Charlie Halleck, in their heart of hearts," said Representative Richard Simpson, "certainly go along with us, not with the White House, on this; and they can swing twenty-five votes, at least, any time they want. We lost by less than twenty-five votes, so they beat us." Martin was the Republican leader, Halleck his likely successor. Is a Congressman doing a better job of representing his district when he keeps in the good graces of such powerful men (and thereby helps to get a bridge or a new post office or a dam for his district) or when he opposes them on an issue, the details of which no one will remember six months later? Mr. Simpson was one of the most persistent enemies of reciprocal trade in the party, and he was probably the most effective in a quiet way. He was opposed to reciprocal trade in part because of its "harmful" effect on his district. However, he cheerfully admitted, "It wouldn't make any difference what I do on this matter," insofar as his reelection was concerned. Afterward he qualified this by saying that perhaps the incumbent ought not to stick his neck out strongly *for* reciprocal trade, but there was no call for activity of any kind. (Of course, Simpson was personally so powerful that he did not need to worry much about crossing Martin or Halleck.)

IV

A Congressman Hears Most Often from Those Who Agree with Him: A Congressman's relationships with his district tend to be maintained through a small group of people he knew before he was elected, or through a group that has since then worked closely with him. Generally speaking, the views of those whom he knew prior to his election tend to be more like his than do the views of the "average" voter. It is a well-known fact that we tend to be like the people with whom we associate and vice versa. Also, most of the people who have worked closely with the Congressman since his election—because he is a Congressman—have a particular ax to grind. They will naturally tend therefore to stress agreement with him on issues about which they are not concerned—just as salesmen typically do not disagree with their customers on politics. For several years, I wondered about the unfavorable references Congressmen frequently made to the League of Women Voters and several times to delegations from labor unions. Ultimately, it occurred to me that these two groups are probably the only ones that seriously, on a face-to-face basis, year after year, go over with a Congressman a series of issues on which they disagree with him. Because their efforts cannot be entirely discounted as "politics," they make Congressmen uncomfortable.

Congressmen may also have a few close supporters upon whom they rely who tend to become "their" men, and who shift as they shift. This is not always just a matter of holding on to a job, but may represent confidence in a man, prestige gained by association with him, or an unwillingness to sacrifice an investment in goodwill that may be utilized for better public or personal purposes in the future. Such supporters are likely to couch any criticism in tactical terms, and ultimately to follow the leader. Speaking as a formerly somewhat active politician myself, I am pretty sure that the men I choose to follow would be *right* from my standpoint on basic issues of international agreement, national defense, civil rights, and public safety and police, about which I particularly care. That is why I am for them. Consequently I can imagine few instances when I would seriously object to or criticize a stand they might take on some other and to me less important matter. This is true in spite of the fact that I am much more issue-oriented than most active supporters and campaigners.

Some Men Automatically Interpret What They Hear to Support Their Own Viewpoint: Senator Green of Rhode Island did not think he heard much about foreign imports. Congressman Forand, also from Rhode Island, said, "It's either the first or second most important issue with me. Unemployment is the other. And, of course, they're really the same thing."

The last sentence is the clue to why Mr. Forand heard so much more than Mr. Green about foreign imports. When Mr. Green heard about unemployment, he heard just about unemployment, or just about the declining industries of the area, or just about the invidious differential effect that accelerated amortization and certain other tax provisions had had on industry in the area. In fact, when I talked to him about the tariff, he advised me that I really ought to study accelerated amortization. Mr. Forand, however, interpreted almost any statement about unemployment as a plea for relief from foreign imports. Sometimes it was, but sometimes it wasn't. So, seeing the same men and hearing the same things said, Mr. Forand "heard" about tariff matters, Mr. Green did not.

The difference between Messrs. Green and Forand was illustrated at a dinner held by a joint labor-management committee from their area. The speaker who represented the trade association was really eloquent when he spoke for protection and against reciprocal trade. He hardly mentioned regional competition. The union executive who followed him sounded as though he were giving a courtesy speech of no importance when he attacked foreign imports; but when he attacked the southern states, which in his view were "robbing the North of jobs and keeping wage rates down," he changed in manner and appearance to a deeply earnest man. Mr. Green turned to the representative of the trade association and asked a searchingly critical question that implied that the latter really knew nothing about foreign trade and its effect on the economy. Mr. Forand, however, stood up to take the bows when another colleague, Anton N. Sadlak, from the adjoining state of Connecticut, assured those present: "Forand and I, you can be sure, will do everything to protect our industries against foreign competition. We will be right in there fighting for you." Almost certainly, Forand actually "heard" strongly held views against reciprocal trade on this occasion, whereas Green did not.

In More General Terms, What Congressmen Hear and How They Interpret What They Hear Depends on Who They Are: Conventional discussion of the relationship between Congressmen and constituents assumes that the kind of man the Congressman is has no bearing on what he hears from the district, and that the question is whether he follows or contravenes district sentiment. The notion of the Congressman representing "the" district at least needs restatement *in terms of a particular Congressman* who represents what he hears from the district as he interprets it. And his interpretation results from his being the particular kind of person he is and is reputed to be.

Of course, Congressmen will hear many of the same things. The similarity is very great, since there are common factors in the careers of American politicians, and since Congress is a continuing social group where habits and attitudes are likely to persist. The old hands (staff, lobbyists, and active constituents as well as members) teach the younger ones. Furthermore, and not surprisingly, within any given district the balance of forces may continue so that several successive Congressmen will belong to the same politico-social group (sometimes even when they are members of different parties). The real test of how successfully the district exerts an inescapable pressure upon the Congressman comes when, without any sharp shift in population characteristics in the district, the Congressman comes from a different social grouping than most of his constituents.

Students of comparative politics have, however, much more manageable ways of exploring this problem than by studying the activities of Congressmen from the same district at different times. For instance, even in terms of our focus upon substantive issues, if I had realized the significance of knowing how a Congressman's interpretation of what he hears is affected by his perception of the job, the constituency, and the facts, I could have tried to find out how

Senators of the same party and from the same state (but representing different factions and obviously looking at the world differently)
understood the reciprocal trade question. It is hardly credible that
Alexander Wiley, Republican of Wisconsin, and Joseph McCarthy,
Republican of Wisconsin, could have heard the same messages on
domestic security and international relations. It would have been
interesting, therefore, to find out whether Wiley was as sympathetic
as McCarthy was to the "need" for protecting Wisconsin's fur-
bearing mammal breeders and trappers against foreign competition.
A. Willis Robertson and Harry Byrd of Virginia, Lyndon Johnson
and Price Daniel of Texas, J. Glenn Beall and John Butler of Maryland, Ed Martin and James Duff of Pennsylvania, Norris Cotton and
Styles Bridges of New Hampshire, Wayne Morse and Richard Neuberger of Oregon, all would have made interesting studies from
this standpoint. As it happened, I did most of my interviewing with
Representatives simply because Senators' schedules are so much
more complex and it is harder to get to see them. (A first-term
Senator may serve on as many as fourteen subcommittees, something unimaginable in the House.)

V

Transaction Rather than Interaction: As long as we think of the
relationship between a member and a district as *inter*actional—
one pressing on the other in a kind of billiard-ball psychology—I
suspect that we will have considerable difficulty in describing or
understanding exactly what goes on. The *trans*actional mode of
analysis, as developed by John Dewey and Arthur Bentley,[1] supplies
us with a leading hypothesis in terms of which political communications can be understood.

*How a Congressman Was "Influenced" by His District: A Trans-
actional Relationship:*   Mr. Serious-Consideration provides a very
good case study of how a particular constellation of factors in the
district may lead to a particular vote. The vote cannot be understood

---

[1]John Dewey and Arthur Bentley, *The Knowing and the Known* (Boston: Beacon, 1949);
and Bentley, *An Inquiry into Inquiries* (Boston: Beacon, 1954).

unless we recognize that both a Congressman, as a personality and at a particular time, and the district, as he understands it, are variables.

During the spring of 1954, my old friend Mr. Straightforward did considerable canvassing in the district with a view to running for Congress in the primary against Mr. Serious-Consideration. Mr. Straightforward, incidentally, had held public office in the area several times before. He told me, in effect, "There's practically no interest in trade or tariff matters in the district. If you're thinking [as we were] of interviewing businessmen and labor leaders about it, don't bother. None of them know anything about it. It just doesn't bulk large in their sight." Mr. Serious-Consideration, however, reported in the same year that in his view it was the most significant or certainly one of the three most significant issues to his constituents.

Why the difference? It can be explained, I think, partly by the fact that Mr. Serious-Consideration was, consciously or unconsciously, looking for ways in which he could appeal to local labor without offending local business. Protection against "low-wage foreign imports" is, as trade association executives pointed out to us, an excellent issue for *uniting* labor and management in depressed or dying industries (of which there were several in the district). Mr. Straightforward, on the other hand, had a program for economic redevelopment and reform of labor legislation which deflected the attention of those whom he met, whether they agreed with him or not, from such issues as the tariff. He therefore probably rarely heard about the tariff as an issue. Then, too, in manner and bearing Mr. Straightforward is clearly an intellectual, and one of the popular conceptions of the intellectual is his belief in free trade, unless evidence to the contrary is supplied. Mr. Serious-Consideration is not at all of this type. Finally, Mr. Straightforward's worst fault as a politician is a rather curt dismissal of anything he regards as nonsense. Mr. Serious-Consideration, on the other hand, might justly be criticized for not being able to distinguish between more or less unmotivated grumbling and serious pleas for effective action. (Mr. Serious-Consideration is, in other words, the kind of man who could be readily persuaded that every businessman who complains about taxes is earnestly desirous of reducing armaments.)

Mr. Serious-Consideration is (rather remarkably among Congressmen) a worrier. He seems genuinely to believe that we must shore up NATO by strengthening trade relations. Therefore, he called a meeting of everyone in his district who might be interested and wanted to come to discuss the problem. After this meeting, his office, which had already received a good deal of mail on the subject, was simply overwhelmed by protectionist mail. This came about because people who had attended the meeting told their friends and business acquaintances about his indecision. Mr. Serious-Consideration had called upon persons who he thought might be interested. Naturally, most of those who turned up were from protection-minded industries. It is much easier for many businessmen who seem to be in considerable economic danger from foreign imports to take a day off to attend a meeting on trade and tariffs called by a Congressman than it is for businessmen who *might* benefit economically if international trade were increased in total. It is more difficult, of course, for professional and salaried people to take such time off, and it is usually quite impossible for them to charge the cost off as business expense.

So this meeting, because of the way it was called, was "stacked" in this particular district. If, on the other hand, Congressman Richard K. Lankford of the Fifth District, Maryland, had called such a meeting, it might well have been stacked the other way. His district is a big tobacco-growing area that is well aware of its dependence on sales to Switzerland, and there had been Swiss threats to cut off purchases unless the U.S. withdrew its trade barriers to Swiss watches. Congressman Serious-Consideration or even Congressman Lankford, however, by some planning could have gotten a more balanced attendance. A different picture would have developed if national or state leaders of those unions in the district whose headquarters favored reciprocal trade had been consulted; and if the several college professors of economics in the district and representatives of the Grange and the Farm Bureau had been invited; and if an effort had been made to get some of the nationally known supporters of reciprocal trade having some ties with the district to present their viewpoints. Or several organizations could have been asked to do what the League of Women Voters has done in some areas—study the dependence of the local industries on foreign trade.

Mr. Serious-Consideration would have had to be a different kind of man to provide wider representation at his meeting. And if the agricultural commodity in which Mr. Serious-Consideration himself has had an interest were on an export basis (as it was prior to World War II), his picture of the situation might well have been altered. He would then have been hearing from his own associates in his own trade association. (The only reason that the commodity was not exported during 1953–55 was that the American market consumed all that was then produced.)

Mr. Serious-Consideration finally decided to vote against the party leadership on the key votes on reciprocal trade. He justified himself by objecting to various procedural aspects of the legislation —for instance, the so-called gag rule, under which the bill was brought to the floor. But he had not objected to this gag rule, which is familiar parliamentary practice, in other cases where it was invoked. He continued to regard himself as a strong advocate of reciprocal trade.

When a Congressman Was Not Much Influenced by His District: Representative Herbert B. Warburton (Republican, Delaware, 1953–55) provided a particularly clear example of the way in which a Congressman may select the kind of communications he hears. In answer to a question from me, he said to his secretary, "Am I right? We haven't received mail from more than five people on this tariff business." I looked somewhat astounded and she replied, "Yes, except of course for the pressure groups." The Congressman had instructed her to segregate all recognized pressure-group mail. And he added, quite offhandedly, that he would discount, "because of his self-interest," one out of the five people who had written him about the tariff. His attitude may, in part at least, explain why the chemical companies and other industries in the state had never given him "any particular specifications" on the tariff. It certainly clarifies his assertion that his approach to the problem of communications had "choked off" pressure-group mail.

Such an approach is relatively easy in Delaware, where Du Pont, because of its tremendous size and consciousness of its own vulnerability, has developed a practice and to some extent a doctrine of self-restraint. In a sense, Congressman Warburton's procedure[2] was made much easier because of the effect upon Du Pont of the munitions investigations of thirty-odd years ago, and the company's

---

[2]Congressman Warburton followed the same procedure on other matters. He was, it is true, rather badly beaten in his try for the Senate in 1954 by the incumbent Democrat, J. Allen Frear, but there is no reason to suppose his handling of communications had anything to do with the outcome. Far more significant political factors, such as the downstate opposition to integration, probably explain that.

For background on Warburton's district, see "Delaware: Where the Elephant Fears to Dance Among the Chickens," in Raymond A. Bauer, Ithiel de Sola Pool, and Lewis A. Dexter, *American Business and Public Policy: The Politics of Foreign Trade* (New York: Atherton, 1963), pp. 265–76; reprinted in, among others, *American Governmental Institutions*, ed. Aaron Wildavsky and Nelson W. Polsby (Chicago: Rand McNally, 1968), pp. 463–72.

subsequent earnest effort never, never, never to get into that sort of trouble again. Thus it could happen, when a prominent Delaware Democrat was asked why Du Pont had not put on a campaign in regard to tariff matters (if, as it was reported, Du Pont was hostile to the Reciprocal Trade Extension Act), that he said in a genuinely shocked voice, "Oh, the company would never allow that, two or three letters at the most."

A Congressman's Reputation Among Those Who Might Want to Influence Him Determines in Large Measure What Actually Is Said to Him: Most lobbyists appear to follow the principle of going to see only those who already agree with them. "Work with your friends, but don't stir up your enemies" is a principle fairly widely held by Capitol Hill lobbyists. (Since each Congressman has his own office and can be approached separately, this is fairly easy. However, in those state capitols where members of a committee, even though they may disagree on a particular issue, nevertheless hang around a lot together, it is reportedly more difficult. Here the lobbyists may use a different technique.) There is a reason for this prudence. Most investigations of lobbying and of particular lobbyists seem to have been started by Congressmen who were annoyed at being continually approached by lobbyists with whom they disagreed. There is also another possible reason: it makes the job easy for the lobbyist. Representatives of the League of Women Voters and of labor-union councils, who do not follow this principle, make themselves unpopular in some quarters.

The tendency to abstain from trying to influence those whom you believe to be against you affects the districts back home as well as professional Capitol Hill lobbyists. The Farm Bureaus in Congressman Mason's district, like most Farm Bureaus, were definitely committed to the reciprocal trade program. Nevertheless, when a delegation went to see him, it made no effort to talk in favor of reciprocal trade (although delegations from neighboring bureaus from similar districts did reportedly do so when talking to *their* Congressmen). Our correspondent in Mr. Mason's district inquired of Farm Bureau representatives why they made no such effort, and he summarized their attitude this way: "The farmers deliberately avoided mention of tariffs. When I asked one of them why he didn't beard old Mason in his high-tariff den, he replied, 'Nothing in the world will change his thinking on tariffs, so why bother? He knows how we feel and can't help but feel a little nervous about the situation. So we can take that nervousness and get him to go along with us on things he isn't so dead set against.' " The probability is that they didn't *change* him on anything, but they may have influenced him to take a more aggressive and effective part on an issue of importance to them—an issue on which he did not disagree, but which he considered less important than they did.

In another instance, the Congressmen from a certain area were inclined to be rather blunt and not to rely on any indirection. Before the 1955 vote on reciprocal trade, the Farm Bureau sent representatives in to talk with these Congressmen. One of them, whom I shall call Congressman Ridge, told me that the farmers said, "National asked us to pass the word along that we're in favor of reciprocal trade—but we shan't be mad if you vote against it." Then, according to Mr. Ridge, one of the Congressmen asked the Farm Bureau men if any one of them really favored reciprocal trade. Anyone who knows the Congressmen present can be sure that at least two of them would look ready to slay on the spot any farmer bold enough to say yes. Apparently no one did say yes, and the reason may have been similar to that advanced by the Farm Bureau member from Mr. Mason's district. So Mr. Ridge, who was not so strongly opposed to reciprocal trade as some of his colleagues, was pushed to this conclusion: Everybody in my state is against reciprocal trade. The only ones for it would be the ultra-internationalists.

Of course, if Mr. Ridge were a devoted supporter of reciprocal trade, or if he were a really sophisticated analyst of interpersonal relations, he might well have felt that the conclusion was not that easy. But he is neither of these, and so he allied himself entirely to his colleagues' opposition to the reciprocal trade program.

Several Congressmen told me that they tell their constituents, in effect, "I want a letter of such-and-such a kind or I won't pay any attention to it." One of the most dedicated opponents of reciprocal trade in the country was a man who had often pointed out that reciprocal trade is really an invention of Karl Marx himself, designed to "make us captives of the Kremlin," developed and implemented by Harry Dexter White. This Congressman stated that he told his constituents that he was interested only in "factual, thoughtful" letters, nothing mass-produced or propagandistic. He also told me that in three months he had not received one single letter opposing his views on reciprocal trade, whereas he had received over 2,000 supporting his position, 1,750 of which were definitely individually composed letters. The very extremity of his position apparently led those who might have disagreed with him to feel, "Oh, what's the use?" Senators who make statements of this kind, however, may simply not know what mail they get, since the mail clerks handle it. Most members of the House do have a fairly good idea of what is coming in to them. Of course, protectionist mail was mass-produced in a way in which reciprocal trade mail was not, and it is far more likely that a protectionist Congressman would receive nothing in opposition to his stand rather than the reverse. (Oil interests on the Atlantic seaboard did mass-produce mail protesting the fuel-oil quota.)

We need more knowledge of the image of a person to whom a communication is sent as it appears in the mind of the sender. By and large, I strongly suspect that the bulk of political communications in the United States today tends to be addressed to those believed most likely to be sympathetic. Exceptions may occur when an issue becomes one of great involvement (as reciprocal trade did *not*, from 1953 to 1955) or of interest to persons politically very unsophisticated who have no image of specific political figures. (Occasionally, too, a writer may regard his request as one for a personal service, but in the recipient's view it may involve an issue. A sympathetic response is expected, of course, to a request for a personal service.)

Some Communications Tend to Be Unclear in Their Meaning: A good deal of so-called lobbying by constituents tends to be nothing more than a social visit and a general discussion. One Senator's assistant said, "You know, many of these guys who come in here from back home never talk about issues at all. I've seen lots of them supposedly lobbying. Now, Roughie [the Senator] takes me to lunch with them and we go out to lunch, but they don't necessarily talk about anything. Roughie just knows a good guy may be going out of business because he doesn't get more trade or so. It's the spirit that influences him." Interestingly enough, some weeks later I found that this particular assistant was completely ignorant of the quite strong feelings (verbalized in other quarters) on tariff matters of an important industry in the state. This is an industry whose representatives had visited him and the Senator, and in whose behalf he personally had spent many hours performing other chores in administrative agencies.

Mr. Personal, as I shall call him, represented a district very much like Rhode Island, and he was home every weekend. He was professedly strongly opposed to reciprocal trade, but when I questioned him, he said he really did not know whether people had talked about the tariff with him or not. At first it seemed as though this might be because of his schedule, which was so heavy that most men could not have stood it, and he must have been, as a result, always fatigued. But the real point appears to be that Mr. Personal's attention in oral conversations back home was focused on requests for personal services. He was the archetype of the errand-boy Congressman, and the only things he seemed attuned to hear were requests for personal services. He shunted comments on issues to one side or regarded them as preliminaries to requests for favors. When Mr. Forand heard someone talk about unemployment caused by foreign imports, he regarded it as a request to fight reciprocal trade. Mr. Green regarded it as nonsense, although possibly nonsense of which he should be cognizant. But Mr. Personal paid only vague attention to it except insofar as it led or might lead to a request for him to perform a service. In this he may well have been correct, for very few constituents talk about an issue with a Congressman just to talk about the issue. I spent about twenty days in the winter of 1956 acting as co-manager of a candidate in a congressional primary campaign, and about half of this time I was actually with the candidate. During the entire twenty days only four people raised any national or international issues whatsoever with him or me. Others who worked for him at the same time and in the same area had similar reports to make, and I have had similar experiences in other campaigns.[3]

VI

Important Instances When Congressmen Were Changed by Their Districts: In the two statistically notable shifts on reciprocal trade in 1955 as compared with previous years, (1) southern Congress-

---

[3]There is a sharp difference between one's experience when handling public relations and mail from interest groups at campaign headquarters and observations when accompanying candidates in the field. In the former case, a good many questions are asked about issues; in the latter, very few.

men, mostly representing textile manufacturing districts, for the first time voted against the Hull reciprocal trade program, in spite of a traditional veneration for free trade in the South; and (2) Farm Belt Congressmen, from districts where isolationist sentiment had been fairly strong, for the first time supported reciprocal trade on the key votes. The latter were presumably influenced by the organized efforts of national Farm Bureau leaders to get their local leaders to understand the (actual or alleged) dependence of farm prosperity upon international trade and the (actual or alleged) values of a program of trade, not aid. But those who were influenced were not, so far as is known, men to whom the issue mattered much one way or another. There is no way of sorting out the relative weight of the constituency's concern from that of the influence of the leadership of the Republican party, President Eisenhower, and Minority Leader Martin.

In the case of the southern Congressmen the matter is clearer. Here "pressure education"—agitation in the district—worked. They broke with the southern tradition and the tradition of Cordell Hull, the father of reciprocal trade. They challenged and to some degree pressured that highly respected southern Senator, Walter George, on his long-standing pro–reciprocal trade position. And they gave, in this case, a weapon to Herman Talmadge, George's potential opponent in the senatorial primary of 1956, in spite of the fact that practically none of them would have preferred Talmadge to George. This breaking with precedent was chiefly the result of the communications they received from their districts, largely from textile interests. Some southern Congressmen received more mail on the reciprocal trade question in a few weeks than they normally did in months on all issues combined. That the mail was more or less synthetic and stimulated is shown by the fact that some Congressmen, whose positions were known to be unchangeable, received not a single letter! For these southern Congressmen, such a flood of mail was apparently like the first engagement in a war for inexperienced troops. They had never seen anything of the sort before. The result: most of the Georgia delegation opposed reciprocal trade on the key votes. Hugh Alexander, successor to Muley Doughton, who as leader of Ways and Means had year after year pushed reciprocal trade through committee and the House much as Cordell Hull wanted it, voted against the program of Hull and Doughton.

This does not controvert what has been said before, except in one respect. Most of these men, although traditionally free-traders, cared very little about the issue one way or the other. If industry and the workers in their district were convinced that reciprocal trade would hurt them, they were willing enough to go along— just as most of them would go along with their farmers if the latter wanted new soil-conservation legislation. In either case, they would regard themselves simply as serving their constituents.

VII

Pressure Is How You See It: "Pressure" and "pressure politics" are regarded by most "sophisticated" people today as explaining a great deal that happens. But it was frequently impossible to find any admission of or apparently any awareness of pressure. That was not because shrewd and worldly politicians were concealing what really went on from this naïve and innocent interviewer and his naïve and innocent colleagues.

The reason is explained by an assistant of a Senator I shall call Mr. Service: "There are very few people actually pressuring us, even if you count all we hear about all issues. Seriously, the sense of being pressured is a matter of reaction. Other people who get no more mail than we do in this office would say, 'See how much pressure is on me.' We don't feel it. Sure, you get mail. It's just that so-and-so makes more phone calls than somebody else. The result is purely physical. It isn't a representation of what or how or when people are going to vote in elections. . . . My personal opinion is that members of most organizations make up their minds on what they read in the papers without reference to organizations."

With this theory of voting behavior, Senator Service's assistant naturally will not be too much worried by a good deal of effort to get him or his boss to change policies; he simply will not regard it as pressure.

Congressman Widesight, to whom I referred in Chapter 6, amusingly illustrated the point made by Service's assistant. Mr. Widesight has moods when he reaches way out into left field looking for things to worry about, things that might possibly defeat him. One day, discussing reciprocal trade, he said that things were very bad indeed. His reason was that he was getting "so much" mail against it. "I, whom they never used to bother at all!" When I checked with his secretary later, I found he couldn't possibly have received more than fifty letters (representing glass, electrical equipment, and two or three bicycle firms) opposing reciprocal trade. This was only a fraction of the mail Senator Service received on the same matter. It was also a fraction of what Congressman Widesight himself had several times received on other matters, such as postal pay increases. However, Widesight was accustomed to communications on that issue, and he wasn't accustomed to them on the reciprocal trade issue.

As a matter of fact, on the reciprocal trade issue, most of the Congressmen interviewed reported that no one had come to see them. Several of them expressed the wish that someone would make the issue clear. (This does not mean, of course, that they were not approached, but simply that they had forgotten the approach or had not realized its purpose.) Some of them tried to question me about the matter in what I think was a serious effort to get some guidance. Generally, as good interviewing technique requires, I maintained complete neutrality. However, in two conversations (after the vote, when it could make no difference) I think I convinced members that a strengthened escape clause results in the worst of both worlds.[4] This is a position I do hold, although I was of necessity neutral on the major substantive issue. It was perfectly clear that no one had ever really explained to the two members I talked to why there is objection to the strong escape-clause procedure, in spite of the fact that one of the two key votes on the issue revolved around this. (Since the key votes were decided by seven or fewer members, every vote counted.)

Even when there is a considerable amount of what the outsider would consider pressure, the point made by Senator Service's assist-

---

[4]Perhaps I should explain this. Escape-clause provisions permit U.S. producers who feel themselves handicapped in certain ways by competition from foreign imports, presumably admitted under reciprocal trade agreements, to appeal to the Tariff Commission, and if they can "prove injury" the Tariff Commission can and is then presumably morally obligated to suspend the harm-producing portions of the relevant agreements. That is, if squeegee manufacturers can show that a reciprocal trade agreement with Ruritania by which the duty on Ruritanian squeegees has been reduced from ten cents a pound to six cents a pound has led to a critical invasion of the U.S. market by Ruritanian-made squeegees and driven good New England squeegee manufacturers into a desperate situation, the Tariff Commission supposedly will take action to suspend that particular portion of the Ruritanian agreement. Of course, the Ruritanian government then has the right to suspend some equivalent portion of the agreement, to the disadvantage of U.S. producers—so perfectly innocent manufacturers of squodunks in Baltimore may suddenly find that the Ruritanian government, to balance the U.S. escape-clause action against Ruritanian squeegees, has raised its tariff rate on squodunks. The net result is that Baltimore squodunk manufacturers and Ruritanian squeegee

ant is entirely valid. What you call pressure, or what you feel to be pressure, depends on how thick your skin is. To many men in politics threats alone represent the only real pressure, because they know very well that few votes are actually lost on any one issue, such as reciprocal trade. But, of course, what is a threat to one man is not a threat to another. (For comparison, we should have studied some explosive issues like McCarthyism or humane slaughtering or perhaps some issues in which the profit-and-loss relationship is clearer, like the question of pay increases for postal employees.)

The most strongly felt kind of pressure on the reciprocal trade issue came, apparently, from Speaker Sam Rayburn and the Democratic leadership against the potentially recalcitrant Democrats. Speaker Rayburn attended a breakfast for freshman Congressmen shortly before the vote and said, in effect, that he'd discovered that those who go along get along. One new member regarded this as pressure—a threat. Another new member, actually probably more vulnerable because of his factional position and his position within the delegation, did not. Both of them failed to go along. Aside from this speech, most of the pressure on the doubtful members seems to have come through the grapevine *or from their own apprehensions as to what might happen if they bolted the party leadership* (the "law" of anticipated reaction).

One reason why fairly few members seem to have felt pressure on this matter is to be explained by reference to their background and associations in local politics. In many states, pressure on matters like highway contracts or patronage or even for or against gubernatorial programs must be relatively heavy—that is, threats are far more common at the state level than they are in Washington. Many Congressmen come from such a background, and a good many are

---

manufacturers, having presumably invested time and effort in establishing a marketing division abroad, and perhaps increased their actual production facilities because of the foreign marketing possibilities, suddenly find themselves forced to cut back.

As a matter of fact, it is generally thought—and was and is thought by me—that the escape-clause provision does discourage many manufacturers abroad from trying to market in the United States. In actual practice, the Tariff Commission has been extremely conservative about admitting proof of injury, and few manufacturers abroad have really been hurt by such actions; but how is a firm that might spend thousands or millions on developing a market to know it won't be the unlucky victim? Even if in the end its operations are not harmed, threats of escape-clause action may drag on for years, and during all this time foreign manufacturers who might otherwise enter the U.S. market will hesitate to do so.

My particular objection to the escape-clause provision is twofold: (*a*) it increases instability in governmental action on foreign trade, when trade is encouraged above everything else by the ability of suppliers to be sure what government will do; and (*b*) the possibility of retaliatory action (as against squodunkers in Baltimore) creates an economically and morally quite unfair hazard to trade development.

still involved in local conflicts about patronage, contracts, and so on. As a result, Washington to them seems very mild.

Nagging may also be called pressure, whether it is done by mail or in person. When a Congressman has definitely announced his stand and does not intend to switch it, he resents being bothered by avoidable pleas (pressures) to change. The resentment point, obviously, is highly individual, so one man's pressure is another man's routine.

It should never be forgotten that most Congressmen respect—although in an inarticulate or almost subconscious way—the right of petition. They have a general feeling that everyone should have a right to talk or write to them about any public issue. That's what they're there for. But they aren't as worried about each communication as college professors might expect. They generally feel they have an equal right to disregard the petitioner's point, once it has been courteously received and acknowledged. Until a Congressman definitely makes up his mind, it isn't pressure—it's communication or information. Much of what Mr. Fourth, for instance, believes about reciprocal trade he learned from his mail.

VIII

Opportunism Is Also Where You See It: Outsiders, nonpoliticians, tend to attribute many political decisions to opportunism. Also, opponents in politics sometimes attribute the decisions of the other party or faction to opportunism. However, in the interviews I conducted, few Congressmen attributed their friends' decisions or their own to opportunism. When friends differ on a particular issue, each may consider that the heat is on the other. It is certainly true that in these interviews many men were amazingly—and often embarrassingly—frank about events, relationships, and personal opinions. But insofar as the acknowledged pictures they have of themselves are concerned, at least as portrayed in their interviews with me, opportunism has little part. Even the Congressman who related his obligation to his district directly to his chances for reelection spoke of his "duty" to get reelected. No one used a systematically opportunistic vocabulary of motives to explain himself or his actions.

Perhaps a different type of interview, some sort of "depth interviewing," would bring out a hidden set of self-images at variance with this surface picture. However, I have no evidence to that effect and am inclined to doubt it.

This report is in contrast, as far as overt self-picturing is concerned, to the views of local politicians whom I have known, notably in Massachusetts and Kansas City, Missouri, many of whom (I am speaking of local Democrats in the 1950s) were far more ready to picture themselves as opportunists than the Congressmen interviewed in these studies. (In Massachusetts there has been some alteration in this regard in the 1960s; I have had no recent contact with local Kansas City politics.)

Part Three

MODELS AND COMPARISONS
FOR THINKING ABOUT CONGRESS

CHAPTER NINE

Models and Comparisons in the Study of Congress

Except for purposes meanly pedagogic, what use may
we make of notions analogic?
—UNKNOWN SOCIAL SCIENTIST, signing himself
"Puzzled Ph.D. candidate," *c.* 1954

I would like to place particular stress upon the dangers of the kind
of approach I have used in this book. In all branches of knowledge,
there seems to be a tendency to *over*emphasize whatever is properly
emphasized. A few years ago, there was difficulty in getting anyone
to pay any heed to the kind of approach that Bauer, Pool, and I
tried in *American Business and Public Policy.* I received a comment
from the *American Political Science Review* on an early draft of
my "The Representative and His District" saying that it was a
"disgrace to the political science profession that [anyone] calling
himself a political scientist" should write such an article; and no
book publisher had any interest at all in my book about Congress.[1]

---

[1] With one probable exception: it was my impression that I was specifically told by a
representative of a prominent publisher at 9 A.M. on a certain morning that his firm would
send me a contract. At 9:45 I received a call saying this was all off, nothing would be
done. It happened that I knew that the representative in question had an appointment at 9:15
with a man who was among the publisher's most prominent authors and who was also a very
bitter political enemy of Foster Furcolo, governor of Massachusetts, for whom I was then
working, and in whose offices I had seen the publishing executive. The inference was plain
enough, although there may have been less here than met the eye.

Yet a few years later, when I had succeeded in getting published, *American Business and Public Policy* was awarded the Woodrow Wilson Prize, and is otherwise sometimes well spoken of. "The Representative and His District" was reprinted a number of times and is a best-selling Bobbs-Merrill political science reprint, and in a single year seven respectable publishers asked me to submit to them a book on Congress!

The fashion had changed.

Emphases, perceptions, and notions of relevance have shifted—possibly slightly influenced by *American Business and Public Policy*, but also independently of it. Our political sociology, our low-key historical conservative-liberal orientation were more fashionable in the mid-1960s than in the mid-1950s. Some of our approaches to the study of social organization and the way in which individual perceptions and preferences modify patterns of role behavior have become far more "in" than they used to be.[2] The increasing appeal in the latter ideas I attribute to ideological and generational changes in the character of the political science audience; and I suspect the tendency I have noticed to bracket my work with that of Ralph Huitt on Congress[3] arises out of specific ideological and generational changes. I suspect that among older political scientists there existed a frame of reference, with some ideological basis, which on the whole tended to place the emphasis upon demand and reaction in political processes. This emphasis could be either populist, in the sense that wicked or corrupt surrender to pressure was observed and emphasized, or democratic, in the sense that congressional and legislative response to the people's will was reported and inferred.

Huitt, Bauer, Pool, and I,[4] on the other hand, present a congressional model in which the characteristics of Congressmen and their personal choices as to how to do the job matter. Individual Congressmen and congressional committees as social systems, etc., according to us, are selective mechanisms that screen out undesired inputs at the same time that particular Congressmen (and Congress as a body), because of the image they have acquired—an image very often closely correlated with reality—exert a stimulus value,

---

[2]But, rather sadly, I must emphasize that the transactional model that organizes all that Bauer and I did, and to some extent Pool's work, is very rarely noticed.

[3]See Ralph Huitt and Robert L. Peabody, *Congress: Two Decades of Analysis* (New York: Harper & Row, 1969).

[4]And, of course, many other scholars, too. See Peabody's review of the literature in *ibid.*

so that some communications are more likely to come to them, and others less.

I have not changed my mind since 1955 on the nature of the system we dealt with. *But* it is worth pointing out that any portrait of reality tends to be accepted and to become conventional not only because of its inherent validity, but because of its congruence with prevailing ideologies. (At the same time, no doubt, accepted portraits of reality may alter to some extent prevailing ideologies.) And the reverse proposition, of course, also tends to be true: prevailing preferences tend to screen away from attention, to stigmatize as irrelevant, actual happenings that are not seen as congruent.

Now, the upshot of all this is merely to suggest that whereas in 1955 writers like Huitt and me had no obligation to stress the dangers of our own emphases—there were enough barriers to our ideas then, without our creating more—the situation now is a bit different. At a practical level, I doubt whether anyone will take us so literally as to suppose that Congress and Congressmen, for instance, are completely autonomous; but there is some possibility now that, because we have pointed out that Congressmen and other politicians often have a considerable amount of freedom, some students, relying upon us, may go too far and ignore the correlated fact that Congressmen, in general, are also influenced by and respond to the environment. There may also be a tendency to generalize findings based on observations made at particular times under particular circumstances and treat them as universally true. While this is to be guarded against, our assertions are nevertheless far more than those of a "mere" case study. This book is in large measure an effort to show that much of what Bauer, Pool, and I first saw as part of our case study is almost certainly characteristic of the institutional system of the current Congress. The kind of thing Bauer, Pool, and I report, and Huitt too, is derived from *current* politics and the *current* sociological patterning of the Congress. The emphasis must be, for the present, on that word "current"; a good deal of analysis and report is necessary to determine whether what is here asserted applies or would apply to other legislative bodies, let alone to other political entities, or whether it was true of the Congress in 1890 or will be true of the Congress in 1990.

As a matter of fact, it is in principle perfectly conceivable that some particular congressional committee or group right now is affected by or pays attention to demands in a fashion not touched upon here. If so, then, of course, appropriate modifications should be made in any general statements about how Congress is influenced, how Congressmen act and react, and how they pay attention. That is, any student of Congress, or anyone trying to understand how to influence Congressmen, should always bear in mind the possibility that the parts of the organization with which he deals may not follow the models here put forth.

To the best of my judgment, the general transactional model, based upon the later work of Arthur F. Bentley,[5] will prove to be generally valid for analysis of any representative-legislative role. *I am interpreting representative-legislative roles as including all those situations in which a group of persons is selected by and is practically, as well as formally, responsible to clients or constituents, on the one hand, but, on the other, has in practice numerous opportunities to allocate values among these clients and constituents, to a substantial degree independently of or in opposition to the desires of a good many of them. A corollary of this kind of representative-legislative specialization is that representatives (1) can very rarely represent completely any one interest or demand because they must broker different demands and different interests and (2) tend to develop their own ethos and reference group, which are different from those of any of those persons whom they serve, represent, or employ.* Congressmen, for instance, often have a reference group in the Congress itself, or in the notion of politicians as occupying a distinct role, or in some subgroup within the Congress. For our purposes, it is likely that Methodist ministers and possible that wholesale salesmen, with their own clientele, perform a representative-legislative function. (This would be most noticeably true of wholesale salesmen during a shortage period, when they allocate rather than sell goods.)

The danger in the kind of research that Huitt, Bauer, Pool, and the rest of us have done, however, lies in the common tendency to turn working assumptions into dogmas of inquiry or theory. It seems to me that several great works of the past on legislative behavior, such as, for instance, Woodrow Wilson's *Congressional Government* or Bertram Gross's *Legislative Struggle*, have made it easy for those who use them to commit this error. Gross, in contradistinction to my book with Bauer and Pool, uses a billiard-ball *interactionist* model, it seems to me; Wilson's model cannot be so easily

---

[5] Arthur F. Bentley, *An Inquiry into Inquiries* (Boston: Beacon Press, 1954).

encapsulated in a phrase, but there are inherent in it, I judge, several assumptions about how rational and responsible and coherent policies are arrived at, assumptions that later writers (such as Herbert Simon, with his theory of satisficing, for example) would not accept, or earlier ones either (such as Edmund Burke, with his great respect for the historical process). Models are necessary, but they should be made matters of hypothesis rather than of unquestionable assertion.

Even if authors do not take their own models as unquestionable, they may—if their ideas become fashionable, or by the cumulative effect of other similar studies—tend to inculcate in readers the notion that their models are naturally true. Arthur F. Bentley, for instance, during his sixty years of scholarly work, never insisted on a given model as *true;* but it appears to be the case (as Mr. Bentley regretted in conversation with me) that some students of his great book on governmental pressures[6] accepted its assertions as scientific truth, which subsequently interposed a barrier to benefiting from later, more sophisticated statements (and incidentally led them to ignore Mr. Bentley's own later work). This sort of danger is especially great when an author's emphasis is, for whatever reason, focused upon a particular case or selection of cases, chosen according to some nonscientific criterion. It would be very easy for naïve readers of Edmund Burke on the American Revolution to interpret what he says about that event as justifying the French Revolution—to which Burke was, of course, bitterly hostile. Concentration on the case and its dramatic aspects might well conceal from many readers the underlying model that Burke was using throughout his political career—a model well analyzed by Gerald Chapman,[7] and which can be summarized, perhaps, as historic liberal-conservative, or, in anthropological terms, as involving a decent respect for the cultural values surrounding any institutional relationship or historical pattern.

I have therefore chosen to conclude the text of this particular book with a discussion of several kinds of analogies and comparisons to the Congress, in the hope that by stressing a number of models I may help us all to remember the danger of undue reliance upon any one model.

---

[6]Arthur F. Bentley, *The Process of Government,* 1908, reissued in 1949 by Principia Press, Evanston, Ill.

[7]Gerald Chapman, *Edmund Burke* (Cambridge: Harvard University Press, 1967).

CHAPTER TEN

Toward an Evaluation of Analogies for Interpreting and Studying the Congress:

AN EFFORT AT HISTORICAL AND ANTHROPOLOGICAL EXPLORATION

I

Some may feel that an exploration into historical anthropology or the nature of analogy has very little to do with the United States Congress. My own belief is evidently contrary; I believe that analyzing Congress in terms of a theory of analogies will provide a helpful perspective within which studies of the institution may be evaluated. I think also such an approach serves as a means of organizing a number of exploratory conceptions advanced by various writers about Congress in particular and politics in general.[1]

Arthur Maass, then chairman of the Department of Government at Harvard University, invited several scholars to present papers at the 1965 American Political Science Association meetings on the use of analogies in our field; he asked me to discuss analogies to Congress, which I did, in a paper called "What Is Congress Like?" This chapter is largely based on that effort.

[1]I personally find, indeed, the study of analogy more fascinating even than the study of Congress, because it seems to me that understanding analogy is basic to a whole set of notions—such is relevance and pertinence—which underlie any kind of useful interpretation of any social event; whereas Congress is, as it functions, a particular product of a particular cultural background, and could hardly exist in many societies.

"Metaphors and analogies ranging from loose correspondences to near isomorphisms are pervasive features of every scientific theory."[2] Indeed, as I. A. Richards, especially, has repeatedly argued, thought itself has a radically metaphoric element,[3] because thought depends upon classification and classification rests upon the assumption that specified analogies may, for the purposes at hand, be treated as homologies, or at least as having homologous characteristics. However, in all fields of thought, we are faced with the problem of deciding under what circumstances characteristics can be treated as "essentially the same." It is obvious enough that in physics, one kind of water and another kind of water resemble each other enough, *for certain purposes,* so that even though one has salt in it and the other does not, they can profitably be classified together. It is likewise demonstrable that in disciplines such as law, it has proved useful to classify together *for certain purposes* things that for other purposes appear profoundly different. The story of the British railway clerk who was immediately able to see that tortoises must, for billing purposes, be insects, is a classic example of the possibility and advantages of legal classification.[4]

Political science has long been concerned with exploring the validity and accuracy of analogies based upon legal classifications. We all now see, if there was ever any doubt, that although legally Great Britain may be a monarchy and France a republic, in substantive political terms both countries are parliamentary democracies. We see equally that although Great Britain is still formally a monarchy, it is not, for our purposes as political scientists, the same kind of monarchy it was in the days of Elizabeth I, still less the kind of monarchy that now rules in Saudi Arabia. Indeed, the early history of political science might be treated as an account of the way in which scholars have discovered that many legal classifications and analogies do not work—are not valid or fruitful—for our purposes. But, of course, one would have to add that more recently political scientists have been reporting that the kinds of

---

[2]Llewellyn Gross, ed., *Symposium on Sociological Theory* (Evanston, Ill.: Row, Peterson, 1959), Introduction, p. 9.

[3]I. A. Richards, *Interpretation in Teaching* (New York: Harcourt Brace, 1938), p. 48. Of course, Richards can trace his conceptual forerunners back a long way. William J. J. Gordon, in *Synectics* (New York: Harper & Row, 1961), quoting also Suzanne Langer, says, "Metaphor is the force that makes language essentially relational. . . . Once language is understood as fundamentally metaphoric, its relational potential can be expanded . . . *not only by making new metaphors, but by revitalizing the old and faded* [*ones*]. . . ." (Italics added.)

[4]Philosophers, concerned with classification, from time to time refer to this old story of a railway clerk who is asked by an impatient customer to arrange for shipping a bunch of tortoises. The railway clerk says: "Tortoises, sir? Tortoises? . . . No, sir, tortoises hain't

classifications and analogies used, discovered, or invented by those who first revolted against legal classifications are not themselves satisfactory for some purposes.[5]

Much analogizing is done intuitively. And, so long as scholars and practitioners are reasonably satisfied with a given set of analogies, they do not usually criticize them; until recently, at least, they did not even criticize the process by which they formulate them. That is to say, analogies are usually regarded—nearly always in the world of political practice, customarily even in the world of political analysis—as self-evident by those who accept them. There is a need for a greater emphasis upon exploring the classifications one uses and showing why they are valuable and fruitful. Of course, those who deal with very large-scale analogies or homologies do sometimes justify their procedures. If we were to analyze the question "Is Yugoslavia 'really' communist?" or "Is Newfoundland 'properly' classified as an underdeveloped country?" we could find some relevant discussion. There is also useful and generally applicable

---

hanimals, sir. . . . No, sir, they hain't birds, neither. . . ." And then, thumbing through the large manual of regulations for classifying goods shipped on railways, "And they hain't statuary . . . nor works of art. . . . No, sir, tortoises hain't reptiles, sir, nor religious goods. . . . Ah, sir, here we has it. Tortoises, sir, is hinsects!" very triumphantly to the customer, who by now is thoroughly cowed and ready to agree to anything.

See T. D. Weldon, *Vocabulary of Politics* (London: Pelican, 1953), for a clear and useful discussion of the difficulties with a vocabulary of political analysis which assumes that in politics we are talking about the same sorts of classes as those fruitfully developed in the study of physics.

[5]It might be desirable, I would guess, to explore the question whether a reaction to a reaction has, in some ways, inarticulately or irrationally, guided us in the kinds of classifications we employ. For instance, Arthur F. Bentley's initial great work, *The Process of Government* (first published in 1908, reissued by Principia Press, Evanston, Ill., in 1949), and the pressure-group interpretation of politics were in large measure based upon a reaction against the conventional quasi-legal interpretation of political processes; in the hands of such would-be followers of the early Bentley as Bertram Gross (*The Legislative Struggle* [New York: McGraw-Hill, 1953]), this reaction against legal formality turned into a presentation of struggle. In later works—of which Raymond A. Bauer, Ithiel de Sola Pool, and Lewis A. Dexter, *American Business and Public Policy: The Politics of Foreign Trade* (New York: Atherton, 1963), is one example—there is a reaction against the struggle metaphor. Now such reactions did not take place without attention to the data: it was rather that the early Bentley found it impossible to classify and formulate ideas about the data he was observing in quasi-legal terms, and we, equally, found it impossible to classify and formulate ideas about the data we were observing in struggle-pressure terms. (It is coincidental that we found ourselves guided in rejecting Bentley's supposed disciples by the later strictly methodological and epistemological writings of Bentley, who had for forty years or so abandoned the study of politics as such.) But would the early Bentley or Gross have couched their conceptions in just the terms they did if they were not reacting against their legally minded predecessors? And would we have couched our findings as we did if we were not reacting against Gross and the early Bentley? Of course, individual cases might be idiosyncratic; but I would judge that many of the scholars of one style, not just Bentley and Gross, were reacting against a legal approach, and that several of our peers, like us, are reacting against the pressure-group model.

treatment by literary critics of political rhetoric and interpretation.[6]

However, most literary critics with such a concern have either dealt with very large problems (how huge entities like societies or salvation schemes are classified) or with quite personal ones (how individuals perceive or react). Relatively little of the analysis of classification, comparison, and analogies that I have seen would apply to specific institutions or subsystems within a general system, such as Congress.[7] Nevertheless, we might profitably carry over the approach of the literary analyst of analogies to works on Congress. Typically, I find it easier to focus on analogies with which I disagree. James M. Burns, for instance, calls his indictment of the present congressional system *The Deadlock of Democracy*,[8] and Richard W. Bolling is critical of the *House Out of Order*.[9] The rhetoric here has an appeal; most of us don't like deadlocks, few of us would be willing to argue in favor of disorderly houses.

But, clearly enough, if we are going to use such metaphors, such figures of speech, at all, they should follow all the way through. There is always a cost attached to eliminating any chance of deadlock; there is always a cost attached to putting a house in order. What countermetaphors would provide useful correctives to the particular perspectives that Bolling, Burns, and many other critics of the Congress want us to adopt?

Here we could use the doctrine of countervailing perspectives as explained by Kenneth Burke.[10] Dissipating deadlocks means also, presumably, destroying stability; what are the advantages of the kind of stability (deadlock) from which we now, according to Burns, suffer? It might be helpful in considering the whole issue to try to list the advantages of deadlock, the positive values of a house out of order. Put another way, people who use such rhetorical

---

[6]Kenneth Burke is the greatest thinker on this issue, particularly in *Permanence and Change: An Anatomy of Purpose* (New York: New Republic, 1935), most especially in the chapter on "Argument by Analogy," pp. 128–63.

A helpful article for political scientists is M. Landau, "On the Use of Metaphor in Political Analysis," *Social Research*, 28, no. 3 (Autumn 1961): 331–53, in which he provides a basis for criticizing the common mechanistic metaphor, as used, for instance, in the well-known text by James M. Burns and J. W. Peltason, *Government by the People*, 5th ed. (Englewood Cliffs, N. J.: Prentice-Hall, 1963).

[7]It is possible—I am too unfamiliar with the criticisms of medieval or early modern political thinking to know—that studies of such ideas as that of the "two swords" have been made which would help, methodologically speaking, in developing criticisms of current intellectual fashions.

[8]Englewood Cliffs, N. J.: Prentice-Hall,1963.

[9]New York: Dutton, 1965.

[10]Burke, *Permanence and Change*.

analogies as those used by Burns and Bolling should also learn the one that says, "What's sauce for the goose is sauce for the gander"; that is to say, they should not be permitted simply to use their particular analogy to argue for their purposes, but should expect, as a matter of course, to have it stood on its head (to use still another metaphorical phrase) and then to have its pockets shaken out to see what is hidden in them.[11]

Actually, of course, the analysis of the analogies of such writers might be much more far-reaching and profitable than the preceding paragraph suggests. We should scrutinize the underlying basic *system* of analogies in work; Landau, in his study[12] of Burns' and Peltason's text, *Government by the People,* has shown us how this can be done with many works of political science. Of course, it should perhaps go without saying, but must nevertheless be said, that the rhetoric of those holding other views should be analyzed with equal care—for instance, the book of James Burnham on Congress.[13] But the fact that there is a clear academic market for such writers as Burns and Bolling, whereas few academicians cite or quote Burnham, is reason enough for stressing the need to emphasize careful consideration of the comparisons used by those who would place "Congress on trial."[14]

Probably the commonest type of intuitive analogizing is through the process of synecdoche, intuitively assuming that the part is representative of the whole.[15] Typically, the political analyst who does this then interprets the whole in terms of the part, and either (occasionally) works out explicitly comparative statements or (probably more commonly) implies or suggests that the common-sense knowledge of the way in which the part process generally functions will, by means of common-sense comparisons, help us to understand all that is going on.

---

[11]Of course, the metaphors are used to explain recommendations that are ultimately justified in terms of substantive policy preferences. See, for instance, Burns's letter to me, quoted in my " 'Check and Balance' Today: What Does It Mean for Congress and the Congressman?" in *Congress: The First Branch,* ed. Alfred de Grazia (Washington: American Enterprise Institute of Public Policy, 1966 [p. 32]; New York: Anchor, Doubleday, 1967). The point is that the metaphors employed may tend to focus attention upon the numerator or denominator of the cost-benefit ratio arising out of the present system, and obscure the other side of that same ratio.

[12]Landau, "On the Use of Metaphor."

[13]James M. Burnham, *Congress and the American Tradition* (Chicago: Henry Regnery, 1959).

[14]The title of an earlier book by Professor Burns. The notion of being "on trial" seems singularly open to question here; a more exact title might be *Congress Ought to Be Severely Criticized,* but somehow this lacks rhetorical flourish.

[15]See Kenneth Burke, *Philosophy of Literal Form* (Baton Rouge: Louisiana State University Press, 1941), pp. 25ff.

In regard to Congress, a fairly good example of this process of synecdoche is the classic work by Bertram Gross, *The Legislative Struggle*.[16] The whole book, as its title suggests, is organized around the notions of struggle and combat. Now, of course, Congress and all other legislative or political entities of which we know do contain a great deal of struggle and conflict. But the net impact of Gross's book is to suggest that we are talking about struggle in almost a neo-Darwinian sense—politics, red in tooth and claw—and that some kind of intuitive knowledge of the nature of severe struggles provides the key to understanding Congress.

Gross's approach was known to me through my work with him (on another project) in 1952; without systematically articulating my feelings, I was somewhat uncomfortable with the notion of bitter struggle and pressure-group politics that I found there. Accordingly, my own interviewing with Congressmen during the trade study of 1953–55 was tipped toward identifying and locating precisely those responses that would show the amorphousness, diffuseness, vagueness, and capriciousness of much of what readers of Gross would be prepared to interpret as struggle and pressure. Bauer and Pool and I also found in our interviews with lobbyists and businessmen that the simple notions of combat and conflict did not seem to apply; but I suspect that one reason we all found this to be true is that we all, for different reasons of temperament perhaps, tended to find the struggle-combat-pressure analogy somewhat unsatisfactory to begin with. That does not mean that we misrepresented or distorted or falsified any data; it simply means that because of our resistance, conscious and unconscious, to a particular perspective and analogy, we observed and detected and found significance in data that we could not have perceived as significant had we accepted the analogy completely. (Of course, we did not reject the analogy entirely, either; but we qualified and modified it. Whereas other scholars would have found the struggle synecdoche *the* significant item in the situation, we merely found it to be *a* significant item.) Presumably, by modifying the earlier analogies, we were able to add something to the capacity to understand Congress and the systems to which it is related.

Presumably, this is the case; but one could interpret the attention that has been given our work in a different way. There are fashions in perspectives; a particular kind of analogy or rhetorical device

[16]New York: McGraw-Hill, 1953.

gets tiresome, or another generation, brought up into a different society, no longer finds old perspectives as realistic and meaningful as its elders did. Perhaps people are simply tired of the older fashions,[17] or perhaps the political science profession now consists largely of men whose careers began after World War II and who have no personal recollection of the kind of society that existed in this country in the thirties and twenties, when struggle may have been more manifest in middle-class life than it is now.

II

This may seem a roundabout way to get to the subject: analogies useful in studying Congress. I have thought it helpful to give *very roughly* a recapitulation of the way my thoughts on the subject developed. Also, I am strongly convinced of the point made by David Lindsay Watson,[18] Leibniz, and Merton[19] that "scientists are human," and that it would be easier to understand, translate, meaningfully reject, or meaningfully apply what they say if they would show how their own efforts and experiences stimulated their ideas.

For months I was more or less aware of the points made in the first section above. I had thought that somehow I would connect them with, for instance, Ralph Huitt's paper on congressional

---

[17]Several letters of congratulation about the book or about my related articles (I now regret it never occurred to me to save them—it is a common phenomenon in my experience, by the way, that what appears to be dross at one time becomes pertinent data after I have conceptualized a set of problems; see my *Elite and Specialized Interviewing* [Evanston, Ill.: Northwestern University Press, 1970] for some other comments on this point) said in effect, "It's nice to see somebody who is not saying the same old thing"; "I get a kick out of the way in which you challenge the conventional wisdom."

[18]D. L. Watson, *Scientists Are Human* (London: Watts, 1938)—a sadly neglected book.

[19]Robert K. Merton, in *Social Theory and Social Structure*, enlarged ed. (New York: Free Press, Macmillan, 1968), pp. 4–5, says, "The books on method present an ideal pattern of how scientists ought to think, feel, and act, but these tidy normative patterns, as everyone who has been engaged in inquiry knows, do not reproduce the typically untidy, opportunistic adaptation that scientists make in the course of their inquiry. . . . The public record of science" (and here Merton is referring as much to reports of specific field studies as to books on method) "fails to provide [an account of] the social matrix needed to reconstruct the actual course of scientific development." (Throughout my *Elite and Specialized Interviewing* I have discussed the need to perceive and to record the actual interview situation instead of merely presenting the formalized account of it ordinarily found, and have cited a number of works that demonstrate the importance of doing this and/or actually do it: by Gregory Bateson, John Dollard, Robert Rosenthal, and Neil Friedman). Merton continues with a quotation from Leibniz (letter of March 22, 1714): "I wish that authors would give us the history of their discoveries and the steps by which they arrived at them." The tabu against being personal is so strong, however, that few scholars in fact make an effort to tell us how things happened; as one whose

reorganization,[20] and with works by Polsby and Peabody and Fenno and Riggs and Davidson and Holtzman and Carroll. I had vaguely in mind that the Vatican, like the Congress, seems to be heavily influenced by seniority; and so do some U.S. trade unions. I thought I could make something of this as an example of a useful analogy. Since I had spent much more time in state government since 1956 than I had on (or in) Congress, and had been concerned with the Massachusetts state legislature, it seemed to me that I would be able to say something significant and meaningful and pertinent and valuable about analogies between state legislatures and the United States Congress. For many years much of my reading for entertainment has been concerned with British parliamentary history—in the letters of Horace Walpole, the novels of Anthony Trollope, and the studies of Sir John Neale and Sir Lewis Namier and those influenced by them—and it seemed to me that this ought to suggest analogies. I particularly thought that this last would be the case because I have often dogmatized, "The British Parliament in the eighteenth century was much more like our current Congress than the British Parliament today is. . . ."[21]

But, with two exceptions, I found myself stymied. In fact, I did not have much to say, except along the lines of the first part of this chapter, and the very last part. The first part has, as I have shown, I hope, some bearing on Congress, but in general this kind of analysis in terms of perspective is more useful in interpreting attitudes toward a whole political system than it is in developing

---

training has been jointly in applied anthropology, sociology, and political science, I am inclined to feel that a bias I have as a political scientist is that I have been slightly influenced by the anthropologist's habit of reporting on the actual messy process of investigation and the characteristics of the investigator. (I also think that one reason for the distaste for my early work exhibited by editorial readers for the *American Political Science Review* (and also for the *American Journal of Mental Deficiency*) arose in considerable measure out of real disgust at the way I had introduced myself, as a person and as thinker and observer, into my account of my research and reflections. There is, of course, great danger of egoism, self-advertisement, etc., in such introduction; but as John Dollard, for instance, makes clear, I think, in his discussions of perceiving his own biases in *Caste and Class in a Southern Town* (New Haven: Yale University Press, 1937), there are as great or greater dangers in leaving oneself out of many kinds of studies. On this point see also the statement of the transactional model by Arthur F. Bentley in *An Inquiry into Inquiries* (Boston: Beacon, 1954). Had Bentley thought himself into the theory of *An Inquiry* before publishing his classic *The Process of Government* in 1908, I suspect he would have done something like what Dollard does in *Caste and Class*.

[20]Ralph Huitt, "Congressional Reorganization: The Next Step" (paper presented at the American Political Science Association meetings, September 8–12, 1964).

[21]It is interesting that one of the other papers in the series that Arthur Maass organized on analogies does indeed focus on parallels between British politics in the seventeenth and eighteenth centuries and contemporary U.S. politics. This is Samuel Huntington's "Political Modernization: America vs. Europe," *World Politics*, 18 (1966): 378–414.

In 1956, when examined by Paul Lazarsfeld and Herbert Hyman on my work on Congress, I insisted that I had learned my "methodology" from Walpole and from Trollope; I was more serious than not, although they thought me merely perverse.

methods of actually studying a subsystem within a larger system. The last part, as will be apparent, bears largely upon the role of the *Congressmen*, the way in which they undergo experiences analogous to those of persons in certain other occupations.

I think these ideas are of value; but it is, I think, clear that there is a substantial difference between understanding Congressmen as social, political, or personality types and understanding Congress as an institution or a process.[22] I would really have evaded the most significant issues about Congress as a system had I devoted most of my space to the understanding of Congressmen; although it would be reasonable to expect that most people find Congressmen more interesting than political processes or tactics.

But the institutional output or effect is not directly validated by an understanding, no matter how detailed, of the social roles or group values of the officers of the institution. Social processes, that is, are not reducible to roles and role norms. Policy may, and sometimes does, evolve from a series of actions and transactions, the end results of which are more or less independent of given social roles, self-perceptions, etc.[23]

For example, Cottrell has a fascinating article called "Of Time and the Railroader."[24] Important as it was thirty-odd years ago to understand the way in which the timetable and the timetable ideology dominated the lives of many railroaders, it would have been very foolish to try to describe the railroading process, its inputs and outputs, in terms of this or any other role characteristic of a given group of railroaders.[25] The railroad as a social organization and a system involved a good deal that it would have been hard to fit into such an approach.

---

[22]A good example of this point is to be found in James D. Barber's excellent book on Connecticut legislators, *The Lawmakers* (New Haven: Yale University Press, 1965), which tells us relatively little about the Connecticut legislature as a legislative body, or as an influence in the policy process, fascinating and valuable as it is as a study in the sociology of the occupational role.

[23]The best discussion of this topic I know is to be found in Robert H. Salisbury's "The Analysis of Public Policy: A Search for Theories and Roles," in *Political Science and Public Policy*, ed. Austin Ranney (Chicago: Markham, 1968), pp. 151–78. See also Geoffrey Vickers, *Art of Judgment* (New York: Basic Books, 1965).

[24]W. Fred Cottrell, "Of Time and the Railroader," chap. 5 of *The Railroader* (Stanford: Stanford University Press, 1940), originally in *American Sociological Review*, 4 (1939). Cottrell's approach impressed me so much that at one time I planned to call my report on Congress "Of Time, Attention, and the Congressman."

[25]One of the few queries I would raise about the great book by Daniel Katz and R. L. Kahn, *The Social Psychology of Organizations* (New York: Wiley, 1966), is precisely on this point. Their notion of social organization as consisting of "holes . . . waiting to be filled" (roles) is likely to mislead in the direction indicated in the text. See my review of that book in *American Political Science Review*, 42 (1968): 1306–7.

This is more or less the point where I was stymied for a time. Then Landau's article on the use of metaphors in political science[26] suggested an effort to try to list uses of analogies that it might be worth considering in connection with the Congress.

First: There is the large-scale metaphor, the perspective, already discussed in section I above. One additional point about this sort of analogy might be made here: Frequently a metaphor, even where the writer or scholar would probably say, "Oh, that's just a figure of speech," directs or reflects the interpretation[27] and even the collection or discovery of data. Edward Bennett and his colleagues[28] have shown, in regard to particular groups of voters, that these voters interpret the Republican and Democratic parties in their state in quite personalized terms—as weak, gentle, inefficient. I strongly suspect that a similar study of words that specific scholars associate with Congress, the Presidency, politics, etc., would show that different ones have quite different and quite value-laden profiles of association; and that we would find that basically these profiles of association constitute metaphors of vital significance. I would like to develop some schedule designed to elicit the metaphors in terms of which different scholars think about Congress and other political phenomena. One simple example: It happens that I am known as a specialist in the sociology of mental retardation ("stupidity") and also to some extent as one who has written about Congress. It happens that some people, including some scholars, think this juxtaposition quite funny, and joke about it, whereas others apparently do not regard it as any funnier than if I happened to be a specialist on Congress and on city planning. So far as it goes (and obviously one association is only a clue and not a proof), people who regard this association as a joke may have a different orientation toward Congress (or possibly toward politics in general) than those who see no reason to laugh.

Not incidentally, it would be possible to make similar studies of people actually in politics, including even Congressmen, ex-Congressmen, and congressional candidates.

---

[26]Landau, "On the Use of Metaphor."

[27]W. Embler, in *Language, Meaning, and Maturity,* ed. S. I. Hayakawa (New York: Harper, 1954), p. 125, put the point in extreme but valuable form: "Thoughts do not select the words we use; words determine the thoughts we have." This is the point made by Granet, Halbwachs, and other disciples of Durkheim: that thought is a social product.

[28]Edward M. Bennett and Harriett Goodwin, "Emotional Aspects of Political Behavior: The Woman Voter," *Genetic Psychology Monographs,* 58 (1958): 3–53.

Second: "*The search* for analogies enables us to see a simple logical form in things that appear quite different . . . [that is] to establish a class [or classes] and [thus] reduce the complexity of the environment."[29]

Of course, reversely, classification may, from a *common-sense standpoint*, increase the felt complexity of the environment, because the logically simple classification may upset common-sense assumptions—as when we discover that whales are not fish, or that Great Britain is a republic.

Third: Analogy and metaphor, "by transferring the actual referent to a new context, stimulate an organization of thought that may be productive . . . [through] reveal[ing] new attributes or disclos[ing] old ones in a new light."[30]

Deutsch adds something worth emphasizing, that the "heuristic" value of analogies and metaphors may be, so far as experience goes, quite independent of their productive power.[31] A good many borrowed analogies are demonstrably misleading, if taken literally, and cannot sensibly be formalized into a set of propositions if they are taken literally; but nevertheless they give people ideas that lead to fruitful discoveries.

We can illustrate the distinction between the productive use of analogies and the merely heuristic by an example from sociology: Students of modern communities have benefited a good deal by (1) ideas borrowed from anthropologists—culture and culture pattern, for instance—and (2) ideas about "human ecology," borrowed from various branches of biology. Nowadays, we do not even regard the notion of culture as borrowed, when we apply it in sociology or political science. The ideas involved have had direct and productive consequences, and we now theorize about community politics in terms of culture. On the other hand, few seriously try to utilize bio-ecological ideas or specific theories of differentiation and selection to interpret the problems of urban government or metropolitan areas; but nevertheless the Chicago school, guided by this biological analogy, made a contribution to our knowledge of twentieth-century cities.

Fourth: In dealing with political systems or subsystems, analogies might be very useful in considering particular parts of the

---

[29]Landau, "On the Use of Metaphor."
[30]*Ibid.*
[31]Karl W. Deutsch, "On Communications Models in the Social Sciences," *Public Opinion Quarterly*, 16 (1952–53): 360–61.

subsystem. Indeed, the awareness of the importance of cliques, work groups, and so forth, derived from the applied anthropologists and the industrial sociologists, has, so far as I can judge, been an important factor leading to the emphasis on committees (work groups), friendship groups, etc. in the Congress. In this case, and as far as I know in every case where such ideas have been borrowed, the borrowing has been merely fortuitous, the result of a general climate of opinion and the fashionableness of particular ideas. I do not know of any systematic attempt to seek out such fertile analogies.

Fifth, overlapping the other three, and particularly the last, but quite different in purpose and focus: Innovations—inventions, if you will—in the governmental and social sphere are often, probably usually, borrowings and adaptations from somewhere else. Many of the proposals for "reforming" the Congress are in fact based upon actual or alleged experience somewhere else. It is dubious, for instance, whether the recurrent emphasis upon a disciplined congressional party would have developed were it not for our familiarity with disciplined European parties. Electric roll calls are of course used in various assemblies; the recent interest in a U.S. ombudsman is a clear case of trying to adopt an innovation tried out somewhere else.

So far as I know, nobody ever has made any wide-ranging effort to locate and evaluate political "innovations" or political practices used elsewhere that could profitably be borrowed or adapted. Yet, to begin with, just in the United States alone there are fifty state legislatures, and it seems likely that at least one of them has discovered some way of doing something better than the Congress. Such an effort should, of course, take into consideration the context within which a practice works; I suspect that ombudsmanship in Scandinavia (or even in Germany or New Zealand) operates within a context too different from the United States to make the idea automatically transferable, without serious modifications. But I know of no reason why the practice of joint committees, as in the Massachusetts legislature, should be unworkable in the U.S. Congress (once the initial obvious obstacles were overcome), though there may be some barriers I have not envisaged.

Such a search for practices that might be borrowed or adapted should of course involve attention to history as well as to current practice, and, among other things, to the history of the Congress. It may be that in the past the Congress had some practices that it might well return to under current circumstances. Indeed, the major burden of Congressman Richard Bolling's[32] prescriptions for reordering the House of Representatives is simply to return to two past practices: a strong caucus and a strong Speaker.

Sixth: In my case, at least, the most important result of trying to locate analogies to Congress has been this: It has forced me to try to think about what Congress is, what it does that is significant. The familiar descriptions do not seem 100 percent adequate. In fact, increasingly, not only in Congress but in the states, important pieces of legislation and appropriations are proposed by the executive, so does Congress make laws? Do I look for analogies in law-making bodies? Congress "represents"; true, but what exactly is representation?[33] Whom does it represent? How? Congress "oversees"; yes, but so do the Bureau of the Budget and the General Accounting Office and the President and a great many other agencies. Congress investigates; again true, but so do presidential commissions, for instance, and foundation-financed groups. My greatest difficulty in thinking about what might be analogical to Congress is that I have not been very clear in my own mind as to exactly what "Congressing" as a process is; and it is hard to formulate analogies to an institution when you are unable to formulate what it does. However, vice versa, seeking for analogies has led me to be aware of my uncertainties, and "to make confusion explicit is the first step toward wisdom"; I used to take it for granted that I *knew* what Congress does.[34]

This may sound too pessimistic; of course, I do know what Congress does in specific cases and specific instances, and I am aware of specific tasks, and I can suggest analogies to such specifics; but I am not certain that I can describe what Congress *as a whole* in practice does.

Seventh: Those who believe that Congress is a Good Thing, that it performs a useful service, or who think it is a necessary institution within the American governmental system, usually in effect say: See, it is good (or see, it is necessary). It does thus-and-so. But such defenses or justifications, common as they are, are quite incomplete. For there may be other institutions that are, in fact, anal-

---

[32]Bolling, *House Out of Order.*

[33]John C. Wahlke, "Public Policy and Representative Government: The Role of the Represented," Laboratory for Political Research report no. 9 (Iowa City: Department of Political Science, University of Iowa, 1967; mimeo).

[34]In particular this reflection led me to an increasing concern with the problem: What difference would it make to the social system if we did not have a separate legislative body?

ogous. The Congress investigates, criticizes, sometimes exposes examples of abuse by the bureaucracy or the executive; very true. But so, in the United States today, do the newspapers and the national magazines and the radio-TV networks. Congress detects, sometimes, waste in the budget, and supervises the appropriations process; but so, in fact, does the Budget Bureau, and so, in fact, do certain taxpayers' organizations.

That is, in understanding the Congress we need to conceive what alternative ways there are of doing some of the things that it does. Obviously, such an approach should encompass practices in other countries, in state government, etc.

And, vice versa, we might profitably think about functions that are in fact performed by other agencies, but which could be performed by the Congress. The executive departments and the bureaucracy have grown substantially, both in the federal government and in the states, because it has been discovered that more and more functions that used to be performed privately can be performed publicly. Although there has been some growth in congressional functions, this has been, as far as I can see, chiefly a response to the growth of the bureaucracy (case service and oversight, predominantly), and, relatively speaking, has been very modest. Are there any services that are performed privately (or which are not performed at all but for which a considerable demand exists or might be created), or which are performed in other countries but not here, which the Congress is equipped to perform, either directly or through delegation to officials actually responsible to it?[35]

Eighth: Our responsibility as teachers and our very involvement with our data probably restrict our tendency to look for another kind of analogy. Most studies of U.S. government, and certainly of Congress, assume that the system as a whole will continue very much as it is now, and, if it changes, will change gradually. Yet so far, most political systems have changed abruptly and violently at numerous points in their history. If the United States had gone through the experiences of France under Hitler or of Germany under Napoleon,[36] would we have reinstituted the same sort of

---

[35]I am, in effect, repeating here the plea often expressed by Charles E. Merriam and Harold D. Lasswell for more emphasis in political science on creativity and political invention. See Lasswell's *Future of Political Science* (New York: Atherton, 1963).

[36]After the Napoleonic occupation some small Germanic states were not restored to the full sovereignty they had formerly possessed. I fancy that, had the United States been similarly occupied for fifteen years by the Japanese, from 1942 to 1957, the states as we know them would never have been re-created; I suspect the Congress would have been. But these are hunches, which I have not yet been able to defend systematically.

Congress we now have? If we had, would we fairly soon have changed it, as the French did in the transition from the Fourth to the Fifth Republic? If the United States were to be subject to severe thermonuclear attack but "survive," (*a*) is there any point in thinking about what Congress might be like, or (*b*) how any of the functions that Congress now performs could be performed?

That is, in terms long ago stated by Lasswell,[37] the job of the political analyst is to specify where we are in the historical continuum. Are there factors that suggest that the Congress will grow more or less powerful? Suppose a very popular President should tell the Congress to shut up shop and go home; what would happen? Are there historic analogies that give us any clues here in the experience of De Gaulle or Hitler or Cromwell or Louisiana under Huey Long or Indiana in the days of D. B. Stephenson? I cannot now imagine a Congress "seizing" the powers of the Presidency and receiving popular support; I can imagine the reverse. We have generally thought of such possibilities, if we have thought of them at all, as due to crisis; are there any analogous cases where people simply preferred a "businesslike consensus" and modified or eliminated the system of separation of powers accordingly?

Most likely, there are not any very clear-cut analogies here; *but I find, and I think others will find, that the effort to locate such analogies and to decide what would be analogical or homologous will help to stretch the imagination and raise questions about the basic developmental processes within our political system.*

Ninth: "Analogies involved in understanding Congress" means, I suppose, "analogies involved in *studying* Congress," at least in part. Substituting the word "studying" calls attention to the fact that there may be analogies between the processes of *studying* two different phenomena, or between the kind of people who study them, even though the phenomena themselves do not resemble each other at all. In view of the emphasis Arthur Bentley and John Dewey[38] and others have put upon perceiving the analyst as part of the field—in view of their leading hypothesis that we can determine the meaning and validity of observations, reports, and inferences much better

---

[37]Harold D. Lasswell, *World Politics and Personal Insecurity* (New York: McGraw-Hill, 1935).

[38]See Bentley, *An Inquiry into Inquiries;* Bentley and Dewey, *The Knowing and the Known* (Boston: Beacon Press, 1949); and Bentley, *Behavior, Knowledge, Fact* (Bloomington, Ind.: Principia Press, 1935). From a quite different starting point, the sociologists of knowledge arrived at a very similar orientation.

if we do not arbitrarily cut the observer off from the observation—
it is of considerable importance to call attention to this kind of
analogy; and accordingly, in a section below, I discuss it.

Tenth: Finally, there is the analogy between Congressman as an
occupation and various other occupations, which is also discussed
below.

III

Everett Hughes has pointed out[39] that almost any kind of professional specialization gives one a license to know guilty secrets,
and also leads one to be blamed for being the possessor and in a
sense the defender of guilty secrets. Note that the emphasis is on
being blamed for being supposed to be the defender and/or the
possessor of guilty secrets, regardless of whether one is in fact
defending anything. I tried to see if any significant analogy along
these lines seems to exist between criminologists, for instance, and
political scientists specializing on Congress. Although the idea
seemed to me an attractive one, I cannot really discern any homol-
ogy; but in the process of trying to work it out, I did begin to notice
that students of Congress find themselves in rather a special situation, one that is worth some thought, in regard to some of the
data (Congressmen) we study. Put more exactly, these data we
study have some special characteristics, which probably affect our
work and work relationships, the impact of which can best be
understood by contrast and analogy.

Erving Goffman, in his *Presentation of Self in Everyday Life*,
reports:

> Society is organized on the principle that any individual who
> possesses certain social characteristics has a moral right to expect
> that others will value and treat him in a correspondingly appro-
> priate way. Connected with this principle is a second, namely that
> an individual who implicitly or explicitly signifies that he has cer-

---

[39]For instance, in *Men and Their Work* (New York: Free Press, Macmillan, 1953), pp.
78–87.

tain social characteristics ought to have this claim honored by others and ought in fact to be what he claims he is. In consequence, when an individual projects a definition of the situation and thereby makes an implicit or explicit claim to be a person of a particular kind, he automatically exerts a moral demand upon others, obliging them to value and treat him in the manner that persons of his kind have a right to expect.[40]

And again:

When an individual plays a part, he implicitly requests his observers to take seriously the impression that is fostered before them. They are asked to believe that the character they see actually possesses the attributes he appears to possess, that the task he performs will have the consequences that are implicitly claimed for it, and that, in general, matters are what they appear to be.[41]

Now for most persons and for most professionals (for us as teachers or consultants, for doctors, for specialists of any sort, in the serious definition of that word), this is obviously a correct statement of the way the social interaction of middle-class people takes place. (Although Goffman does not say so, one possible operational definition of "lower-class people" might be to say that they are so *un*important that they cannot get their claims taken at face value; and of upper-class people, that they are so important that they can refrain from making claims or can make bizarre claims and still be treated seriously.)

It is in general true that bureaucrats and judges will be able to get claims of prestige and competence taken at face value. To be sure, *as candidates,* the topmost members of the executive branch may have their claims consistently and systematically challenged in a way that most of us never experience; but as Presidents (or as governors, for that matter, in several and perhaps in all states) they are surrounded by ceremonial and by subordinates.

Congressmen and state legislators, however, can be and are subject to the constant *likelihood* of open criticism of a sort that few professionals meet from their equals on a day-to-day basis. To be sure, in a good many cases no such criticism takes place, but a Congressman must nearly always anticipate that it may take place,

[40]Erving Goffman, *Presentation of Self in Everyday Life* (Edinburgh: University of Edinburgh Press, 1956), p. 6 (also published in the United States by Doubleday, 1959).
[41]*Ibid.,* p. 10.

unlike a judge, a college professor with tenure, or even a middle-class suburban housewife.

Such criticism comes, first, from congressional colleagues, beyond the limit of what is characteristic of most professional groups; but, aside from this, in our particular society, Congressmen may expect to be—and often are—exposed to rather constant negative remarks from their clienteles and from the public. As an example, I remember a Congressman whose credit card was challenged by a garage mechanic he'd never met before because it said "Honorable . . ." What right, the mechanic wanted to know, did a *Congressman* have to be called honorable? As another example, at one time I was using Congressman Bolling's office over a vacation period, and was expecting a visit from the science editor of the *Saturday Review*. I suggested for reasons of mutual convenience that we meet in the Congressman's office. "No," he said vehemently, "I can't be associated with any mere politician in such a way." But he was perfectly willing to see me in an office in fact financed largely by defense contracts.

Legislators are among the very few professional or quasi-professional groups in the United States of which it is almost taken for granted that almost anyone may momentarily challenge any claim for immediate deference their members may make. (The nearest parallel I can think of is policemen.) And they are probably among the few groups that have a substantial public ready to reward them for exposing their colleagues' performances. Similar criticism by a doctor of a fellow-physician would be regarded as absolutely unethical, and teachers are certainly running grave risks (in most schools and colleges) of losing respect[42] even from students if they engage in what in their case would be called "backbiting."

If I am correct in these observations, they are of course relevant for comparing the sociology of the congressional occupation with other occupations, and may indeed be even more significant in that context than in this, which is concerned with analogies (and contrasts) to *studying* the Congress. But the importance of the point for *studying* the Congress is chiefly that it explains how and why it is so much easier in some ways to study the Congress (or more properly put, how much easier it is to study some parts of the congressional subsystem of the U.S. government) than it is to

---

[42]The rise of the New Left movement among the junior faculty of colleges and universities has modified this situation to some extent, but in general the statement is still true.

study various other professions and occupations and governmental groups. I suspect that when one gets into that aspect of the congressional subsystem concerned with money-raising and money-raisers, it would be more difficult, for instance, and we can think of other aspects of the subsystem that are difficult to study.

In one important respect, studying the Congress is analogous to most studying of most institutions and social groups, only probably somewhat more so. In the nature of the case, anyone who studies a social group enters into social relationships with the members of that group, and is to a certain extent "rewarded" or "punished" by them. Not infrequently, he adopts their definitions of situations and identifies with them as against the uncomprehending outside world, partly because this is the easiest way to obtain acceptance for himself and thereby to obtain access to the information he needs; partly because his concentration of attention upon the values and points of view of the particular group with which he is working tends to shut out alternative definitions of the situation, so that their way of looking at things comes to seem to him natural; and partly because he really does learn things that other people overlook. One danger of participant observation, of studies undertaken by people who in fact have a role other than that of scholar or scientist in a system, is generally and correctly assumed to lie in the fact that the adoption of such a role will tend to lead the scholar to focus only upon the views that go with the participant role. But even when the observer is not a participant in fact, he may be led to adopt the views and viewpoints of participants by a wish to defend them against unmerited criticism—as the scholar who returns from a visit to some foreign country and tries to "explain" what its people are doing that appears odd to Americans finds himself cast as a "defender," and in fact, in order to get his point across at all, sometimes becomes one.[43] Congress, indeed politics in general, is an alien territory to many of those with whom we come in contact, and I strongly suspect that most specialists on Congress do, in relationship to their students and even to their colleagues, in fact defend Congress.

I suspect that a considerable contribution could be made, not only to the study of Congress, but to the study of political science in

---

[43]The experience of the businessmen who go abroad and willy-nilly become defenders of the U.S. position (whatever their initial views), reported by Bauer and Pool in our *American Business and Public Policy*, is quite relevant. See pp. 167–73.

general, if we had many more detailed accounts and analyses of the effects of identification, the tendency to defend, etc. upon our reports and emphases. To some extent, anthropologists and sociologists, as they engage in community studies, have made a serious effort to report on the relationship of their predispositions to their findings and observations;[44] but in political science I know of little such effort.

Of course, to those who believe that the point of view of the great Marquis of Halifax in the immortal *Character of a Trimmer* contains an essential application of Aristotle's emphasis on balance and the golden mean, the current biases of the relatively small number of congressional scholars have been so far a welcome offset. For the tendency of the academic profession, for obvious enough reasons, has been to identify itself with the active and vigorous chief executives or with the bureaucracy—here are its sources of patronage, here is hope for the kind of change a New Dealist group favors, here is efficiency instead of "time-wasting." So the fact that the congressional intern program—plus the increased number of congressional staff positions open to scholars, plus the increased popularity of Congress as a subject for study—has created a group of scholars whose evaluations and associations and hopes and friendships and reference groups are congressional rather than executive or bureaucratic is all to the good, as far as it goes; but it would obviously be desirable to be ready to redress the balance the other way if need be.[45]

One point that students of community behavior have discovered is the great effect that may arise from a scholar's early contacts in a group he is studying. If he identifies with one moiety, class, group of kinfolk, or one set of any sort, he may find great difficulty in winning acceptance from other groups in the same community. He also runs the risk of unconsciously learning to report his findings about the whole institution in terms suggested by the perspective that is ideologically (but not necessarily factually) appropriate for those people with whom he associated himself first.

---

[44]See Dollard, *Caste and Class.*

[45]It would be an interesting venture in the sociology of knowledge to try to ascertain whether the greatly increased popularity of the Congress as a subject for study is simply the resultant of the first two factors, or whether there is some other aspect of the climate of opinion in the period since 1955 which has affected this development. If we had a clearer understanding of the role of fashion in the selection and treatment of social science studies, we might have a better basis for evaluating systematic biases in a particular group of scholars. See my "Selective Inattention in Social Science," *Social Problems,* 6 (1958): 176–83.

Oddly enough, I am not aware of any great attention to this problem of research technique by political scientists. Yet political science, above every other profession, should be aware of the importance of *faction*. By way of analogy with community studies, we might at least raise the question whether political scientists who study Congress do not quite disproportionately work with the liberal-intellectual members of Congress and the liberal-intellectual staff employees, thus reinforcing the predispositions with which they generally start. To some extent, this may handicap them in obtaining access to the Tuesday–Thursday Club,[46] or to men like the late Senators George Malone[47] and Pat McCarran; what is probably more dangerous, it can mean that the frame of reference within which they approach non-liberal-intellectual members of Congress may be to a considerable degree created by the vigorously liberal intellectuals, men like Bolling and Thomas Curtis and Bradford Morse and Lee Metcalf.

One other analogy that presumably applies to studying Congress is the value that scholars in various fields have found in rejecting the obvious definitions of a system, definitions suggested by the data. That is, there is no particular *a priori* necessity to assume that the Congress is separated from the rest of the political system by barriers and boundaries that make it helpful and desirable to regard the Congress as in itself a segregated subsystem. Griffith[48] has made this point very cogently in his picturing of "the whirlpool" as possibly a basic "legislative" unit. Presumably we should try to systematize our awareness of the misleading quality of seemingly obvious barriers, using analogies from other branches of social science (such as clinical psychology, where "milieu" therapy replaces individual therapy, or the study of the interrelationships of culture and personality) and also from the biological sciences (where, for instance, it is more and more realized that the external environment and the genes are actually part of the transactional system).

---

[46]Some members of large urban delegations are in the habit of taking very long weekends, and reportedly are in Washington only on Tuesday, Wednesday, and Thursday.

[47]Senator Malone cross-questioned me for a period of time longer than it often took me to complete an interview with other members as to who I was, where I came from, and so on. He ultimately agreed to talk freely to me when he learned that my grandfather was a Baptist minister. "Well, God bless you, you're all right, then."

[48]Ernest Griffith, *Congress and Its Contemporary Role*, 2nd ed. rev. (New York: New York University Press, 1956), pp. 37ff. Katz and Kahn, in their presentation of the nature of "open system" inquiry in *Social Psychology of Organizations*, provide a theoretical basis for refusing to let the data define the system—that is, for refusing, in principle, to believe that the barriers defined by the people under observation in fact necessarily represent meaningful system dividers.

IV

If time, space, and patience permitted, it would be possible to develop at length each one of the ten points on types of analogy made in section II. Since time and space, at least, are limited, I shall concentrate on just two of them.

First, contemporary consideration of reorganizing Congress is essentially a discussion about the *adaptation, diffusion, and acceptance* of innovations. There is a substantial literature on this topic,[49] but little of it bears explicitly on the adoption, adaptation, and diffusion of *political* innovations. Yet there is in fact an enormous *experience* of the adoption and diffusion of political innovations. The Congress itself, for instance, adopted the "lame-duck amendment"; many states have recently adopted new constitutions with provisions that were more or less inconvenient to some members of important political groups. Fifteen years ago, I fancy that most of us would have been much surprised had anybody predicted the changes that have (apparently) taken place in the Roman Catholic Church; twenty-five years ago, few would have foreseen that what Morton Grodzins calls the marble-cake type of federalism would replace much of the layer-cake system of federalism on which we were then brought up.

There is, however, no comparative study of how such changes take place—of how resistances are overcome, of how perspectives are altered.[50] Yet it is only in terms of such analyses that we can determine whether recommendations or proposals for reorganizing the Congress are likely to be adopted or not. My guess—and it is simply a guess based upon impression and some slight factual knowledge—is that one of the two most important factors in the kinds of changes that are being proposed for the Congress is the point so cogently made by Schattschneider, that "the most important strategy of politics is concerned with the scope of the conflict. . . . Every change in the *scope* of conflict has a bias. . . . It must be assumed that every change in the number of participants [comes about because] . . .

---

[49]See Everett Rogers, *Diffusion of Innovations* (New York: Free Press, Macmillan, 1962); George M. Foster, *Traditional Cultures and the Impact of Technological Change* (New York: Harper & Row, 1962); and G. K. Zollschan and W. Hirsch, eds., *Explorations in Social Change* (Boston: Houghton Mifflin, 1964).

[50]There are, of course, comparative studies of revolutions both violent and nonviolent, and there are how-to manuals on social action; see, for instance, my forthcoming manual on community action, to be published by Rand McNally.

newcomers have sympathies or antipathies that make it possible to involve them."[51] So far as I know and can judge, the majority of persons actively and continuously involved in Massachusetts politics did not want to see the powers of the Executive Council clipped; yet they have been clipped and perhaps will be clipped more. I also am pretty sure that the preponderance of active, involved, professional political opinion was against the four-year term for governor; yet we got it, beginning in 1967. On both matters, *additional participants, not normally politically active,* entered the arena. These items may be contrasted with the failure of Senator John F. Kennedy in 1958 and of Governor Endicott Peabody in 1963 to clip the wings of "The Iron Duke," Speaker John F. Thompson. (The public functioned simply as a passive audience in the latter case, and did not know about the affair in the former.)

The other factor that I judge makes previously inconceivable innovations happen is the simple fact that people who are important and influential either (a) change their perspectives or (b) lose their self-confidence.[52] The French Revolution, it seems to be widely thought, was as much as anything else produced by this factor; some of the governing class, that is, lost nerve and belief.[53] For that matter, the civil rights revolution going on right now in this country is due (a) to a change of attitude and (b) to a loss of nerve by respectable segregationists.

Accordingly, I am disposed to doubt whether on the basis of experience we can say categorically that "there is a great toughness in [all] established ways of doing things," as Ralph Huitt apparently does in his treatment of "Congressional Reorganization: The Next Chapter."[54] I am more disposed to feel, with my old teacher Charles E. Merriam, that we ought to pay quite a bit of attention to the "poverty of power,"[55] for once the perspective is changed, once nerve is lost, once the new elements are brought into the arena, power often does become ineffective. Perspectives in the United States are changing rapidly and new groups are entering the political arena, and it

---

[51]E. E. Schattschneider, *The Semi-Sovereign People: A Realist's View of Democracy in America* (New York: Holt, Rinehart & Winston, 1960), pp. 3–4.

[52]Or the men who ascend to powerful positions lack the self-confidence of their predecessors: Louis XVI instead of Louis XIV, Senator Mansfield instead of Lyndon Johnson, etc. And I would add the present generation of college presidents as contrasted with predecessors.

[53]See Crane Brinton, *Anatomy of Revolution,* rev. ed. (New York: Prentice-Hall, 1950), esp. chap. 2.

[54]Paper read at the American Political Science Association meeting, Chicago, September 8–12, 1964.

[55]Charles E. Merriam, *Systematic Politics* (Chicago: University of Chicago Press, 1945).

may therefore be that currently incredible changes will take place in the Congress within the next few years. The very facts that Huitt presents to support the argument that the Congress does not do so badly—and I thoroughly agree with him *on the facts*—seem to me also to suggest that a good many people (including the poor and the Negroes) are acquiring the notion that Congress is an obstacle to what they want. This may lead to innovation; it may mean simply that the Congress will engage in ritualistic gestures that seem like innovation, but which are not really substantive in nature; it may mean some mixture of these two; or perhaps the Congress can successfully reinterpret its mission and function, but in so doing (the analogies that come to mind immediately are the Counterreformation, when the Church did successfully fight back, and the imposition of the Black Codes in the South, *circa* 1901, when the well-to-do southerners also successfully fought back), it will willy-nilly, as in any other counterreformation, change its own nature.

I should add that I smuggled in that word "all" in my quotation from Ralph Huitt above; but if his statement is to be read "some," then we need to consider the entire set of issues raised here, because to say that "there is a great toughness in *some* established ways of doing things" means that we have to find out (by analysis or analogy) what differentiates the ways toughly resistant to change from the ways less resistant to change.

V

The second type of analogy on which I propose to make some further comment is congressional role performance and occupation. Congressmen work in Washington most of the year, but they are chiefly dependent for continued employment upon their constituents back home. Their major work group is not therefore the entity to which they are responsible. Now, we have here a set of problems generally associated with the familiar names of Edmund Burke and John Stuart Mill, but which might be looked at in terms of different (and possibly competing) reference groups, different (and possibly conflicting) primary groups, different (and in some crucial cases conceivably conflicting) definitions of the situation and the role. So far as I am aware, there is no schematic treatment of the sociology of the Congressman's job in terms of the sociology of occupations[56] and the general problems of multigroup affiliation. Yet there is a considerable amount of sociological comment (for instance, the conception, in abstract terms, of "marginal man," the notion of "reference group," and so on) which is pertinent. And what is equally valuable, there are other occupations that involve the same sort of mixed relationships. For example, the trade association executive in Washington may similarly be torn between his constituency and those with whom he actually works on a face-to-face basis, the government bureaucrats or the congressional staff, with whom he has much more interaction than with most of his constituents.[57]

And there are other comparisons: *industrial salesmen* who know customers far more intimately than they know most people in the firm's offices, and who constantly act as intermediaries between clients and headquarters; *Methodist ministers and Catholic priests,* who are (I understand) in practice ultimately responsible to the bishop and the hierarchy, but who must work on a day-to-day basis with the parish (and who frequently have been trained in a much more sophisticated fashion than most of the parishioners); *members of commissions,* representing different interests, when the commission members interact closely with each other over a period of time; *labor-union officers,* who have acquired the viewpoint of professional negotiators and have left the shop behind them; *the public relations executive,* who must preserve long-term goodwill for all his clients and himself, but who is subjected to justified demands for short-term results from particular clients. Indeed, more and more in our society, professional men are coming to have a mixture of reference groups. Perhaps there are some who have about the same mix of orientations as the Congressman—who are both locally and professionally oriented—and would serve as close comparisons.

This is just one example of the contribution that the sociology of role performance might make to our understanding of Congress. Even more generally, almost every page of Goffman's *Presentation of Self in Everyday Life* suggests a comparison or analogy with the role of the Congressman. For example, it would be possible—and

---

[56]But see Barber, *The Lawmakers.*

[57]This point has been made in several studies of lobbyists, and it crops up repeatedly in Bauer, Pool, and Dexter, *American Business and Public Policy;* see esp. pt. 4, "The Pressure Groups," pp. 321–400. It is a major theme of my *How Organizations Are Represented in Washington* (Indianapolis: Bobbs-Merrill, 1969); see esp. chap. 8, "Characteristic Tensions Between Clients and Free Professionals," pp. 137–51.

valuable—to write a lengthy essay about Congress using these two sentences of Goffman's:

> Finally, we find performers often foster the impression that they had ideal motives for acquiring the role . . . that they have ideal qualifications for the role, and that it was not necessary for them to suffer any indignities, insults, or humiliations, or make any tacitly-understood "deals" to acquire the role. . . . Reinforcing these ideal impressions we find a kind of "rhetoric of training" whereby labor unions, universities, trade associations, and other licensing bodies require practitioners to . . . foster the impression that a practitioner is someone set apart from other men.[58]

The first sentence, of course, suggests many analogies to the congressional role performance. Goffman refers, *inter alia*, to aspects of academic life. The second sentence suggests, vice versa, a contrast between the congressional role performance and professional role performance in general. Congressmen sometimes glory in stressing that they have no special training—they are ordinary fellows!—and although the majority probably do make a claim to professional skills, they are more subtle about it than members of many professions. That is to say, although candidates for election or reelection or members in their legislative capacity may in some fashion call attention to their special expertise and how they acquired it, they will at the same time in many instances stress the fact that they are more or less ordinary individuals. The late Mrs. Robert Taft, as a campaigner for her husband in his first successful senatorial campaign, made a point of the claim that her husband was "a very extraordinary man"; the bold assertion provoked a good deal of comment, precisely because it ran so contrary to the normal effort of American political figures to appear in some significant ways ordinary—in the tradition of Jacksonian democracy.

---

[58]Goffman, *Presentation of Self*, p. 29.

WHY CANDIDATES
FOR REELECTION TO CONGRESS
MUST DEPEND ON THEMSELVES
Why Coattails Cannot Be Depended Upon

There has been a good deal written, of course, about presidential and party coattails. From the standpoint of this book, that places the emphasis the wrong way around. For, since every Congressman or Senator who is running or may run for reelection knows that his electoral margin may vary a good deal from that of the President or others on the ticket, he strives to advertise himself, build his own constituency, get his own following.

In 1953–55, in order to demonstrate what seemed to me to be fallacies in the work of Malcolm Moos[1] and Louis Bean[2] on presidential coattails, I prepared a seventy-two page set of tables of votes *for other offices*, organized by congressional districts, for 1946 through 1954. The point was to show that in many elections there is very great variation among candidates on the same ticket, and that this variation is the rule rather than the exception. Further, it does not point any one way. I called the set of tables "How Candidates Lend Strength to Tickets: Contestable Congressional Districts—A Table of Variation in Party Strength in U.S. Congressional Districts,

---

[1]Malcolm Moos, *Politics, Presidents, and Coattails* (Baltimore: Johns Hopkins University Press, 1952).

[2]Louis Bean, *Midterm Battle* (Washington: Cantillon Books, 1950).

1946–54."[3] Were I to redo the analysis now, I would leave out the first six words, and I would leave out the words "in Party Strength," for all I actually do is show the variation in percentage of votes cast for different offices.

But the following illustrative cases from these ·tabulations will show why members of the House of Representatives feel that they can, independently of candidates for other offices, increase or decrease their own chances of reelection by pleasing or displeasing somebody. If I had had or had supplied fuller data on the following points, the argument I made would have been even stronger that it is:

1. I lack any information on counterbalancing shifts; on the face of them, the voting figures deal only with net variations, and there is of course every reason to think that net variations grossly underestimate actual variations. That is to say, Mr. A and Mr. B vote for Congressman X, Democrat, and State Treasurer Y, Republican, while Mr. C votes for Congressman X's opponent, Mr. Z, and for the State Treasurer's opponent, Mr. F.

2. Information on closely contested primaries, which some incumbents also experience, was not included.

3. Information was not obtainable on New York City or Greater Los Angeles congressional districts, since their election figures could not easily be compared from election to election.

4. Information was not included on candidates for local or county offices; if this had been done, even more cases of variation would have shown up.

5. I omitted the Eisenhower-Stevenson figures in 1952, since they had no bearing on my purposes at the time I prepared the tables.

It should also be pointed out that there were no two-party contests in the South during this period, and that some short-ballot states, like New Hampshire, provide very few pertinent contests. For the sake of convenience, the following examples are taken entirely from states that did not redistrict from 1946 to 1954: In the First Colorado (Denver) in 1950, Byron G. Rogers, Democrat, carried 51 percent of the two-party vote, while the Republican candidate for governor in the same district received 51.6 percent of the two-party vote. Two years before, in 1948, John A. Carroll, Democratic candidate for

---

[3]The set of tables was privately published and is available from me at 536 Pleasant Street, Belmont, Massachusetts, 02178, for $1.80, plus any post-1969 rise in postage rates.

reelection to Congress, had run about 11 percentage points ahead of Truman in the two-party vote.

In the Second Colorado in 1950, William S. Hill, Republican candidate for reelection to Congress, ran 4.2 percent ahead of the Republican candidate for treasurer, while in 1946 he had run 12.4 percent ahead of the Republican candidate for governor.

In the Third Colorado, J. Edgar Chenoweth, Republican incumbent, received 49.3 percent of the two-party vote in 1948, nearly, of course, winning reelection, while the Republican candidate for President got only 40.5 percent of the two-party vote in the same district.

In the Second Connecticut in 1950, Chase Woodhouse, Democratic incumbent, was defeated for reelection, getting only 49.2 percent of the two-party vote, whereas the Democratic candidate for the Senate in the same district actually got 51.8 percent of the two-party vote. And in the state as a whole, the Democratic candidates for both long term and short term in the U.S. Senate were elected, while the Democratic candidate for U.S. Representative at Large was beaten.

The same thing happened in Delaware in 1948: the Republican candidate for U.S. Representative at Large was elected, but so was the Democratic candidate for U.S. Senator.

In 1948, in the First Idaho, the Democratic candidate for Congress carried the district, but Truman lost it to Dewey.

Similarly, Democrats carried the Fourth, Seventh, and Eleventh Districts of Indiana for Congress, while Truman was losing these three districts. But in the Sixth Indiana, the Democratic candidate for Congress was beaten, while his Democratic running mate for governor carried the district by 2 percent in the two-party vote. And in the Tenth Indiana, the same Democratic candidate for governor carried the district, running 4 percent ahead of the Democratic candidate for Congress, who was beaten.

Iowa shows particularly large variations. In the Second Iowa in 1950, the Republican incumbent Congressman got 62 percent of the vote while the Republican candidate for governor lost the district by almost 1 percent; in the Third Iowa, H. R. Gross ran 10 percent ahead of Dewey on the Republican ticket in 1948, Gross winning, Dewey losing. In the Fifth Iowa in 1950, the Democratic candidate for the Senate carried the district, running almost 9 percent ahead of the Democratic candidate for the House, who was beaten. About the same proportions prevailed in the Seventh Iowa in 1948, in regard to House and Senate; and in the Eighth Iowa in 1948, the Democratic candidate for Congress got 44.6 percent, while Truman got 52.1 percent and the Democratic candidate for the Senate 61.3 percent!

In the Fourth and Fifth Kansas, the Democratic candidate for Secretary of State carried both districts in 1948, while the Democratic candidate for Congress got only 35 percent in one district, 44.4 percent in the other.

In Maine, Governor Edmund Muskie (Democrat) got 52.71, 55.13, and 56.60 percent in the three districts in 1954, as compared with candidates for Congress on the Democratic ticket, who got respectively 47.93, 46.03, and 39.46 percent. Similar results can be cited from most other states. In general, congressional incumbents usually do better than the ticket, but a few incumbents do worse.

People seem to pick their Congressmen the same way they pick many of their purchases in a department store. They tend to vote for the familiar name, or failing that for one that is attractive for some reason (ethnic connotation, for instance). But *some* familiar names have acquired negative connotations (as, for example, the late Congressman John Taber [Republican, New York] in sections of his Finger Lake district), so, while some constituents may still vote for the familiar, more vote against it in such cases. Some Congressmen—like some products—have broken through the barriers of inattention and indifference that affect most voters and purchasers, and do considerably better than the ticket for positive reasons. The late Congressman Merlin Hull, Ninth Wisconsin, received 70.8 percent of the two-party vote in 1950, while Senator Alexander Wiley got only 52.5 percent of the two-party vote in that district on the Republican ticket, and the Republican candidate for governor did about 1 percent better than Wiley. Hull no doubt was positively identified as an old-time Progressive in an area where that mattered; Wiley did a little bit worse than the governor or the ticket because he was so absentminded he did not do a good greeting and handshaking job; he remembered few names.

More common, perhaps, is the candidate for higher office who has become an institution or an image—John F. Kennedy, Democratic candidate for reelection to the Senate in Massachusetts in 1958, is an example, as, in many elections, were Thomas Buckley, Massachusetts Democratic auditor (who did better than Kennedy in 1960, and has done about twice as well as the bottom of the ticket), and, in earlier years, Fred Cook, Massachusetts Republican Secretary of State. In 1946 Cook got 52.8 percent in the Third Massachusetts, while the Republican candidate for Congress got only 37.8 percent in that district. On the other hand, Buckley got 59 percent in the First Massachusetts in 1948, while the Democratic candidate for Congress got only 42 percent.

My figures were prepared for 1946–54; there is every reason to suppose that variation—split-ticket voting or failing to vote at all on some positions while voting on others—has increased during the succeeding years.

Incumbents know that they may run ahead of or behind the ticket; they also know, as some of the above cases show, that an election may be very close indeed. Incumbents familiar with cases of this sort, as most politicians are, may always have the nagging feeling "If I do a bit more to please some groups . . ." "If I avoid displeasing some others . . ." Of course, different politicians have different theories of what counts; some swear by case service (handling individual complaints), other stress the advantages of publicity in the mass media, still others think of workmanlike help on community and constituency matters. Some are chiefly retailers of votes at heart, while others regard vote-getting as a wholesale job. But whatever a man's chief emphasis, knowledge of close elections like the following[4] may make him more eager to please or avoid displeasing.

Lyndon Johnson won the Texas senatorial primary runoff (which in that state was in that year in effect the election) by 87 votes out of almost a million cast in 1948. He was jokingly called in consequence "Landslide Lyndon." Although suits and countersuits were filed, Johnson was officially declared the winner by the Democratic State Executive Committee by a vote of 29 to 28!

In the Maine governorship race in 1962, John Reed, Republican, beat Maynard Dolloff, Democrat, by 483 votes out of almost 300,000, while in the South Dakota senatorial election in the same year George McGovern, Democrat, beat Joe Bottum, Republican, by 597 votes out of 250,000. Well known is the Georgia 1966 gubernatorial election, in which Howard H. Callaway, Republican, led Lester Maddox, Democrat, by 1,848 votes out of over 850,000 cast, but since no candidate received a majority, the election was thrown into the Georgia House of Representatives, which chose Maddox.

In the Nevada senatorial election of 1964, Howard Cannon, Democrat, beat Paul Laxalt, Republican, by 48 votes out of almost 135,000; the matter went to court, and Cannon was declared the winner.

---

[4]These figures were kindly obtained for me, at the request of Congressman Bradford Morse of Massachusetts, by Mr. Richard Malow of the Government Division of the Legislative Reference Service, Library of Congress.

In the Minnesota governorship contest of 1962, the first "final" report showed Elmer L. Andersen, Republican, the winner, but after two recounts the results were changed and Karl F. Rolvaag, Democrat, was declared the winner and later certified as governor, with a majority of 91 votes out of a million and a quarter cast.

INTERVIEW PROTOCOLS

Interview with SAMUEL JACOBS,
Staff of Senator Patrick V. McNamara, Democrat, Michigan

[*This was an interview of special importance to the study that Ray-mond Bauer, Ithiel Pool, and I were conducting on foreign trade, because* (a) *we had been concentrating on and conducted a number of interviews in the Detroit business community,* (b) *Sam Jacobs had recently been appointed executive secretary to the newly elected Senator from Michigan, and* (c) *earlier, when he was international representative of the United Automobile Workers, I had interviewed him several times about reciprocal trade activity and that union's part in the 1954 fight; and, in any case, I knew him pretty well through cooperation in Maryland politics.*

Jacobs was formerly a schoolteacher and an old-line moderate Socialist. He worked for the OPA during the war, and later became active in union matters. Though he spoke to me off the record, there is no longer any need to keep his words confidential, as Sam is dead now, killed with his wife in an automobile accident, and Senator McNamara has also died.

The "wheels" figure referred to in the text is this: I had developed the conceit that on the one hand there is legislation—one wheel on an unsteady base; side by side with it is mail and communications

*about legislation—another wheel on an unsteady base. Once in a
while, because of the slight unsteadiness, one wheel hits and affects
the other, but mostly they just whirl around independently, close
enough together so that the unobservant watcher thinks they are in
continual contact.*

*This interview, like those that follow, was written up in haste im-
mediately after it took place, with little attention to the niceties of
punctuation and sentence structure, and no immediate checking of
facts. My uncertainties have been retained for all to see, along with
my asides to my colleagues, for whom the interview protocols were
written. For the sake of those who will read them here I have tidied
up an awkward sentence or two—but not many, and not much, and
never in any way that alters the meaning. In all essential respects,
these are the original interview protocols, except for two matters:
(1) For reasons of space, about a quarter of the Jenkins interview is
omitted. (2) Originally I made frequent contrasts between statements made during the interviews and statements made in earlier
interviews. Naturally, some of these contrasts point up a lack of
perceptiveness or accuracy on the part of some interviewees. When
comments of mine reflect unfavorably on interviewees who are still
living, I have deleted them.]*

N.B. I am going to look next week at the McNamara correspondence
file on trade, and will probably have dinner with Sam and wife. Any
questions?

SAMUEL JACOBS, —th interview
Present: Lewis Dexter
February 25, 1955

> Note: As stated on cover, please to regard as con-
> fidential.

Sam is now Executive Secretary (Legislative Assistant) to Senator
McNamara; was formerly UAW International Representative.

Significance: I interrupted Sam with very few questions, I think. He
told me largely about his experience and observations, as a result of
which he seems to have reached a viewpoint similar to mine. He has,
to be sure (unwillingly at my recommendation), read Bentley's
Knowing and the Known, about four or five months ago. Also the
business about CIO-AFL failure to approach the Senator is very
significant!

"What I've learned in this job above everything else is how unimportant a lot of the things I used to do are which I used to think very important. They are just the beginning of things! Before God, one thing I *never* will do again is to give a speech to a UAW local saying, 'Write your Senator.' " I chuckled. "No," he said, "you laugh because you think it's to save us work. There's that; but the main thing is how little difference it makes. The *only* argument you can make in a case like that is to get the guys, the UAW members, themselves involved in the process, and that kind of approach, really, after seeing all the other things that go on, it's kind of dishonest so far as they're concerned—you're asking them to do something, saying that it matters. . . ."

"One of the questions which bothers me is: How much does a Senator or his assistant need to know? There are a few things about which you need to know a fairish amount . . . but how little about a lot of others! Most things you catch on the fly, talking to people, interested, trustworthy lobbyists, etc. . . ."

I said, "Well, isn't that what you were doing at UAW, being that sort of a lobbyist?" "Well, I suppose so, but I would have rejected the term lobbyist. Service agent. Bringing people on the Hill who already agreed with me information they needed to know."

Abruptly: "You know, I'm kind of frightened, frightened for myself. . . . I don't think there's going to be any time or chance for reflection. I feel now that any time I take from what is properly my job, helping the Senator on direct things, is sort of stealing. . . . Yet I'd like to . . . Nobody is trying to reach a satisfactory modus vivendi on a certain problem [which he described off the record] in school legislation, on which you know I have some background. I haven't got anybody, haven't found anybody who's tackled that problem. . . . I could . . ." I said, "Well, how about, say, an economist like John Miller at Yale? Wouldn't he . . ." He said, "That's just it. I ought not even to take the time to find that out; it won't pay off to the Senator. And I couldn't honestly recommend we hire another professional staff person to work on things like that. If we were to hire another professional staff person, I'd recommend a good press person; but that would mean cutting down on our clerk hire money. I feel myself under moral pressure to work on the things that will pay off [in votes]."

"I see how little impact this mail has on Senators because of the way it's handled. The Senator hardly ever sees any of it. Now I've worked out a way by which *I* don't see much of it." (Of course, in this case, anyhow, and certainly if I pushed him, and could honestly say I thought it worthwhile, they *might* try out a system of devising tables of incoming mail! See below.)

"I'm worried in terms of my Democratic commitments as I look at the kind of mail people send. Testing it against the effect on the legislative process, these people aren't writing about anything that could have any effect on that usually. It's mostly almost random comment."

I told Sam my figure of speech about the wheels (cf. my MS) and he said, "Yes, that's it; they're very rarely in alignment," and then went ahead to describe one case, the proposed civil rights rider on school legislation, where the mail actually has been related to the issue and the Senator is to some extent in the middle. "But that's an exceptional case—mail oriented to the legislative process."

"When you think about the complexity of issues, that raises a whole new field of thought about the possibility of effect of pressure. That must be true particularly in the House, where the Rules Committee sets the whole context within which things are considered. Senators have more freedom of initiation."

"On the other hand, of course, if you want to introduce some legislation, you have to have public support. Yesterday, for instance, I had some representatives of the veterans' group of the CIO in here. I sent for them—they hadn't tried to see me. We had thought about some changes in veterans' legislation which we think desirable, but where would a Senator's office be if we initiated some such legislation and no veterans' group supported them? They hadn't even seen the possibilities or need we saw."

"You know, I was very much surprised at how few representatives of organizations came around to make themselves known. You know there is the CIO Government Workers Union; the Senator's on the District of Columbia Committee and a union man; nobody came around from there to see him, or from any other CIO union interested in government employees. I raised hell with them about that; but some of them who should have been haven't been up here yet. I'd have been up here the first week."

"So this story you hear about vigorous effective lobbying just falls down. It isn't so." (Emphasis mine. L.A.D.)

I asked about the AFL. "No, even fewer came around from them than from the CIO. This must be absolutely confidential. I raised hell with them, too. They may have thought he was sore. There was lots of ill will left over from the campaign that I didn't know about. A lot of these guys here in Washington had tried to get him to withdraw. As a matter of fact, he wasn't sore, and would have been willing enough to see them. If they felt hesitant about it, they could have made a courtesy call or thrown in their hats by— Well, I don't need to tell you all the different ways to throw in your hat. And if he were sore, he would have tossed the hat out. Listen, I just don't see how you could disguise that about the AFL, any way you published it; it must be kept confidential."

"The government people I've brought in here, the experts, have made me pretty sick. The Senator—well, I guess he's sort of unique. He had less preparation than most people who came to the Senate." I said, "Oh, hell, John Williams, and a lot of those Republican businessmen, and after all, the Senator was in a big union and on the city council eight years," just as Sam was correcting himself: "No, I guess I'm wrong. Anyhow, he isn't an expert, and they come in, from the educational groups, for instance, in which the Senator's really interested, and they insist on talking to him either as an expert or an ignoramus—they can't get any in-between."

"On reciprocal trade and tariff, I've not myself had any contact with anybody at all who's talked about it. There's been a lot of mail, the bulk of it high tariff. But some small businessmen are concerned with increasing their exports. I don't know who's been around here, doubt if anybody has. And after all, that's a matter on which the Senator did have and has a pretty strong position and commitment. I don't show him the mail on that. He doesn't particularly want to see it. It won't change his commitment. And people who come and see him, why should they bother about that?"

Then he made some general and in themselves interesting and significant comments about the mail, but not pertinent to our topics that I can see.

"I haven't seen Mr. Hettler of the Detroit World Trade group around here; nor have we heard from him. Of course, this may be a matter of timing. The matter's not up yet in the Senate."

"Yes, I think the Congressman who told you that they usually write too late was right; the debate produces news stories which produce mail. Now, on reciprocal trade, most Senators are committed. But

Formosa was a new issue; their views were unstructured. But the mail came too late for the vote. And then again, after McNamara had publicly challenged Secretary Mitchell on the civil rights rider, how much give did he have left on it?"

I said, "Well, suppose, for example, Andy Brown [the UAW community man in Detroit] should write in and say, 'Look, this is making the guy look ridiculous.' Wouldn't it have weight? Not that McNamara would exactly back down, but—"

"Yes, it would. When it gets to some committee consideration, the Senator might just say, 'Well, I've made my pitch,' but not press it—under that influence.

"But even there, actually, what he does in committee will depend upon what Paul Douglas and one or two others do. Of course, they in turn are subject to influences. But I am contrasting the picture we used to have when we say or said, 'Flood your Congressman with mail,' which assumed more or less a one-to-one relationship between pressure and legislation, with the terrifyingly complex, freely moving motions and factors which enter into this sort of thing; what Paul Douglas does might be affected by what the Senator does." (I swear to God that I had not put any questions more leading than those reported. L.A.D.)

"You know, one of the things you should study is the staff here on the Hill. It's a very interesting business. It has admirable and contemptible aspects. It's completely amoral. They regard it as a racket pure and simple, a racket even, a lot of those clerks, on their own Senator. And they show a servility to him and an arrogance to outsiders which they often wouldn't if they had a real personal loyalty to him. It's a completely amoral business with them." I gave a hypothetical example of some United Rubber Workers regional directors. "No," said Sam, "you're wrong. Those URW guys—sure, in the example you gave they don't see very far, but they are performing a real service to the members, or trying to, on grievances, hours, things like that. It isn't as completely amoral as a lot of these. The patronage employees, I think, are the worst—the elevator operators and stuff. The admirable part is they form a self-aiding community in a lot of ways, get each other jobs, go to bat for each other, help éach other out. Most of these people here, or a lot of them, look on the whole business as a game with perquisites."

(I may add at this point that Sam was extremely acceptive to Dick Brown's eagerness to meet him [see Brown interview], said,

"Sure, any time," and a little later I arranged for the two of them and have lunch Monday—I think that is indicative; see Brown interview.)[1]

I had to leave at this point, but Sam took me in to the mail clerks, told them to lock up the silver any time I came in, but to haul out any mail folder I wanted to see.

Interview with Representative CLEVELAND BAILEY, *Democrat, West Virginia*

Present: Lewis Dexter
June 24, 1954

Mr. Bailey does not state his age, but is obviously an elderly man. He is a member of the Education and Labor Committee, but is generally regarded as the leader of the high-tariff forces in the House, together, perhaps, with Simpson.[2]

Significance: 1. Mr. Bailey's entire attitude led me to feel that, together with Mr. Holmes, he would be more likely to adopt a kind of paternal attitude toward our study if it should be repeated than any other member.

2. Mr. Bailey's statement on how he exerts pressure on the pressure groups rather than the other way around. ("I tell them to get off their fat asses.")

3. The report that the House Ways and Means subcommittee on this matter is already planned.

---

[1]Brown was a newly appointed assistant to Senator Thomas Hennings of Missouri; I had known him previously in Kansas City politics and I had recently interviewed him for the project. I have not included his interview here.

[2]As pointed out in Chapter 2, Congressman Bailey was regarded by some knowledgeable observers on Capitol Hill as worth fifteen votes to the opponents of more liberal reciprocal trade in the House. He was one of the very few men—perhaps the only man—in the House who in terms of expenditure of time made reciprocal trade a top-priority issue. (Of course, members of the Ways and Means Committee who spent less time on the matter were in a better position to exert influence.) Bailey, to some extent, illustrates the proposition: "One man with a principle (a concern) is worth a dozen with an interest."

"Leader" was perhaps the wrong choice of word for him. Richard M. Simpson, on Ways and Means, and Henderson Lanham, off Ways and Means, were really leaders, because other men deferred to their judgment and had a feeling that they were wise and shrewd; I do not believe anyone felt this way about Bailey. But Bailey was an effective *agitator*. He kept reminding people about the feelings of the industries for which he spoke, calling to the attention of members the possibility that people would be hurt by more liberal trade measures.

4. Reiterated insistence on not "basically against" reciprocal trade.

Mr. Bailey gave me a very long lecture, really, punctuated insistently by "You understand?" or "You begin to see the picture?"

"It's the number one problem"

"The tariff and foreign imports are the number one problem in all the districts of West Virginia. Out of forty-one thousand miners, fifty percent are unemployed. Let's enlarge on that. I am not basically opposed to reciprocal trade. All I want is equality of treatment."

Cordell Hull's chicanery

"Now, let me give you the picture. The Smoot-Hawley Act is still the basic tariff law. Cordell Hull, when he started out, had difficulty selling his idea to Congressmen individually. Of course, I wasn't here at the time, but I've been told about it by men who were.

"So, he started out dealing with blocs. He found sixty-nine members from the cotton states and districts—traditionally free-traders. He approached them with the proposition 'We will guarantee to keep all cotton out under the Agricultural Act if you'll go along.' And they did, and it is out to this day, except for a little Egyptian long-staple cotton. They wrote an embargo on cotton.

"Then he looked around and saw twenty-seven tobacco Congressmen. He used the same argument—he said they could have a law, which they now have, which imposes a thousand-dollar fine and a year in jail on anybody who imports any tobacco. You begin to get the picture? The same thing with sugar" (and he described the sugar acts).

"He did the same thing partly, not to a full extent, with wool. He was still short of the necessary votes, so he said to the steel industry: 'What Europe needs for the next twenty-five to fifty years is heavy equipment.' Overnight he made free-traders out of these heavy protectionists."

Henry Ford

"And that's why Henry Ford leads this free-trade lobby group today. Thirteen out of thirty-eight Ford plants are abroad. There's a ten percent tariff on foreign trucks. If this thing goes through, he'll just make those trucks abroad in places like Stockholm, where the labor cost is only forty-two percent of Detroit's, and he will expedite cheap foreign labor. It's not patriotism with Mr. Ford; it's strictly the pocketbook."

"Then who did Mr. Hull overlook?"

"Then who did Mr. Hull overlook? Well, he overlooked a hundred and thirteen basic U.S. industries. A hundred and thirteen industries which aren't especially interested in international trade. That's the group I'm pleading for. Ninety-one percent of all the unemployment in this country today is due to the discrimination of the Truman and Eisenhower administrations on trade policy. Now, I want to prove that to you."

"In my state, there is unemployment"

"In my state, there is unemployment in pottery, hand-made glass, clothespins, chemicals, electrical appliances, and coal. There are a hundred and ten thousand unemployed in the coal industry."

Escape clause

"Now, you'll find I'm the author of the escape clause." (Incidentally, everybody seems to be that. L.A.D.)[3] "I wrote it in the bill in '51. The object was to relieve unemployment. But the Tariff Commission has set up criteria which make it difficult to apply and has totally misinterpreted the intent of Congress. If a company produces three items, and it makes a profit on two, the Tariff Commission takes into account the overall profit and won't give it tariff relief on the third."

Coal

"Now, sixty-eight percent of the economy in our state is tied up with coal. You understand now that I'm a Democrat. But I started the fight against reciprocal trade in the fall of '45 and I kept it up under Truman—and now I find that Eisenhower is adopting that part of the New Deal philosophy.

"Now, two years ago, Acheson got the idea of setting up a new reciprocal trade agreement with Venezuela. He cut the import duty from twenty-one cents a barrel to five and a quarter cents. I protested this first to the Tariff Commission and then to the White House. Truman gave me fifteen minutes to tell him about it; and it ended up in my staying there forty-four minutes in a wrathy

---

[3]In other interviews, a number of Congressmen had told me flatly that they individually were responsible for the escape clause.

argument with the President of the United States. I was trying to tell him:

"In 1929, the oil companies had no foreign oil concessions, and they supported Smoot-Hawley. Since then, they've acquired them and support reciprocal trade.

"In 1936, we exported thirty-six million tons of coal. Maybe we've lost all this now."

I asked whether he'd heard the discussion between Sparkman and Gore in the Senate that afternoon, in which they maintained the coal marketed had been regained.

"Yes," he said, "I was there. But they'll have to do more than talk to show that. Now, let's go ahead." He then gave me a series of figures far too fast to get down, on how oil can undersell coal. The gist of them may be summed up: One coal company in his district in 1952 sold a million tons to Boston Edison. Now B. E. takes oil. It would cost the coal company $10.45 a ton to lay down the coal on the Boston wharves, *without any profit*, whereas the same number of BTUs in oil can be purchased at the wharves for $6.40. "Now you understand why we have idle men in the mines. The captive mines are the only ones operating." (And he explained why this is; something to do with sulfur content and coking.) "Sixty-seven percent of our coal has too much sulfur for coking. We have no market for the ordinary coal now."

"Major railroads are in difficulty"

"The major railroads are in difficulty, too. The B and O did furlough twenty percent; they've now taken back nine percent. The C and O and the N and W are worse hit; and the Virginian, too. Seventy-two percent of the B and O's business is coal." (Note considerable exaggeration of B & O's own figure—see B & O interviews.[4] I checked this and Mr. B. repeated it.) "The only reason the B and O hasn't suffered as much as the other roads is that it ships to the lakes, where oil hasn't been a competitor, as well as to the East Coast.

"Now, preserving the railroads in a good financial situation is essential to the national security in case of emergency. Otherwise, they will not be able to make use of them." At this point he interrupted himself and said: "Let's go back. Make a notation that fifty-three percent of all the fuel in the country . . ." (something or other).

---

[4] Not included here.

"I've lived it"

I said to him then, "The thing that interests me more than anything else about this is the ease and certainty with which you quote figures here, and facts."

He said, "Well, hell, man, I've lived it—lived it for years."

Later on I asked him about districts, and he said, "Two of the districts in the state are even harder hit than mine by these foreign imports."

I said, "And yet you take the load?"

"Well, man, I'm the dean of the delegation. They weren't up here when I started making my fight."

Pottery

"In my district there is the largest manufacturer of vitrified [something or other] in the world. Thirty-six percent of all [something] produced is produced in my district. Our wage scale is $1.56 an hour, the foreign scale is, Britain forty-two cents, others lower."

Glass and William Oates, the newspaperman

"Handmade and hand-blown glass plants are important, too. Then I have three window-glass plants, Pittsburgh Plate Glass. Eighteen percent of hand-blown glass comes from abroad. Out of nine plants, only five are open; two are open part time. Had I not succeeded two years ago in getting the Czechoslovakian trade treaty abrogated, *none* of these glass plants would be open.

"You remember the fight two years ago over William Oates, the newspaperman. To hear me talk about it [he winked] you would have thought Oates the greatest person who was ever captured. The bulk of it was that all the time I had my glass workers in mind; fifty-five percent of the glass came in from Czechoslovakia."

Clothespins

He then discussed clothespins of Swedish manufacture. The gist of it was that Sweden pays 28 cents an hour, West Virginia 61.4 cents an hour. Sweden can undersell at the wharf in New York.

Chemicals, electrical equipment

Only in recent months have chemicals and electrical equipment suffered from competition; they filed a brief or tried to appear before the Randall Commission.

More on glass

He returned to glass, giving me more figures.

"Coal and glass led me to . . . the St. Lawrence Seaway"

"Coal and glass led me to lead the fight against the St. Lawrence Seaway. Fifty-eight percent [I think he said] of West Virginia coal and glass go to the lakes. Today tankers can't get into the lakes. If you build the Seaway, tankers will sell [oil, I think he said] at $3.95 a ton at Milwaukee and Chicago. Now do you understand why I was forced to leap into the fight against the Seaway?

"And Belgium will be able to sell glass throughout there at less than Pittsburgh Plate Glass. At present Belgium undersells PPG in New York; but fortunately the rail freight rates eat up this differential as you get into the center of the country. But the Seaway would change all this. It would knock out the PPG factory in Clarksburg, West Virginia, althogether. And then the Seaway will take Ford cars back to Europe for twenty-two dollars less per car than before, and will take every damn dollar away from Pittsburgh Plate Glass."

Sums it up

"Well, I guess that about sums it up. Do you begin to see now why I take the lead in these things?"

"Listen, I'm a reasonable fellow"

"Listen, I'm a reasonable fellow—I know we have to have trade. What I object to is the gross favoritism to a select few American products. Give me equality of treatment and I'll shut up."

His background

I asked him about his background, and he said, "No, I hadn't had any special interest in the tariff before I came up here; but my background might show you why I took the lead in this kind of thing. I was chief clerk of Jones and Laughlin [Steel] for fifteen years; and you absorbed by osmosis from the big men you dealt with ideas about economics. Then some of my friends back home persuaded me to run for superintendent of schools. I did, and learned a lot there. Then I ran a daily newspaper. Then I was assistant state auditor from 1932 to 1940, and director of the state budget from 1940 to 1944. So far as I know, I'm the only member of the House who doesn't live in his district; I haven't lived there for twenty-three years. And listen, don't put this in, but if they had cross-filing like in California, I'd get both party nominations."

Farm surplus proposal; stockpiling

He talked about a piece of legislation for disposal of surplus farm products. "Congressman Judd of Minnesota added an amendment to authorize taking 'goods and services' as well as 'foreign currencies' for the surplus. I proposed a substitute amendment to his amendment, substituting 'crucial materials' [critical, I guess—L.A.D.] and I beat him in a floor fight. That has a lot of bearing on reciprocal trade. If we had an emergency, we'd need glass and textiles too."

Budget and Truman

At some point in there, he told me how his experience as state budget director had enabled him to foresee certain errors in the 1945–46 budget (dealing with recaptures on the excess profits tax), and he had warned the President and budget directors about what would happen, and they got sore, but he was right, as events showed.

Why he'd started on the tariff

I pushed further on my question as to why he'd started on the tariff, and he said, "Well, shortly after I got here, my glass plants were meeting too much competition at the end of the war. My first crack after it was in connection with the Geneva Conference of GATT. I started raising hell in order to help the handmade glass industry. I lost, but I came back to fight again in '49, '51, '53 and '54."

"The President looked right at me"

"Last night, the president of the West Virginia Association invited me to the dinner where the President spoke, and he talked about building up Japanese trade. I was invited because I used to be a newspaper editor. The President was looking right at me—I sat right in front of him—and I was suspicious he had me in mind." (The President here is Eisenhower; reference is to his Japanese trade speech—L.A.D.)

Dexter: "But he didn't convert you?"

Bailey: "Oh, hell, no."

"In sixty days . . ."

"In sixty days, the Japanese treaty will be signed—they've got it all worked out now—and that's going to hurt a hell of a lot of industries—glass, pottery, ornamental glassware. I just don't know to what extent it will affect us. Their wage structure is so far out of line, nine to seventeen cents an hour. It looks gloomy as hell. But what are you and I going to do?"

"I'm going to spend the summer here"

"Well, one thing. The Ways and Means subcomittee will start hearings in late July and early August. I can't see any other approach for them than to make a careful survey of each industry and see what percent of domestic production we can give to foreigners. Ten percent in some cases, fifteen percent in others, possibly a few times twenty percent. That's a quota basis. We'll say to them, 'We'll give you fifteen percent of the domestic market instead of the thirty-five percent you now have.' I'm going to spend the summer here to keep after those boys and see they stay in line."

One hundred and thirteen industries

"Of course, this harm is not only in my district. There are one hundred and thirteen industries. New England, fisheries, boots, shoes, watches, clocks, safety pins, motorcycles, jukeboxes, hats. Western New York, pottery, aluminum, motorcycles. Pennsylvania, glassware (also in New York), pottery, aluminum (now they've built an aluminum plant in Canada). Independent oil in Louisiana, Texas, Oklahoma. All three of these states conserve their oil supply. Now, on account of foreign oil, they've had to withhold forty percent of their oil in Oklahoma; and since ten cents per [?] goes to schools there, you'll see how it hurts them. Texas depends pretty heavily on its severance taxes, and that's dropped."

Taft; Ford; stockpiling jobs; Bailey's day for getting his ass kicked

I said, "Well, I bet Charles P. Taft would write you a letter of criticism if you asked him."

He said, "Taft? Huh! You know who he was. Just a lawyer for the Venezuelan government. That's all. And Ford? I took him apart on the floor of the House. I love to needle these fellows. They talk all the time about stockpiling. Well, I'm going to ask them: Can they stockpile jobs?"

Then he told me about a conversation he had had before the vote on June 11, in which he said to someone, "Well, it's just the annual day for Bailey getting his ass kicked."

Reciprocal trade politically

"Outside Rhode Island, we've been injured more than any other state. But I tell you this: If this Eisenhower administration keeps up reciprocal trade, there'll never be another Republican elected in the state of West Virginia. The present policy cannot be continued. It breeds unemployment."

Pressures; "I just reverse that"

"Now, what are you going to do with all this?" I explained about our interest in communications and pressures, and he said: "Well, I just reverse that. I call up the National Coal Association or some of these guys and say, 'What the hell are you doing? Why don't you get off your fat ass and get a move on?'"

Democrats are shifting

"You know the chairman of the Ways and Means, Mr. Cooper, and Mr. Gore[5]—they think everything Cordell Hull did was sacred and should never be touched. But I hope you noticed in the debate that the gentleman from Rhode Island [Forand] said he was very reluctant about supporting the bill. And the gentleman from Kentucky [Gregory] has headaches about it. In fact, Kentucky suffers more than any other state except West Virginia from this foreign oil. And Eberharter, you know he has the Pennsylvania railroad and so forth, and you know how they feel about this. Yes, sir, things look a lot better for us."

"I'm a crusader"

"You know, these lobbies and so forth aren't pressuring me. I raise hell on this, just because I don't call myself a politician. I don't like that idea. I'm a crusader, a crusader for the little guy, his representative in Washington."

"Come back"

Perhaps six times Mr. Bailey told me, "Come back any time. Be sure you do. That's an invitation." From this, and also from the way his

---

[5]Both Congressman Jere Cooper and Senator Albert Gore were from Tennessee. Gore, still serving in the Senate, had at that time (1954) taken the lead for stronger reciprocal trade legislation (see Raymond A. Bauer, Ithiel de Sola Pool, and Lewis A. Dexter, *American Business and Public Policy: The Politics of Foreign Trade* [New York: Atherton, 1963], pp. 354ff), and Cooper, as ranking Democrat on Ways and Means at the time, was, to a considerable degree, formally and actually responsible for the pro–reciprocal trade activities of the Democrats on his committee. Hull himself was from Tennessee, and his concern for reciprocal trade has sometimes been said to spring from his Tennessee background.

secretaries treated him, I sort of received the impression he might basically be a lonely old bachelor; but it turns out he has six children.

Needling

He also told me some stories about his campaigning, ·of how he needled the Republican Unionists back home in West Virginia. He even had some pictures of Stonewall Jackson to show me. These stories depend for their effect upon details of the West Virginia locale and the Civil War, so I won't take the space to repeat them here; but they are psychologically interesting for the picture they conjure up of the old campaigner teasing his constituents, raising hell with them, so they go around and say, "Ay, gorry, old Bailey's quite a card!" "They love it," he says; "they love it."

Interview with Representative VICTOR KNOX, *Republican, Michigan*

[This is one of many interviews that were not in themselves particularly exciting or revealing, but which cumulatively added to the sense of pattern. (I thank Mr. Knox for permitting me to use it.)

A note on my particular interest in seeing Mr. Knox:

Chapter 15 of American Business and Public Policy *is called "Detroit: Hotbed of Free Traders." This title was chosen because business groups in the rest of the country (and people in the administration) often said that Detroit was the city above all others where the agitation for lowering trade barriers originated. In general, there is a feeling, probably well founded in fact, that members of any committee, and especially of Ways and Means, speak for and represent their states as well as their own districts. The member from Kentucky on Ways and Means, for instance—and Kentucky generally has such a member—is supposed to speak for whisky and racing, whether they matter economically in his district or not. It is generally believed that at that time the Republican party in Michigan was heavily influenced by and financed by the automobile companies, which were supposedly strongly in favor of liberal trade. One would have supposed under these circumstances that Michigan's only Republican on Ways and Means would have heard something significant from Detroit—particularly when he was, as Congressman Knox appeared to me to be, a responsible, sober person, the kind who might well exert influence among his colleagues, and when the general feeling about the Democratic member on Ways and Means, the late Congressman John D. Dingell,[6] was that he was a lightweight (see the interview with Thomas Jenkins). (I have made the point before, but let me repeat it: This judgment in no way represents the feeling about the younger Congressman Dingell, who now serves in the House.) Just as Sam Jacobs said, the reciprocal traders in Detroit had not done what seemed obvious; and the Knox interview confirms Jacobs' words.]*

Present: Lewis Dexter
June 29, 1954

Congressman Knox is in his fifties. He was for a number of years a member of the Michigan House of Representatives (Ways and Means Committee) and for six years its Speaker. He was first elected to the U.S. Congress in 1952. He is a member of the House Ways and Means Committee. It may be significant that both he and Utt, added in 1952 to the Republican side, are strong protectionists, supposedly.

Significance: Here is a guy who with just a little explanation, I'd bet, might see some of the reciprocal trade standpoints, a guy from Michigan, on the committee, who reports or recollects being approached by Detroit protectionists but not by Detroit free-traders, and a guy from a district with a lot of agriculture.

I had the feeling that a different interviewing technique might have provoked better answers from him. He responded to leading questions by saying, "Yes, that is correct," except in the one case I have indicated. Most Congressmen and Senators elaborate or

---

[6]The late Congressman Dingell was one of the members who apparently would have been a key figure for our inquiry, but I never did get to see him. He turned us down initially on the ground that all these matters are reported in committee hearings, etc.! Later on, when I could have got introductions to him, I had already reached the conclusion that his reluctance to see us was a simple matter of feeling that he might look foolish to academic interviewers (or that his staff felt this way), and that, in sober truth, he would have had nothing to add to what I had already learned. When, later on, I was working for Senator McNamara, also of Michigan, I could easily enough have seen him, but I did not bother to do so.

It should also be added that I never actually talked with Congressman Jere Cooper, then ranking Democrat on Ways and Means. I did see him for a minute or two, long enough to make it clear that he was unwilling to answer any questions about anything. Later I learned from members of the press that this was his usual treatment of unknown newspapermen, and their comments fitted my hypothesis that he regarded me simply as a newspaperman, to be brushed off. (At the time, it was said there was no daily newspaper in his district.) Through a Congressman's wife with whom I was friendly and to whom Cooper was under an obligation, I could have met him socially in circumstances that probably would have resulted in an interview, but she put it to me: "How important is this to you? If I ask him for this, I may not be able to ask him for something else," and I couldn't honestly say it was very important.

qualify such leading questions. I probably asked him more questions in less time than most other interviewees because of the brevity of his answers. I don't think his terseness sprang from hostility, although it may have indicated disinterest. Note his discussion of housing.

Agricultural problems most important

"I wouldn't say that this is a particularly important matter to my district, judging from what I hear. There are so many more agricultural groups than any others, which I hear from on agricultural problems."

Who he hears from in district; state; country

"Usually I hear from an industry which says it has been injured. I have heard in my district chiefly from the woodworking industries. I have just heard from management; I have not heard from labor or do not recall doing so." (See his remarks on clothespins, below— a branch of woodworking.)

"Of course, the Farm Bureau in my state is in favor of extension of the reciprocal trade act for three years, and I've heard from reciprocal trade. . . . Yes, it is correct that I hear from outside my district, not only from the state, but from the rest of the country. I have not heard so much on free trade or reciprocal trade from Detroit, but mostly from outside the state. (Of course, you know the automobile people are reciprocal traders.) The people from Detroit often drop in and see me; some write me, too. No one from my own district has come to see me about this." (He has been back only twice, briefly, this session. He has no opposition in the primary and apparently feels fairly confident about the general election.) "The people from Detroit who come to see me are largely people who want to [talk about][7] several different industries, not just one."

Clothespins; protectionist views

"Of course, in my district an industry had to close shop. The clothespin industry. This was a matter of quotas. The problem was to control quotas allocated to other countries. I appeared before the Tariff Commission in behalf of more limiting quotas two or three weeks ago."

---

[7]The words in brackets represent a guess at what I probably meant to put here. The fact is, there is nothing between "to" and "several" in my original notes, and I'm not going to pretend now that I remember what Knox actually said.

(At this point we were interrupted by a prolonged long-distance call about housing for boys at an air base in his district. He questioned his caller very closely and intelligently, and showed a detailed knowledge and a decent attitude about the problem, I felt.)

"Of course, I have also called the attention of my committee [Ways and Means] to the problems of the clothespin people. They could reopen if quotas were changed."

I asked, "Have you been able to do anything else for them?"

At this point he abandoned briefly his businesslike manner, and said with some feeling, "I know we must have foreign trade—I know if we don't buy from western Europe they'll sell elsewhere—but nevertheless I feel we should not destroy U.S. industries to raise foreign standards of living. I am cognizant of the fact that a million people enter the labor market each year" (He included in his calculations 200,000 under the DP Bill for 1954!—L.A.D.)[8] "and only half a million retire, so I believe a grave question is set up with regard to the way reciprocal trade destroys industries. . . .

"You can fly over this country anywhere and you may see a little town in the mountains or in a valley which is the center of people's livelihood, where they have their being, a little town with a small industry perhaps—when you destroy that industry you don't only destroy it, you destroy the town and the life of the people."

I asked, "Is the town where the clothespins are of this type?"

He said, "Yes. They closed up shortly before my election in 1952. Munising, Michigan. The thing got so bad that people had to sell their houses. And you know what happens when people have to do that, and then they go elsewhere for work and have to pay inflated prices. . . . I have certainly brought to the attention of the Ways and Means Committee what is happening there and what is taking place in the woodworking industries."

Plywood

"I have particularly brought to its attention what is happening in my district because of the sale of foreign plywood from Japan." (He did not give any specific answer to my query as to whether the Japanese trade treaty would make it worse.)

---

[8]Since the Refugee Relief Act of 1953 authorized only 214,000 special-quota immigrant visas altogether, to be issued during the three years 1953–56, and since some of these went to wives and dependent children who did not enter the labor force, the Congressman's figures here are not to be taken seriously.

Michigan House vs. Federal House

In view of O'Neill's[9] interesting comments comparing the Massachusetts House of Representatives with the U.S. Congress, I asked Knox if there were any ways in which he found Congress different from the Michigan House. He said, "Well, as Speaker, people came to my office for all sorts of things, since the individual members don't have offices. And in general I think in the Michigan House the members learn each other's views better, because they don't have offices. So a businessman may invite them all to dinner on a comittee and they'll each hear the others question him; whereas up here, I don't learn my colleagues' views to the same extent. And knowing those views is an advantage."

Interview with Representative THOMAS A. JENKINS, Republican, Ohio

June 10, 1955

Mr. Jenkins, of the Tenth Ohio (East Liverpool), is one of the half-dozen senior representatives in point of service. He is acting senior Republican on Ways and Means while Mr. Reed is ill, and will presumably succeed as chairman if the Republicans take over. He is an exceptionally amiable, healthy-appearing man, talks in a low voice, very friendly smile and handshake, full head of hair. He said again and again, "Don't take this down," so afterward I had to write up an interview that had taken about an hour with few notes to jog my memory.

"I think the conference report was pretty good. Of course the Senate bill had substantially the amendments we'd offered in the House" (we Republicans) "and been beaten on."

"The Republican members of the Conference Committee from the House agreed with the Senate conferees, so that the Democratic House conferees really had no chance. They kept putting things off and so forth, I suppose because Sam Rayburn had asked them to, and they didn't want it to appear that they were clasping the Senate bill in their arms like a long-lost child, and then sometimes

---

[9]Congressman Thomas O'Neill (who is still serving in Congress) had been Speaker of the Massachusetts House, just as Mr. Knox had been Speaker of the Michigan House. When I interviewed Mr. O'Neill, he made some interesting comparisons between the Massachusetts House and the federal House, which was what led me to ask Mr. Knox these questions.

we couldn't get hold of the Senate conferees and one thing and another, too trivial for you to put down, and that's why the delay."

"All the Senate members supported the Senate amendments, Kerr particularly. Byrd had his proxy the couple of times he was absent. Kerr was very friendly and amiable to the House Republicans. Of course, our House Republican amendments were added and supported by Senate Democrats. The textile fellows, etc., are strong for the changes, and the conference report will go through the House."

"Mills is a very able fellow, very bright, very well educated, quick to grasp things, and on close terms with the House leadership, so they give him all their information, etc., much smoother and easier to get along with than Jere [Cooper]. Jere is a pretty pontifical and stubborn fellow, fussy about details. However, we're a very harmonious and outstanding bunch on Ways and Means, and get along very well."

"Of course, I don't think the conference report bill is nearly as good as our real Republican bill." (The Simpson? Bill of '53?)

"All members of the Conference Committee will sign the report except old John Dingell [second Democrat]. Old John just doesn't care about anything except beer.[10] He's always raising fusses. That's because he's been a sick man for a long time. Why, ten years ago, Mrs. Jenkins and I were in Sarasota—we have no children, so we go south for Christmas—and old John was at another hotel there, and he called me and said, 'Tom, if I get real sick in the middle of the night, is it all right if I call you?' And I said, 'Yes, I'm strong and vigorous.' Well, that was ten years ago. As I said, we're a pretty harmonious bunch!"

[*Here a section is omitted. Later on Mr. Jenkins got to discussing the fact that women, in particular the League of Women Voters, support things like freer trade.*]

"The menfolks are realistic, and now, of course, it wouldn't do for me to say this, but the womenfolks are more naïve and trusting, you might say gullible, and some agitator comes along and talks about 'trade, not aid,' and they believe him."

---

[10]This should not be misread! What Mr. Jenkins meant (and it can easily be checked against Ways and Means hearings) is that Mr. Dingell was tremendously worried about the importation of Canadian beer into the Detroit area, a matter about which he asked several witnesses.

"Now, I've taken two long trips around the world recently, and I learned a lot on these trips." He explained how "old" Russia (just as he said "old" John) has interior lines, whereas America has an expanded "perimeter." "One of these trips was as a member of the Joint Committee on Atomic Energy" (on which he served last Congress, but not this). "I was impressed in Calcutta with this: Those women hold babies in their arms and cuddle them and nurse them" (he gave a rather vivid and poetic description) "just exactly as ours do—just exactly the same. But after that everything else is different." (He described women lying on sidewalks, waiting for a bull to walk over them.)

"Now, in this country the Fords, rich as they are, don't look down on poor people—there in India nobody tries to help the poor people or to aid them. Sure, I want to aid the poor people there, but I don't see how trading with their rich manufacturers is going to do it. When they have a six-cent-an-hour-or-so wage scale, it doesn't help those people at all."

"Of course, we must have friends now, old Russia is reaching out and reaching out, and we are supplying all sorts of aid. Aid is very much better. Because when it's aid, everybody pays; it doesn't reach just into the pockets of the workingman in my district, the coal people, the pottery people, who have to drive fifty or seventy-five miles to get a job. Now they say under this Republican administration that there are a lot more jobs than there were before; but all I know is that in my region there are a lot of people out of work, and as long as that's so, we'd better spend our money on aid."

"Now, I don't hold with those people who say we shouldn't spend money abroad; we've got to spend a lot of money. But it should be aid."

Somehow from here he got into the Ford UAW contract. "Personally I'd like to see each of the Ford brothers taxed a million dollars out of the business and then turn the company over to the sons-of-bitches. Within a year they'd be bankrupt. But who am I to say what should be done? . . . Reuther, they say he's well educated, but they forget to add, educated in Moscow."

Then he went ahead to tell me about how in Johannesburg, "a city about the size of Cleveland," they expect the Americans in Casablanca to defend them.

"Now about workers. Supposing the Japanese with their low wage rates can produce something which they can sell at twenty-five dollars. Here it costs seventy-five. What happens? Some American buys it and sells it at sixty-five. Well, I guess that money goes to Americans who get it, but they get it simply by cheating and I don't like that." (Cheating: an inordinate markup.)

"I voted for an international road the other day. I hated to do it. Still, we'll have it if we get into trouble there, unless they dynamite it. But when have any of those countries ever helped us when we were in trouble except for Puerto Rico [sic] and a very little from Mexico and Brazil to give us soldiers. We've supported them through the Monroe Doctrine; of course that was for our own sake too."

"A lot of these countries run to Russia whenever they have to." (I think the reference here was to countries throughout the world, not merely to Latin America.) "And Argentina . . ." (The comments were scathing.)

"Bicycles—now in Rome and a couple of other countries, everybody rides bicycles." (I didn't see the tariff point, but there was one.)

"Watches—when has Switzerland ever done anything for us? And national defense skills are very important. In fact, to my mind, war is the paramount question; everything else must be secondary to that."

"The manager's report [conference report] has all these things in it, goes on and on, whereas if lawyers didn't write it, we could have a fifteen-to-twenty-line report, just saying Congress intends this, and if a man doesn't get justice he can go to court. We could declare war and kill a million people in a lot less space. It's full of words, words" (something about old Jere splitting hairs).

"Now, what will you say about me? That's right; that's right. Let me see your report. I want to see it. You may have some ideas. As you have learned from listening to me, I need to learn a lot about this. Let me know if you have ideas as to what we should do."

(Conceivably the last point suggested by imminence of chairmanship?)

Earlier I had asked him about KWEH.[11] He apparently had not remembered the idea clearly, although it frequently appears in

---

[11] The Kennedy-Williams-Eberharter-Humphrey proposals to help industries and workers who could demonstrate injury from foreign competition—government loans, guarantees, allowances for retraining, etc. See Bauer, Pool, and Dexter, *American Business and Public Policy*, pp. 43, 75.

the testimony. "Well, I don't know. I'm afraid that sort of thing can spread. Now, look at social security. You know I voted for social security at first, because we already had it in Ohio, and then I felt it should be extended to the blind. So I pushed that and made a heartrending speech about it, which they still make fun of me about —but look what we have now, all sorts of social security everywhere."

He commented on customs simplification. "Now they have another customs simplification bill coming up. I sponsored the last one. But every time they simplify it, they make it more complicated. Just because of all those words."

Probably the most important point was Jenkins' report that everyone from the House except Dingell (who was always absent) and from the Senate except Kerr attended every conference committee meeting.

APPENDIX C

THUMBNAIL SKETCHES OF SOME
MEMBERS OF CONGRESS, 1959,

With a View to Showing How They Might Be Influenced to Vote Favorably (from the Standpoint of a Particular Client) on Trade and Aid Matters

[*In 1959 I was employed by an organization with considerable interest in liberalizing foreign trade and increasing foreign aid coverage to report on the ways in which it might influence Congress. (This report served as the basis for my* How Organizations Are Represented in Washington.)[1] *I also prepared specific statements about how members of the House Committees on Foreign Affairs and Ways and Means and the Senate Committees on Foreign Relations and Finance might stand on issues of concern to the ultimate clients.*

As a preliminary to these reports, I prepared the following notes for the officers with whom I directly worked:][2]

---

[1]Indianapolis: Bobbs-Merrill, 1969.

[2]Some minor modifications have been made here, for clarity and to avoid hurting some feelings.

It is important to note that any report, such as this, which focuses on *individuals* leaves out some of the important characteristics of a group or an institution—for a group or institution is often much more than the sum of the individuals, because within the group individuals act in terms of roles and perceptions arising from their relationship to the group and to each other. Readers will probably find this point illuminated in John Manley's book tentatively titled *The House Ways and Means Committee* (Boston: Little, Brown, forthcoming).

NOTE ON COMMITTEES AND
COMMITTEE LEADERSHIP

I am reporting in the accompanying document on the Ways and Means and Foreign Affairs Committees of the House and the Finance and the Foreign Relations Committees of the Senate. It should be borne in mind, however, that on matters affecting trade and aid, mutual security, and the like, the Appropriations and the Rules Committees of the House and the Appropriations Committee of the Senate may be more important than the Foreign Affairs and Foreign Relations Committees. It should also be borne in mind that it is sometimes possible for an astute and determined legislator to claim and obtain jurisdiction over some aspect of a field that would normally seem to belong to Ways and Means or Foreign Affairs. For example, the so-called Trade Agreements Adjustment Act (the Kennedy-Williams-Eberharter bills) was originally prepared as a series of amendments to the Tariff Act of 1930, the basic tariff law; but these proposals could also be referred to Education and Labor in connection with distressed-areas bills, or special applications of them could be handled by Merchant Marine and Fisheries or by Interior (for mining). Also, almost any committee may *investigate* something that leads to criticism of foreign aid, reciprocal trade, and the like. The Government Operations Committees are specifically set up for this purpose; and the Labor Committee of the Senate on several occasions, most recently in the Pastore subcommittee, has been used as a sounding board for complaints about so-called cheap foreign labor and the effect of foreign imports on U.S. unemployment.

Some members have on occasion professed and voted views different from those here attributed to them; the explanation under Frank Ikard and John Watts as to how this may happen should be borne in mind in evaluating formal professions "for the record"; see also Edna Kelly for a somewhat more intuitive guess as to why the record does not always serve as a guide to what members will do when the chips are down. These points probably must be stressed because a commentator as acute as Mrs. Roosevelt has consistently misinterpreted the situation—or rather ignored it—in her comments on Senator John F. Kennedy and the McCarthy censure, and therefore misinterpreted the significance of his abstention. If she does this, it is to be supposed that others may misinterpret the record. It is particularly important *not* to suppose that in the clinches someone like Watts or Ikard will not realize the significance of overall U.S. foreign policy[3] simply because on other occasions he has spoken or voted otherwise; and a fairly large number of the Congressmen who protested the mistreatment of this or that local commodity in the great debate of 1955 before the vote on extending reciprocal trade were speaking purely for the record, and were glad that procedure and party organization made their protests ineffective. In a good many other cases, members perform local services to their districts (for example, some members who voted several years ago for the amendment to the Defense Appropriations Act requiring the use of U.S.-produced instead of foreign textiles for certain purposes) without realizing or envisaging the fact that there is a contradiction between some local services and overall foreign or military policy objectives, because no one has clearly explained to them wherein the contradiction lies. Few Congressmen have time to study the large field of legislation, and they must necessarily rely upon what somebody tells or does not tell them.

It is not now likely that either the House Foreign Affairs Committee or the Senate Foreign Relations Committee will take any drastic step early in the Congress even to consider legislation that may materially affect our client. The Senate committee is definitely committed to a series of studies, which are not yet (January 10) officially contracted. The House committee has a subcommittee of senior members on foreign aid; and it is my understanding that Chairman Thomas E. Morgan is seriously entertaining the possibility that this subcommittee should hire its own professional staff, whether for temporary or permanent purposes I'm not certain. No word is likely on this till early February. If it turns out that a permanent staff is contemplated (as it well may be), the staffing of the group may be the most important item to affect our client in these committees in this Congress.

The general constitution of the House committee is described in Holbert Carroll's excellent book *The House of Representatives*

---

[3]Since the entire report was prepared for a client in favor of trade and aid, I naturally wrote it in terms of the client's basic assumptions and interests. Vice versa, when at the same time I was preparing a report for some aluminum interests, the quasi-protectionist assumptions of those interests were taken for granted. In other words, although every statement about Congressmen and their orientation represents my best judgment, there is sometimes no occasion in such a document as this for the writer to assert his own views on the basic policy issues that led the client to come to him.

and Foreign Affairs (University of Pittsburgh Press, 1958), which in my judgment should be in the hands of everyone concerned with this committee. His discussion of the greater weight of the Committee on Appropriations on foreign affairs (Chapters 8 and 9), and of six other committees sporadically (Chapter 5), is highly useful.

It is often maintained that John M. Vorys of Ohio and Brooks Hays of Arkansas really ran the committee under the previous chairmen, Robert B. Chiperfield and Thomas S. Gordon. Neither of them is in the Congress this session; but in any event, Mr. Hays did not take a very active part in the committee last session (except for the special subcommittee on Canadian affairs), presumably because of the Little Rock situation. Mr. Morgan, as reported, is an enigma; if he does not run the committee himself, who will? The outstanding members of the committee in terms of personality and their colleagues' image of them appear to be Frank M. Coffin of Maine and Walter H. Judd of Minnesota. Mr. Coffin is of course quite junior, and there is considerable talk he may go on Ways and Means in 1961. (I doubt he would want to. But neither Lee Metcalf nor John C. Watts, new Democratic members this session, wanted to, either; they were drafted, not invited.) And Mr. Judd is tagged as Chiang Kai-shek's Congressman. But unless Morgan and Clement Zablocki have more leadership characteristics than is superficially obvious, Coffin may become the spark plug of the committee. He certainly would be more heeded outside the committee than most senior members, as of now, by the more alert, active liberals in Congress. And Judd may decide that Chiang Kai-shek is a lost cause and shift his allegiance to Japan as the best bulwark against communism. Consequently, these four members seem the most important for those interested in our clients' concerns to establish good contacts with, plus, of course, the staff.

Bourke Hickenlooper and Mike Mansfield are reported to be the Far East specialists in the Senate committee. But new Democratic members of the committee, if any, could do far worse than establish themselves as Asian experts. Fulbright and, because of his Presidential potential, Kennedy are equally important. Because of the general lack of clarity on Asia and the Senate's general uncertainty about the administration's foreign policy, the contractors, whoever they may be, for studies of the Senate committee might be very influential. (I am assuming this is one area in which a contract will definitely be consummated.)

Since, as I indicated in my preliminary statement, Ways and Means and Finance are generally much more important than Foreign Affairs or Relations on matters of concern to our clients, I have devoted less effort to formulating statements here on members of these committees than on the former two; and some statements are made with less certainty here. Since it is generally easier to get expanded biographical material from library research on Senators than on House members, I have spent more time on the House than on the Senate, believing that, within the limitations of time, I could be of more use to you by trying to reconcile conflicting views of Mr. Morgan, for instance, than of Senator Long.

REPORTS ON INDIVIDUAL MEMBERS

[*These reports will probably better indicate the way in which individual personalities and perceptions interact with district interests than an abstract discussion of the topic. I believe they are also of some value in showing the difficulty that one fairly well-informed congressional observer had in getting hard information on some points of moment. In some ways, no doubt, I was at a disadvantage as compared with the average lobbyist: I did not actually carry out discussion with members about an operative proposal. But I had some advantages, too—wider academic and journalistic contacts, and six years of concern with the reciprocal trade issue. On balance, I doubt if most lobbying groups with which I have been in touch do much better in amassing extensive and relevant information (except for a few that keep up continuous contact over years). So even the errors below (and there are some) and the guesses help to show how persons trying to influence Congress act on uncertain or faulty perceptions of individual Congressmen. It would be possible for me to correct some of these statements now; and with careful study I might add to and modify a number of them. But then readers would not have a typical example of the way in which guesswork, knowledge, impression, and ignorance mingle in determining legislative evaluations. (I may say I don't know if my clients actually used this material. I believe it was sent to headquarters, and it may have influenced actions—or it may not.)*

I include only some of the reports I prepared; these will serve to indicate what the others were like. (I also wrote reports on Senators, not included here.)

The committees at the time I wrote included:

HOUSE OF REPRESENTATIVES

Ways and Means

DEMOCRATS	REPUBLICANS
WILBUR MILLS, Ark.	DANIEL REED (died), N.Y.
AIME FORAND, R.I.	RICHARD SIMPSON, Pa.
CECIL KING, Calif.	NOAH MASON, Ill.
THOMAS J. O'BRIEN, Ill.	JOHN W. BYRNES, Wisc.
HALE BOGGS, La.	HOWARD H. BAKER, SR., Tenn.
EUGENE KEOGH, N.Y.	THOMAS CURTIS, Mo.
BURR HARRISON, Va.	VICTOR KNOX, Mich.
FRANK M. KARSTEN, Mo.	JAMES UTT, Calif.
A. S. HERLONG, JR., Fla.	JACKSON BETTS, Ohio
FRANK IKARD, Tex.	
THADDEUS MACHROWICZ, Mich.	
JAMES B. FRAZIER, JR., Tenn.	
WILLIAM J. GREEN, JR., Pa.	
JOHN WATTS, Ky.	
LEE METCALF, Mont.	

Foreign Affairs Committee

DEMOCRATS	REPUBLICANS
THOMAS MORGAN, Pa.	ROBERT CHIPERFIELD, Ill.
A. S. CARNAHAN, Mo.	FRANCES BOLTON, Ohio
C. J. ZABLOCKI, Wisc.	CHESTER MERROW, N.H.
OMAR BURLESON, Tex.	WALTER JUDD, Minn.
EDNA KELLY, N.Y.	JAMES FULTON, Pa.
WAYNE HAYS, Ohio	DONALD JACKSON, Calif.
ARMISTEAD SELDEN, Ala.	MARGUERITE CHURCH, Ill.
JOHN PILCHER, Ga.	ROSS ADAIR, Ind.
BARRATT O'HARA, Ill.	ALVIN BENTLEY, Mich.

Foreign Affairs Committee

DEMOCRATS	REPUBLICANS
L. H. FOUNTAIN, N.C.	LAURENCE CURTIS, Mass.
DANTE FASCELL, Fla.	STUYVESANT WAINWRIGHT, N.Y.
FRANK COFFIN, Me.	
LEONARD FARBSTEIN, N.Y.	
D. S. SAUND, Calif.	
CHARLES C. DIGGS, Mich.	
LINDLEY BECKWORTH, Tex.	
HARRIS McDOWELL, JR., Del.	
WILLIAM T. MURPHY, Ill.	
WILLIAM H. MEYER, Vt.	
CORNELIUS GALLAGHER, N.J.	
CHESTER BOWLES, Conn.	

The reports are here presented in alphabetical order; when first presented to the client, they were, of course, given in order of seniority by party.]

Representative Howard H. Baker, Sr., Tennessee
Fifth-ranking Republican, Ways and Means

The State Department, there is some reason to believe, made quite a special effort this last year to persuade Representative Baker to adopt a more liberal position on reciprocal trade; but, although he did seem influenced to some extent in committee, his floor position remained protectionist. There are in his district several small industries, and in Tennessee a fair amount of textiles and coal, which are quite apprehensive about foreign imports, and Mr. Baker has always been effected by these groups. His son-in-law was Representative William Wampler, a one-term Republican (1953–55) from the Ninth Virginia, whose defeat in 1954, some felt, was partly due to the unsympathetic attitude taken by the administration toward the problems of the coal industry in that area on imports, and it is a reasonable inference that this background may reinforce Mr. Baker's attitudes. There is nothing of which I know in Mr. Baker's attitudes or district to make it particularly likely that he would be materially swayed more effectively than in 1958; and he impressed me as the kind of man who would "go along" to a very considerable extent, and therefore the increasingly protectionist cast of the Ways and Means Committee might even make him more difficult to sway. The best guess is that any strong Democratic effort could unseat him and that he stays in because of a bipartisan deal or Democratic factional conflict; understanding of such a deal might provide a key to influencing him.

Representative Lindley Beckworth, Texas
Sixteenth-ranking Democrat, Foreign Affairs

Mr. Beckworth is reported to have become gradually but not very emphatically more liberal over the years. The possibility that despite some previous votes against the type of program that is favored by ICA, etc., he will follow the leadership when on the Foreign Affairs Committee is believed to be fairly good. He has a kind of suspicion of this type of effort, more or less as a "goody-goody" sort of thing; but he is said to be a man who can be convinced by a straight factual argument, which, as a member of the committee, it is to be presumed he may hear. He is hardheaded in all senses of that American term. His district is less Texan than old southern, I am told, although oil is probably the most important product, small farming next.

Representative Alvin Bentley, Michigan
Ninth-ranking Republican, Foreign Affairs

Mr. Bentley is a member of what is sometimes called the radical right; it is generally asserted that he and his then wife were close to Senator Joseph McCarthy and others of that ilk, personally as well as politically. He was formerly in the Foreign Service but did not carry out of that body typical Foreign Service attitudes on such matters as mutual security. The continuum along which he measures events is probably quite different from that of other members, and one would have to talk with him at some length or read and analyze his speeches as an exercise in itself to determine just what his frame of reference is; but without such painstaking analysis the assumption is that he would not be amenable to any of the ordinary arguments for mutual security, and the only aspect that would appeal to him would be something that might roughly be denominated as "American imperialism." On the other hand, on such matters as Foreign Service legislation, he is reportedly cooperative enough with the Department; and there might be wedges on particular aspects of mutual security similarly based upon his experience. His perspective plus his district would not make him a strong candidate for helpfulness on reciprocal trade, again unless it could be demonstrated that somehow some particular item in the reciprocal trade program helps American nationalism.

Representative Hale Boggs, Louisiana
Fifth-ranking Democrat, Ways and Means

Boggs has committed himself as strongly to the foreign trade field as any member of Congress; and if he should turn strongly against reciprocal trade, the likelihood is that there would be no hope left.

As a Louisianan, Boggs is committed to protection for sugar, but that, fortunately, is handled by the Agriculture Committee and does not limit his free-trade views on other matters. The Port of New Orleans, which he represents, has probably done more to try to develop and dramatize trade than any other port in the country; Louisiana also sells rice.

Boggs wears two hats, being also of the Subcommittee on Foreign Economic Policy of the Joint Committee on the Economic Report; this is not a legislative committee but can undertake investigations of moment (as it did when Mr. Bolling was its chairman).

The only need or concern in regard to Boggs that I can see or foresee is the chronic one of most Congressmen—times and occasions may develop when help or publicity back home will be of use to him.

Representative Frances Bolton, Ohio
Second-ranking Republican, Foreign Affairs

Mrs. Bolton's major concern is with Africa. Basically, she is internationalist; although she will be glad to have her hand held, be congratulated, flattered, etc., once in a while on these issues. Cleveland, of course, has many industries that are export-oriented; but like any big industrial city, it has dying industries too. Since Don

Pryor, the new executive director of the Cleveland Council on Foreign Relations, and his wife, Barbara Pryor, are politically quite experienced, in a way that is relatively uncommon among such executives, and have many friends in Bethesda and Washington who possess legislative sophistication, I would think that it would be useful to get them to get the appropriate members of the council to congratulate, thank, and praise Mrs. Bolton for her presumptively favorable stands on mutual security, trade, etc.

Representative Chester Bowles, Connecticut
Newly appointed Democrat, Foreign Affairs

Mr. Bowles is so well known and his statements on Asia and the Far East have been so numerous that it would probably be several weeks' work in itself to determine the significance of everything he has said; but there can be little doubt that he will take a leading part in the public eye, at least, in favor of mutual security and Point Four programs for the eastern nations, and he will probably seize and develop the initiative shown by Senators John Cooper and John Kennedy. To the extent that there may be any actual or potential competition between India and Japan, in textiles, for example, I suppose his inclinations would be pro-Indian.

It is never safe to assume that a distinguished public figure who enters the Congress will thereby become of much influence in the House of Representatives or the Senate; Herbert Lehman was possibly one of the least influential of Senators *in* the Senate, and no one can guarantee that Bowles will "fit." However, the weakness of the Foreign Affairs Committee in general (see Carroll's *The House of Representatives and Foreign Affairs*) and Bowles's general reputation would lead one to suppose and hope that he will be one of the more influential committee members.

His district, like Rhode Island, with which it is economically more identifiable than the rest of Connecticut, is an area that suffers from foreign imports all over. Take, for instance, screws, textiles, fish, and a score of other New England industries that have fallen on hard times. Bowles would therefore probably be politically unwise to take a firm stand for reciprocal trade, or to identify himself with Japan, which *is* a competitor, rather than with India, which is not recognized as selling in the U.S. market competitively, and if he simply doesn't vote against reciprocal trade, that would be the shrewdest thing; however, he may well go further, and support liberal trade actively.

One of the ways run-of-the-mill organization Democrats explained his defeat in his bid for reelection as governor was by pointing to the young crew-cut brain trusters he picked out to help him; evidently, he has not himself believed this allegation, as he has selected as his assistant Thomas Hughes, who was with him in India, and who has since been legislative assistant to Senator Hubert Humphrey, but could not stand the "torture" there and is glad to return to Bowles.

Representative John W. Byrnes, Wisconsin
Fourth-ranking Republican, Ways and Means
(De facto third-ranking Republican, owing to illness of Daniel Reed.)

Mr. Byrnes is an Irish Catholic from Green Bay, Wisconsin. He is sometimes spoken of as a candidate for Speaker or Republican majority leader, and may end up in that position, though this is unlikely.

He is concerned with plywood and also with fountain pens, so far as his area goes. More important than this, he is apparently a protectionist and a suspecter of foreign aid, as are many midwestern Republicans. He is considered to be "more intelligent" and "capable" than most of the people who hold this position by some of those who oppose and deal with him, and less "religiously" devoted to protection than Simpson or Mason. It is not believed that he is dependent upon or particularly under the influence of any one person or group, and it is strongly emphasized that he is one who makes up his own mind—a leader, not a follower; it is probably the characteristics referred to in this and the preceding sentence that led the Committee for a More Effective Congress to call him a "more progressive" Republican than Charles Halleck or Joe Martin, but I do not really see the justification for such a statement, except that as a committee chairman or leader he might be more prone to listen to facts.

There is particular irritation against him just at present among Wisconsin Democrats because he is regarded as the hatchet man for the conservative wing of the Republican party in Wisconsin, the one who invented the nasty stereotype of William Proxmire as a spender, etc. On the other hand, quite certainly William Van Pelt and probably Melvin Laird, also from Wisconsin, will follow Byrnes's leadership on trade matters. (Gardner Withrow, Alvin O'Konski, and Senator Wiley, however, would be uninfluenced by him.)

The St. Lawrence Seaway has had considerable influence in Green Bay and surrounding areas, and if I were to attempt to develop counterfire of an international sort from the district on Byrnes, I would try to locate the members of local business organizations who worked hard for the Seaway.

It is suggested that Byrnes is a member with whom it would be worth having informed people talk dispassionately; ideally, some Irish Catholic economist who knows something about Wisconsin. Two other points should be borne in mind: (*a*) Wisconsin is dairy country, and dairymen generally tend to be suspicious of foreign trade; and (*b*) there is a vocal minority in Green Bay against the Seaway, for fear it may be bringing in more "cheap" goods, etc.

Representative A. S. Carnahan, Missouri
Second-ranking Democrat, Foreign Affairs

Representative Carnahan is a convinced, but not particularly effective or influential, member committed to mutual security and related matters. There is not likely to be any great agitation in his district on mutual security. In the state of Missouri, chemicals, lead, zinc, and glass are the strongly based industries most likely to oppose reciprocal trade, but they are not particularly crucial in his district or oriented against our clients. Mr. Carnahan recently made a nationwide speaking tour, together with Chester E. Merrow of New Hampshire, speaking on mutual security, and this reinforced his feeling of its importance. I would suppose that some of those who arranged the trip would be good contacts if anything in particular were desired of Mr. Carnahan on which he could not be approached directly. On some particular matters affecting mutual security, Mr. Carnahan might well become convinced enough to make issues of them; but as I have indicated, I doubt very much that such a need will develop during this Congress in this committee, and Carnahan lacks entirely the kind of weight that would permit effective opposition to other, more powerful committees.

As a senior member, he is automatically a member of the sub-committee concerned with foreign aid, and thus of particular importance at the moment.

Representative Robert Chiperfield, Illinois
Ranking Republican, Foreign Affairs

Representative Chiperfield has never apparently exercised the leadership to which his seniority would entitle him. He has been persuaded or coerced, depending on the interpretation, to go along with the Republican administration on things that really mattered to it, and presumably will be so persuaded again, if the need arises; although of course the administration is now politically weaker. One would almost guess that when, as, and if Senator Everett Dirksen goes along with the administration, Mr. Chiperfield can be persuaded to do so, too; and necessarily great efforts will be made, if needed, with Mr. Chiperfield.

It seems improbable that anything will develop or that anybody exists in his district that would materially add to administration influence; although of course there are some farmers affiliated with the Farm Bureau in his area.

Representative Marguerite Church, Illinois
Seventh-ranking Republican, Foreign Affairs

Mrs. Church is reported to share the general foreign policy orientation of the *Chicago Tribune;* nevertheless, she represents the North Shore area, from which enthusiasm for Willkie came, and where a lot of wealthy Republicans would do anything for Stevenson except vote for him. The treasurer of the Illinois State Republican party, Charles Percy, a strong organizer of the Committee for a National Trade Policy, lives in her district, and, it is said, by considerable "pressure" has been able to shift her on trade; no similar concentrated effort has been made on mutual security, to my knowledge.

A careful and very interesting article by Kenneth Adler and Davis Bobrow in the *Public Opinion Quarterly,* 1956, describes the tremendous number of contacts between well-to-do Republicans in one of these North Shore suburbs (I think it was Winnetka) and the executive on international programs, and asserts their great activity in local politics also. I suppose they do not concentratedly realize Mrs. Church's stand in Congress or write it off as "just politics," but I suspect there is no Congressman on either of the committees whose views (or rather votes) could be more readily changed than Mrs. Church's if some key person, with enough prestige or acumen, should try to make the effort to get these people to think about her and get in touch with her.

Representative Frank Coffin, Maine
Twelfth-ranking Democrat, Foreign Affairs

Mr. Coffin is one of those members who can always be counted on to think of the national and international interest ahead of district or personal concerns. He is an able and competent man, and may turn out to be, if not immediately, at some time the spark plug of the committee. He suffers, however, from plywood, textiles, and to a lesser extent, potentially at least, shoes, electronics, and fish, which compete or may be competed with by Japanese products. He has made efforts (as in the Coffin amendment to last year's Mutual Security Act, an attempt to remove the handicap U.S. textile exporters are under in third markets because they have to pay more for raw cotton than foreign purchasers) to help the district where he can with no perceptible threat to larger issues, and will no doubt continue to do so; and, of course, some of these efforts might hurt specific foreign business interests. But he will weigh very carefully the issues involved before doing so, and always be willing to listen to any bona fide argument that he has neglected their implications, although I would be much surprised to find he ever did.

He is far ahead of the district on these matters (like Lee Metcalf of Montana), and all that could possibly be desired is that college (Bates, Colby) groups in which there is a strong missionary and Point Four orientation should be helped to realize that here is a Congressman who is actually thinking in world terms. (Coffin later became a judge of the U.S. Court of Appeals for New England and wrote a minority opinion in the case of the "Boston Five.")

Representative Laurence Curtis, Massachusetts
Tenth-ranking Republican, Foreign Affairs

Mr. Curtis is almost uniformly reported by the professional people I know who have talked with him not to be very quick; yet it is hard to imagine Justice Holmes would have selected or tolerated a secretary who was not quick. But whether as protective coloration or not, this aspect of his personality has made it hard for a great many people to know what Mr. Curtis' real views are on many topics, including foreign affairs. He will almost certainly vote for mutual security programs, because of the many liberal suburbanites in Newton and Brookline, and he will similarly be likely to want to place himself on record as not having become internationalist. I suspect this latter factor, if he calculates the odds, might matter differently now, because in 1954 and 1956 and 1958 he had (and could look forward to having) opponents who really were internationalists. The likelihood is that his 1960 opponent, on the other hand, will come from one of the groups in the district rather suspicious of internationalism, and may likely be Councillor Edward McLaughlin. On trade, he once told me (in 1954 or 1955) that he did not know of many specific people in the district hurt by foreign imports but imagined that there must be fishermen and textile employees and employers who are; he did not bother to make the converse point. Because of the fact that he might wish to appeal in 1960 to liberal ADA-type Democrats who supported Jock Saltonstall and Jackson Holtz but will not necessarily support McLaughlin, I can conceive he might go further toward explicit and identifiable internationalism now; Brookline and several wards of Boston are heavily Jewish, and Newton has a number of upper-income internationalists, as have, of course, a couple of wards of Boston itself. The small number of Japanese in Boston live in his district, I believe; there are also groups of Chinese and Filipinos.

Representative Thomas Curtis, Missouri
Sixth-ranking Republican, Ways and Means

Mr. Curtis (from suburban St. Louis, chiefly) is one of the more difficult members of Congress to characterize. Some of his friends might and would say that he is an exceptionally conscientious man, who sees both sides of a question and its many ramifications, and therefore seems disposed to pursue an independent course, while some of his critics have said to me, "The only question you have about the s.o.b. is when he's bought, will he stay bought?" This kind of independence or waveringness, depending on the point of view, is apparently as characteristic in party organizational matters in Missouri as it is in tariff matters in Washington; and for this reason, if Mr. Curtis should live to become chairman of Ways and Means, I would anticipate that both protectionists and reciprocal traders will sigh for the day when they knew more or less where the chairman stood!

He has adopted an extremely esoteric position, so esoteric that he himself did not remember a few days after the key vote in 1955 how he had voted upon it. Roughly, it depends upon two conceptions, not usually so strongly stressed: (1) that reciprocal trade is no good unless it encourages democracy; (2) that basically the Reciprocal Trade Act is procedural, rather than substantive. He can thereby oppose reciprocal trade legislation as benefiting oligarchies rather than democracies in some countries, and he can oppose it because of the rule-making power it lets the executive have. However, unlike most people who stress this second procedural point, he is also explicitly much concerned about foreign policy, development of international cooperation, etc., and consequently his votes waver. Several years ago he drew up a proposal, which I think he himself took seriously, for granting reciprocal trade concessions only to democratic countries. He got eight or ten votes for the amendment based upon this proposal in committee in 1955, but all these votes were from Republicans, some of whom certainly regarded it as another protectionist gimmick (although Mason of Illinois, I suspect, was willing to go along with Curtis' idea for its own sake—once wage rates move toward equalization, freer trade is possible). Democracy is defined essentially in terms of the ratio of wages per hour to gross national product in the country from which imports come and the same ratio in the U.S.A.; the proposal was clearly unworkable as legislation, because figures are simply not comparable, and some international organization would have to be obtained to prepare comparable figures. But by this device Curtis was able to reconcile his interest in United World Federalists, his church background of international concern, his reputation as an internationalist, and his committee and district situation.

In his district live a large number of Monsanto junior employees, who evidently were instructed in 1955 to press their Representative and Senators for protection; many of them in fact wrote to Senator Hennings urging his support of the Curtis proposal, perhaps at company instance. Mr. Curtis also maintains that "some pretty high-ranking CIO officers sat on that couch and argued against extension or at least for substantial amendment," although he had heard from their national leadership *for* reciprocal trade. He points out that Monsanto in St. Louis, as of 1955, paid $2.10 an hour, whereas in Italy the same labor got $ .45 an hour, and the Curtis amendment would have "guaranteed" Italian labor $1.31 an hour instead under reciprocal trade agreements. For similar labor Japan would have had to pay $ .84 an hour the first year, working up to $1.31 an hour ultimately.

In 1958 Mr. Curtis got alarmed about his prospects for reelection and appealed to all sorts and conditions of people for help. One such letter is in the files of Standard Oil of New Jersey, I am told, and others are no doubt in the files of other big international firms, some of whose officers probably did support him. He also has said that Charles Taft is a personal friend of his; but that made little difference in 1955, as far as I know.

I suppose Mr. Curtis might be influenced by evidence that foreign labor is receiving a higher proportion of the gross national product than it used to, and by evidence that the effect of reciprocal trade agreements, etc., might be to increase such a tendency. Actually, his basic legislative proposal, although not without the germ of an idea from which something could be made that would really meet its professed purpose, is economically and anthropologically rather foolish; and I am reasonably certain that he has not been exposed to an extended dispassionate academic analysis of the difficulties in its path. Such an analysis could do him no harm, coming from scholars.

The preceding two paragraphs indicate possible approaches to influencing him; I would strongly suspect that there will be in his suburban St. Louis district a rather vehement Rockefeller-for-President group, similar to the Willkie groups of 1940, and I would look to the people most likely to start such a group (which could probably be found out from the political editors of either of the St. Louis newspapers) to try to persuade Mr. Curtis to go along with Republicans like Javits on foreign trade matters. (His background and contacts are such that I think he will be OK on aid.)

I have devoted this much space to a relatively junior member because I think that his gross national product scheme might have some appeal to Democrats from textile, mining, etc. districts in the event of any substantial increase in unemployment (which can happen even with a boom), probably in a simplified form, as a means of reconciling protection and liberalism.

Representative Charles C. Diggs, Michigan
Fifteenth-ranking Democrat, Foreign Affairs

Mr. Diggs, according to the closest informant I could get, is likely to tackle foreign policy in terms of the old elephant story that concludes with the winning Polish essay being on "The Elephant and the Polish Question." His approach to foreign policy is likely to be in terms of race relations, pure and simple. It is not known that hitherto he has shown any interest in problems of foreign affairs. He is regarded by colleagues in the House, however, as on the whole "reasonable," willing to take half a loaf if he can't get a whole one, and not offensively preoccupied with race. He is naturally concerned with the views of the United Automobile Workers, and if I needed to influence him on any specific mutual security or reciprocal trade matter, I would consult Samuel Jacobs,[4] who is personally a very strong and intense believer in reciprocal trade.

Representative Leonard Farbstein, New York
Thirteenth-ranking Democrat, Foreign Affairs

Mr. Farbstein is reported by most people to be considerably above the average of ability of the metropolitan members; New York, Chicago, Baltimore, and Philadelphia have typically produced Democratic members whose forte was not legislative work so much as organizational loyalty. Some report him as a man of real ability, fully cognizant of and interested in the Development Loan Fund and similar matters. He represents a rather heavily Jewish group, and concern with Israel would be expected. He is said to be proud of the fact that institutions like Secretary Dillon's banking house are in his district and to be conscious of the international banking role of New York City. On the other hand, the following statement from an intensely devoted follower of reciprocal trade matters, familiar with New York politics, may be borne in mind: "I anticipate that Farbstein would follow the generally protectionist views of Dubinsky et al. Yes, the answer is that Dubinsky, like Potofsky and Rose,[5] for a couple of years past has been protectionist, though they do not brandish these views as yet. Still, the alarm felt about *Japanese*

---

[4]See the interview with Jacobs in Appendix B.
[5]David Dubinsky, International Ladies' Garment Workers; Jacob Potofsky, Clothiers; Alex Rose, Hatters—big political unions in Farbstein's area.

imports has been very real. A public relations aide of ILGWU with whom I talked acknowledged its real concern, although expressed its desire to maintain a liberal pose. But one will find many tirades by rank-and-filers against 'Japanese invasions.' Indeed, this new tone has influenced the *New York Post,* which ran a series about the 'destruction' of some New York towns by our oriental pals. However, the *Post* preserved its liberal views by getting quite exercised about escape-clause action on violins!

"Farbstein would at present mouth the 'liberal' slogans on trade, because they are characteristically New York liberal Jewish; but the garment-center manufacturers or the textile unions could heavily influence him the other way, and would on Japanese matters, I would guess."

Obviously, anybody with liberal Jewish backing has a number of acquaintances who are strongly interested in matters like development loan funds. Import-export business is concentrated in New York. But I would rate my informant's honesty 100 percent and his accuracy 80 percent, and if he is correct on these points, as he states them, some stress by some of these local people on the bread-and-butter aspects of international trade, mutual security, etc., to Mr. Farbstein would be helpful to supporters of the administration program.

Several people, on the other hand, have reported that he has shown real interest and enjoyment in regard to membership on the committee, and real skill in handling Development Loan Fund matters; and it should be added that he is evidently entirely independent and free to be creative on any matters except those nationality ones of special concern to Israel. If, as looks to be the case, the ILGWU, etc., definitely align themselves soon with Rockefeller, it is hard to see what the influence of these groups on Tammany Democrats will be.

But because of Farbstein's intelligent concern with DLF matters, etc., I would suspect that factual presentation of needs and problems would be useful.

Representative Dante Fascell, Florida
Eleventh-ranking Democrat, Foreign Affairs

Mr. Fascell is also a member of Government Operations; I suspect he has been more active on the latter committee. He does not recall any proposal affecting mutual security, or hearing anything much about it. He thinks that there will be a switch in this Congress from emphasis on military assistance to more concentration on economic assistance. He does not believe that the Congress will have to initiate this, as he thinks the President's State of the Union speech gave a tip-off to the Executive Department's intention to make such a switch.

He hears very little about our client; nothing "yet anyhow, thank God," about the sort of competition our client would provide, "although we are a light-industry area." There is, he thinks, a good deal of support for and some active opposition to mutual security; but few people have actually initiated conversations with him about these problems.

He has the reputation of being a man of considerable liberality and ability, a man who would like to play the traditional role of the border-state compromisers within the Democratic party, and is equipped to do so. In talking to interviewers and such, he interrupts extremely; but he has grasped the point, so far as I can see, and is just very quick.

The city of Miami (Fascell's district), Senator George Smathers, and Congressman Fascell, all are particularly interested in Latin America.

Representative Aime Forand, Rhode Island
Second-ranking Democrat, Ways and Means

Mr. Forand, it is believed, plans to retire at the end of this Congress; apparently this is quite definite. Another New England Democrat will presumably be appointed in his place. Frank Coffin of Maine or Torbert Macdonald of Massachusetts would be the two most likely possibilities, but Coffin would find himself needlessly on the firing line and give up some interests he has developed on foreign affairs, and Macdonald may decide to run for governor, or just conceivably Senator, in 1960. (Neither was appointed; instead, James Burke of Massachusetts was chosen.)

By starting off with the discussion of who may replace him, I am indicating what is perhaps the most important thing about Mr. Forand, so far as one can foresee probable developments in the present Congress. The entire committee will be concerned with social security matters and taxes, Mr. Forand particularly with the former, and it is not too likely anything of great moment will happen on reciprocal trade; if it does, it is more likely to be in the second session than in the first.

It is, however, not at all improbable that for the record Mr. Forand, in support of Senator John O. Pastore's efforts to protect the Rhode Island unemployed, will introduce or support proposals for textile quotas by categories, etc. I do not believe he would fight for them in this session, unless a lot of strong support comes from other members of the committee and the House.

Mr. Forand has, reportedly, on one or several occasions, made remarks about "I too can be patriotic," when in the last round, so to speak, he has supported reciprocal trade or consented to the emasculation of his proposals to cripple it, and presumably, if this is his last session, he would be more likely to be patriotic.

However, it must be remembered that Rhode Island suffers much from foreign imports—textiles, lace, toys, cheap jewelry, etc.—and that in recent years Rhode Island has been an area of heavy unemployment. Probably no other state in the union would benefit as much from the enactment of a viable distressed-areas bill.

Forand has several times—comprehensibly—been burned up because the Providence newspapers and other worthy supporters of foreign trade, etc., have attacked him for supporting protection when in fact he was setting up a lightning rod that harmlessly dissipated protectionist sentiment from New England. For this reason, I'd be very careful indeed about calling on the "goo–goos" to tackle Forand on trade or aid; they might make him annoyed. And I'd try, if I could, to prevent the League of Women Voters, etc., from seeing him on the issue! Probably the best local approach to him would be through some of the Providence businessmen and bankers who are intelligent enough to express appreciation of what he has done for Rhode Island and on the committee, and yet who realize that their interests and those of their employers are tied up with foreign trade. Henry Dexter Sharp comes to mind as a probable example (machine tools, family interest in candy, also conservative well-established family, but personally and industry-wise believer in liberal trade, etc.), and other such names could be suggested with some local inquiry.

Under no circumstances, however, would it be wise to try to dissuade Forand from sponsoring or introducing proposals. The only point would be to try to be sure he didn't fight for them effectively, or to get him to modify them so they would be less repugnant. Although Forand's impending retirement is widely known, such things are never certain until they're certain; he can change his mind.

Representative L. H. Fountain, North Carolina
Tenth-ranking Democrat, Foreign Affairs

Representative Fountain has but rarely attended committee meetings and in fact regards this as very definitely a second committee; his Subcommittee on Intergovernmental Problems of Government Operations is of considerable interest to him and takes a great deal of time. There is nothing of which I know that is likely to change his unfavorable votes; but if he became a key person or his vote the decisive one, he is a man of evidently real ability and insight who could be persuaded as to the facts. I do not know anything about his district, beyond the obvious economic and social facts, but in regard to influencing the man, if it were really a crucial issue, I would make the acquaintance of two of the staff men on his subcommittee, Del Goldberg and Jim Naughton, both of whom are highly esteemed by the community of liberal, professional staff men around Capitol Hill, and whose sympathies and desires might be expected to be toward support of the mutual security and reciprocal trade programs. I have not asked either of them about the matter at present, because I am so sure that their response would be that the Congressman simply doesn't devote too much time or reflection to foreign affairs. A factor in his votes—probably the major factor—is the disenchantment of many southeastern Congressmen with mutual security and reciprocal trade; but he is perfectly capable of being independent of his colleagues, if he focuses attention on the topic. Mr. Fountain was *not* a member of the International Operations Subcommittee of Government Operations in the 85th Congress.

Representative James B. Frazier, Jr., Tennessee
Twelfth-ranking Democrat, Ways and Means

Mr. Frazier was apparently put on the committee to follow the lead of the chairman and the Speaker, and there is little likelihood that he would deviate from their positions on substantial matters when the chips were down, although he might vote protectionist on amendments when it didn't matter, because of textiles in his neighborhood, etc. Senator Albert Gore has at various times documented the extreme "pressure" he is under from Tennessee coal, textiles, and other industries to vote protectionist; and no doubt this pressure to some extent may be directed against Mr. Frazier, so that Mr. Frazier is somewhat inclined to talk about "live and let live," "we don't want to overreach ourselves," and generally utter rather meaningless equivocal sentiments. Mr. Frazier does not reportedly have the temperament or disposition to become a leader on any side.

If there were at any time any situation where the leadership so lost control that members would act as they thought their districts wanted, Mr. Frazier might go along with some other southern textile members. If such a development took place in this Congress and affected Mr. Frazier's position on the committee or a key committee vote, I would suspect it would be more meaningful to consult Senator Gore and probably Senator Estes Kefauver's office as to who in Frazier's district would be most effective in presenting the basic interests of Tennessee in foreign trade than to make any other approach, because they both are likely to know who counts there, and to be 100 percent sympathetic with foreign trade policies acceptable to our client.

Representative James Fulton, Pennsylvania
Fifth-ranking Republican, Foreign Affairs

Mr. Fulton and Mr. Judd are generally reported as the strong members—willing to work—on the Republican side of Foreign Affairs. Mr. Fulton's general views and sympathies are reported by all as being in the internationalist direction; and he is not apparently seriously hobbled by the fact that Pittsburgh has been an area of relatively heavy unemployment or that Westinghouse and Pittsburgh Plate Glass are among the firms in the country that most concentratedly have fought reciprocal trade. But he is somewhat limited by the fact that the Republican House majority and some of the leadership have been unsympathetic to internationalist programs, and he lacks the effective self-reliance and independence of a Javits. Some people report of him that his views are much influenced by the last person he talked with, and it is generally agreed that someone in the higher levels of Pittsburgh business and society is the right person to approach him. Because of the unique and unprecedented position Chancellor Edward Litchfield of the University of Pittsburgh has established in Pittsburgh and national business, and because of the fact that he is a professional political scientist, still head of the Government Affairs Institute in Washington, I would certainly inquire from him first and foremost as to which of the prominent Pittsburgh industrialists would be good people to con-

tact Fulton. Of much less importance probably in Fulton's evaluation, but significant electorally, is the fact that David McDonald of
the Steel Workers was a member of the Randall Commission and
signed the appendix on adjustment programs for depressed areas,
and that William Batt, Jr., who wrote that appendix, is now Secretary
of Labor in the Commonwealth of Pennsylvania, and that consequently special information might well be obtained about the impact
in actuality of trade, mutual security, etc., on Fulton's district, if it
ever mattered, far beyond what one could hope to get for most
districts.

Representative William J. Green, Jr., Pennsylvania
Thirteenth-ranking Democrat, Ways and Means

There was considerable objection to the selection of Mr. Green
for one of the vacancies on Ways and Means because he is just un-
dergoing trial for what amounts to bribery and conspiracy to defraud
the United States; he was able to delay the trial for some period of
time by the argument that the judge had been so close to him personally and professionally that the judge would be forced to lean
over backward against him. However, Mr. Green's seniority and
control of the chairmanship of the Philadelphia City Committee gave
him sufficient influence so that his bid for the vacancy was not
turned down. Were he found guilty, how this would affect his
committee or congressional position is hard to foretell. (Congressman Thomas J. Lane of Massachusetts was renominated while in
jail!) In the meantime, Mr. Green unquestionably has more influence
on four other Philadelphia Congressmen than almost anybody else.

On reciprocal trade matters, he has been influenced by textiles and
the other Philadelphia industries subject to foreign competition. No
doubt, Philadelphia as a whole profits from trade; but the intensity
of the hurt on those hurt is great. Were I engaged systematically in an effort to influence Mr. Green and still more his Philadelphia colleagues, I would ask William Batt, Jr., secretary of the
Pennsylvania Department of Labor and Industries and formerly
staff economist for the Randall Commission, to inform me what
specific interests in Philadelphia, ward by ward, would be hurt by
any reduction in foreign trade or mutual security expenditures.

Mr. Green is on very bad terms with both Senator Joseph Clark
and Mayor Richard Dilworth, and consequently with the liberal,
internationalist type of Democrat prominent in Philadelphia.

The *Philadelphia Inquirer*, as you probably know, has for many months been full of the problems created by a foreign firm that "threatens" to be the low bidder for some city business (trolley construction, I think) against a Philadelphia firm, and this is probably a matter of some interest to all Philadelphia Congressmen at present.

Mr. Green is basically a municipal politician to whom politics is a business, a difficult person to approach on such matters as reciprocal trade and mutual security; patronage for his friends would rank very high with him, one supposes, as an argument.

Representative Burr Harrison, Virginia
Seventh-ranking Democrat, Ways and Means

Mr. Harrison, like Messrs. Mills and Herlong, has written his own statements and questions about reciprocal trade, and they are on the whole favorable. He has in his district, however, velveteen, rayon, and viscose, all of which are subject to foreign competition. On the other hand, a more central industry is fruit (apples particularly, also peaches), which is historically, if not necessarily in any given year, on an export basis.

The Virginia delegation is perhaps more subject to organization influence than any other group except that from Chicago, so that Senator Byrd's position and stand would presumably have some importance with Mr. Harrison, who in any case is supposed to be desirous of becoming governor of Virginia at some time, a position that in the last sixty years has always (with one exception) been under the control of the Byrd organization and its predecessor.

Mr. Harrison is reportedly a genuinely educated man, one who reads widely, almost in the tradition of the early Jefferson-Madison leadership of Virginia, and would probably be far more susceptible to a reasoned presentation by scholars, without any ax to grind, than to "pressure" or "counterpressure."

Representative Wayne Hays, Ohio
Sixth-ranking Democrat, Foreign Affairs

Mr. Hays is reportedly the most vociferous member of either committee in objecting to such things as cheap Japanese labor. This is no doubt because he represents a section of eastern Ohio that contains a number of dying industries, subject or seemingly subject to

Japanese competition—pottery probably is the most prominent. Mr. Hays has at various times on the floor protested foreign imports from some places.

On the other hand, Mr. Hays in general regards himself as a progressive or liberal, has an academic background, and won the esteem and goodwill of various foundations by his participation in the Cox-Reese Committee investigation *against* the Cox-Reese viewpoint. It is reported by people who may know that he is quite vain about his own accomplishments and influence, including his academic ones, and that he is the type of member who might be influenced by an invitation to get an honorary degree.

Mr. Hays has stated at various times, I believe, in answer to requests from CIO national leadership that he moderate his protectionist stand, that it is the CIO *locals* that force him into the position he adopts.

Representative A. S. Herlong, Jr., Florida
Ninth-ranking Democrat, Ways and Means

Mr. Herlong represents central Florida, which has at the present time relatively few problems of manufacturing competition with Japan or western Europe, although the Florida development schemes may be in the process of altering this. The main concerns a representative from this district has with foreign competition are citrus, citrus juice, and early vegetables from other Caribbean areas; and on all these matters Californian and Texan competition is a lot tougher than any from abroad.

Mr. Herlong gave, and, it is believed, wrote himself, a graceful, well-composed speech on and in favor of trade agreements last session; there was no particular necessity for him to give it and none whatsoever for him to write it (since the staff could easily have written it). Last Congress, because of early fruits, etc., he may have been somewhat more timid about all-out support for reciprocal trade than he would be this session, because his electoral position is now much better than it was in 1957.

Insofar as a member represents a state on committee, as well as his own district, plywood is of some concern in Florida.

Although I do not believe Mr. Herlong is well known at all to them, it is perhaps worth knowing that in Winter Park and to a much lesser degree in De Land (at Stetson University) there are a high number of people who have strong internationalist sympathies and interests; they are not on the whole the kind of people who in the normal course of their concerns would know what is going on in Congress, however.

Representative Walter Judd, Minnesota
Fourth-ranking Republican, Foreign Affairs

Mr. Judd's position and views are well known; he is unquestionably the most aggressive and hard-working member on the Republican side of House Foreign Affairs, and his main interest has been Chiang Kai-shek.

Minneapolis and St. Paul, the Twin Cities, probably have as high a proportion of sympathy with international causes as any city in the country, and I doubt much organized district support is necessary. If anyone is ever interested in the way a Congressman can make a particular foreign situation an issue, the report on the 1950 elections in Judd's district and in the adjoining district, prepared for the Bureau of Applied Social Research, Columbia University, under the direction of William McPhee, shows how Judd seemed to do this. (It's possible that Mary Goddard, CIO PAC, or Bob Bower, Bureau of Social Research, Washington, might have a copy of this report, which was never printed, just dittoed or hectographed.)

Although probably not relevant, Judd's evangelical religious background is very interesting; as a member of the executive committee of a refugee-serving organization, to aid mostly non-Christian Chinese, in, as I recollect, 1953, he explicitly vetoed the selection of an executive director, who had been accepted by most other committee members, simply and professedly because the man was Unitarian!

Representative Frank M. Karsten, Missouri
Eighth-ranking Democrat, Ways and Means

Mr. Karsten was formerly a congressional secretary and evidently has more of the congressional secretary's orientation toward his job than many Congressmen—that is, he is solid, hard-working, undramatic, writes his own speeches, does his own evaluation. His general viewpoint is said to be thoroughly "liberal" on trade and aid matters, and it is hardly likely that he would switch.

His district is St. Louis. Monsanto, which is St. Louis–based, and other chemical companies have of course made a particularly strong pitch in this area to influence their Congressmen and Senators; and there are some small industries, toy manufacturers of various sorts. I recollect a rather vociferous though very small marble manufacturer in St. Louis who was worried about Japanese competition in "this most American of games."

Representative Edna Kelly, New York
Fifth-ranking Democrat, Foreign Affairs

Representative Kelly is described by several persons who know her as having the kind of temperament that makes it easy for her to be rather hostile and suspicious of out-groups; she has made some statements about Puerto Ricans, for instance, that made me (a former employee of the University of Puerto Rico) quite resentful. She is, however, glib enough at using the approved Democratic party language of international cooperation when desired. She represents a district many of whose citizens are being rather "invaded" by newer immigrant groups, Puerto Ricans particularly, and who by the same token are likely to sympathize with Zionism, freedom for Ireland, etc., as a displacement of their own resentments.

She is reported by people who have had contacts with her office to be unusually reluctant to allow her assistants any leeway or independence; and it would be unwise, it is said, to ask their views on anything as representing her. However, a well-informed person tells me (and I have some confirmation of this) that her assemblyman and district leader (whose name, as I recollect, is Stanley Steingut) "is a pretty fair liberal" and could in a crisis tell her what to do. On the other hand, she was extremely friendly with Wayne Hays, whose views are protectionist; so far as I know, this friendship continues.

More than with most members, it is my guess that the personal aspect of a presentation would affect her. If I needed further leads on her, in addition to Steingut, I'd go to Angela Parisi, formerly head of the New York State Workmen's Compensation Board and vice-chairman of the New York State Democratic Committee.

Representative Eugene Keogh, New York
Sixth-ranking Democrat, Ways and Means

I postponed writing the sketch of Representative Keogh because I could somehow not think of anything central and simple to say about him. "Of course," said one of the people I recently talked with about him, "that's because he always has an angle." And another earlier had said, "He's a politician's politician, the kind of guy who always has an angle but never meets himself coming down the street." Typically, he has introduced at least two, I think already more than that, bills for special treatment of commodities. One of them was clearly protectionist, the other was almost certainly designed to liberalize trade, and each was clearly a favor to an individual business firm, according to analysis by the State Department. On the basis of recent experience, Keogh is not expected to fight for them, and certainly not for the protectionist measures, but will get enough credit by introducing them.

Still another informant tells me, "I don't know who or where they are, except for the American Institute of Accountants, but Keogh probably has more strings on him than any man on Capitol Hill, more business ties." Keogh and former Representative Thomas Jenkins, at the behest of the AIA, pushed the Keogh-Jenkins Bill, which would benefit most of us professionals who are self-employed by permitting us to acquire large credits in retirement set-asides; this may well pass the new Congress.

One other group should be added for which Mr. Keogh has done a good deal of work: the Spanish lobby.

He has, despite the particularity of his business approach, said on several occasions, apparently without any immediate interest being involved, "The difference between the parties is, more than any one thing, their attitude toward protection," with the implication that's why he's glad he's a Democrat.

Keogh supported James Farley for U.S. Senator in 1958 and is rumored to be close to Farley politically and personally. Since Farley is an officer of Coca-Cola International, one assumes he would tend to favor reciprocal trade, etc.

Representative Cecil King, California
Third-ranking Democrat, Ways and Means

Since Mr. King will now be eligible to participate on conference committees, and since Mr. Forand already is, four of the five House conferees (these two plus the two leading Republicans) are by no means necessarily certain to stand strongly for undiluted reciprocal trade. Mr. King is concerned with plywood, and particularly with tuna fish; tuna is a very strong issue in his district, and it is by no means inconceivable that he could be persuaded into some sort of log-rolling arrangement on the matter. Tuna is important for two reasons: (1) According to Mr. King's own statement, the independent tuna packers are the first or second largest source of campaign contributions to him. (2) Tuna has long been an issue about which people get really excited, march on City Hall, etc. (This is quite rare on import matters in this country; I have never heard of its happening on textiles or toys, for instance.) In addition, some of the tuna fishermen in Mr. King's own area are Japanese-Americans.

On the other hand, Mr. King himself is not by conviction or temperament inclined toward protectionism. His political orientation is generally described as that of an almost anachronistic New Dealer of the Olson days in California, a man to whom foreign economic policy would not be vital, but who certainly would not sympathize with Simpson or Mason. Mr. King is also said to be one who does not really delight in the kind of hard legislative work that may be necessary to get through special-interest legislation, and consequently he would be quite willing to settle for a newspaper victory on tuna, regardless of whether there were any actual decrease in Japanese imports to the U.S.

On the other hand, Mr. King's district and area contain a number of high-level intellectual, well-to-do Democrats, whose inclination would be to support reciprocal trade. These people probably provide a disproportionate number of the organizers and financers of his campaigns. For instance, in the 46th Assembly District (which contains probably roughly one-quarter of the district's population) Mr. King's campaigns in 1956 and 1958 were largely run by two women who had been prominent in the League of Women Voters, and the League, of course, attaches very high priority to reciprocal trade. League members in his district may know of Mr. King's stand on tuna, etc., but it is by no means certain that they are aware of his potential key position on such matters because of his greater seniority. In the same general area live, for instance, the Warshaws, machine-tool manufacturers (and, if they're like most machine-tool people, on an export basis), heavy contributors to the Democratic party in California, although not particularly to King, so far as is known. There are also a number of Japanese-Americans resident in the district (though on trade this cuts both ways).

I have not verified another allegation: a Democrat who knew King well when he started out in politics says that he "was and is" a protégé of Mr. Edwin Pauley, the big California oilman-Democrat.

If so, no doubt Pauley's concerns on oil and trade would be worth checking.

King will presumably support mutual security.

Representative Noah Mason, Illinois
Third-ranking Republican, Ways and Means
(Because of Mr. Reed's ill health, will probably generally serve as second member, and therefore on conference committees.)

Mr. Mason is a stubborn man, who prides himself on being even more stubborn than he is, and particularly on being stubborn about reciprocal trade matters. The Farm Bureau people and others in his district long since gave up any thought of changing or influencing him on reciprocal trade matters, hoping that if they left that alone, they might do better with him on other issues.

The net economic interest of the district is clearly in foreign trade. I am reasonably sure few industries in his district suffer from any foreign competition; but this is not relevant to Mr. Mason's principled protectionist position.

Mr. Mason is not an acute or skillful maneuverer or the like, and is therefore a far less effective enemy than someone like Simpson.

He has voted "wrong" on aid votes, too, out of the same general nationalist point of view. If I were resident in his district and trying to influence him at all, I'd try to change him on aid, rather than on trade, even though his views on aid are less important committee-wise.

I suspect that some of those who oppose him on trade and taxes and co-ops and many other matters would be glad to change him on *anything*, he is so proud of being "set" in his ways, and perhaps therefore the Farm Bureau or Caterpillar Tractor, which is in his district, would be willing to tackle him on aid.

Among the small industries that the Congressman believes are hurt by foreign imports in the district are Illinois Zinc in La Salle and a sewing-machine company in Belvedere.

The Congressman was one of the members of the committee to support Representative Thomas Curtis' proposal for using reciprocal trade as a means of raising wages of foreign countries to a higher proportion of the GNP (see under Curtis), and I suspect the only member except Curtis who really believed in the idea. I think he would probably be willing to accept reciprocal trade in regard to any product or country where the real wage rates, as measured in terms of purchasing power, were no lower than those in the U.S.A., and that his devotion to protection is really to high wages and the full dinner pail.

Representative William H. Meyer, Vermont
Nineteenth-ranking Democrat, Foreign Affairs

There were several articles in the *Boston Globe* about a week after election (probably obtainable from the Washington correspondent of the *Globe*) about Mr. Meyer, which went into considerably greater detail on him than any other Boston or New York paper.

The most significant point, possibly, is that during his campaign he argued for the recognition of Red China, and this did not prevent his election as the first Democrat in a hundred years or so to be sent to Congress from Vermont; he may believe it helped him. He was also a conscientious objector during World War II and apparently is still a conscientious objector.

He is apparently inordinately naïve politically, and both he and his wife are personally very unsophisticated. It is my understanding that when they appeared on TV shortly after his election, there was some alarm by those around whether she would consent to wear makeup. The probability is that he will be simply unaware of the significance of the "political pressures" that most Congressmen take into account, and also will conscientiously resist them. On mutual security matters, it is harder to calculate how a man of this orientation will go. It is likely that unless military aid can be separated from economic aid, he will be predisposed to oppose them both. It is unlikely that he will be much affected by representations from the state *per se*, although he might be responsive to the idealistic viewpoints of several Bennington faculty members. I would anticipate that he would be particularly concerned about the "guilt" of Hiroshima and Nagasaki.

In general, on military aid issues, I would think that the thing to do is simply to get the best available person who sympathizes with but does not share his views—if in fact he is recalcitrant on anything that matters—to talk to him. Barbara Luther of the Women's Division of the Democratic National Committee was stationed in Vermont during the last month of the campaign and assisted him; she probably would know as much about him as anyone in Washington. It should be added that he is a professional, and apparently a dedicated, forest conservationist, and I suppose it would do no harm for any visiting foreign forest conservationist who is politically "hep" (if there are such people) to be introduced to him.

Representative Wilbur Mills, Arkansas[6]
Chairman, Ways and Means

Mr. Mills's general views and preferences on reciprocal trade are generally in the classic Doughton-Hull-Cooper southern liberal trade tradition, reinforced in his case by the fact that he is one of the members of Congress who reads (or at any rate creates the impression of reading) contemporary economic literature with judgment. He believes he does guide his district, and in large measure has in fact shut off communications expressing a viewpoint different from his own; in part, he has done this by persuading the few interests in his district vividly worried about foreign imports that stockpiling and similar administrative devices are more useful to them. The only kind of pressure campaign from the district and area to which he would be likely to succumb would be a carefully planned grass-roots one of the sort put on by the movie excise people a few years ago for Ways and Means; and there, I'm inclined to think that the mere revelation that he was being "used" would incline him to react negatively. (*Mutatis mutandis,* I think that any visible effort at district pressure *for* reciprocal trade would annoy him also as unnecessary.)

Mr. Mills, however, differs from his Democratic predecessors in the chairmanship, Jere Cooper and Muley Doughton, and from Albert Gore of Tennessee, his predecessor as the southerner's choice to succeed Sam Rayburn, in that he probably does not have the same unquestioning *moral* commitment to reciprocal trade that they have (the same kind of moral commitment that Messrs. Mason, Utt, and to a lesser extent Simpson have to protection). To him, it is a political issue to be weighed against other political issues; and since he is chairman, this is worth a little speculation. One can imagine, for example (as one could not with Cooper), that some by-products of

---

[6]In addition to the account of Mills in John Manley, "Wilbur Mills: A Study in Congressional Influence," *American Political Science Review*, 43 (1969): 442–64, a good discussion of Mills's later development is found in Murray Seeger, "The Most Powerful Man in Congress," *Washingtonian Magazine*, 4, no. 11 (August 1969): 41, 81–82.

the Faubus–Alford–Southern Manifesto business[7] might force Mills into a position where he might go a lot further than he would like in the protectionist direction in order to preserve some freedom on segregation and civil rights, etc. I would anticipate that any such influence on him would come, not from the district directly, but from leading Democrats in the state or region, contributors conceivably, but particularly from other prominent southern Congressmen, who could make use of Mills's known ambition to be Speaker, plus the protection–civil rights situation, to sway him in their direction. Whether such a development is likely will depend in part upon how far Mills recognizes (what I think is the case) that Faubus and Alford have fairly effectively washed out his chances of the Speakership, and how far he still can conceive of himself as competing with Francis Walter types for the conservative Democratic votes if Mr. Rayburn retires. In a sense, the best thing from the standpoint of reciprocal trade would be for Mills thoroughly to realize that he could not become Speaker for the next three or four years (if in fact this is the case, or if it is not), because then he would have little occasion to soften his reciprocal trade viewpoint (except, of course, that on specific issues within the committee trading is always conceivable, although such trading does not appear very likely this session; by this I mean that some members who are inclined to disregard the leadership on some issue of taxes or social security might conceivably be brought into line by a local commodity concession on the tariff).

Those concerned with influencing Mr. Mills on a principled basis on foreign trade (or aid) matters would, I suppose, be able to get most of the information they would need from Rachael Bell and the Committee on a Foreign Trade Policy, because he must necessarily be a special topic of concern to them. I believe that it would perhaps be worthwhile to establish contact with Charles H. Davis, a tax attorney in Chicago, who was formerly chief clerk of Ways and Means under Mr. Doughton, a very conscientious man, who would

---

[7]Arkansas politics in the late fifties was much influenced by the widely publicized stand of Governor Orval Faubus against desegregation in Little Rock and by the correlated defeat of the widely respected U.S. Representative Brooks Hays of Little Rock by Dale Alford, a write-in candidate, the issue supposedly being desegregation. Nearly all southern members of Congress had signed a "Southern Manifesto," which was in effect a protest against the desegregation decisions and policies of the federal government. Representative Mills had also signed it; but having signed it, he had weakened his appeal as a potential Speaker to some northern (Negro and liberal) Democrats. He would have been reluctant, one assumes, to alienate them altogether by stronger segregationist stands, so long as he hoped to become Speaker.

probably be familiar with previous stands and positions of Mr. Mills's also, if one anticipated having to make any particular approach to him. Beyond this, I would suggest two possible approaches, which as insurances might be considered:

1. I have the distinct impression that Mr. Mills wants to be respected and known favorably by professional economists, economic commentators, etc. I would suspect that on any trade or aid matter, a distinguished economist, familiar with the general issue, *and prepared to study the specifics of a particular piece of legislation under consideration,* or several such, would be the most influential people for him. The italicized portion of the sentence should be heeded; any generalized statement by someone who manifests ignorance of the specific would merely provoke contempt from him.

2. You will probably have more general information on this point than I, but I have a hunch that "decent" moderate southerners are now going way out of their way to show that they are not prejudiced. I would suspect Mr. Mills might be vulnerable in this respect (as perhaps also Mr. Harrison), and that in any instance where an issue could with reasonable legitimacy be presented as involving potential prejudice against our client's sort of people, this possibility should be borne in mind.

Representative Thomas Morgan, Pennsylvania
Chairman, Foreign Affairs

Representative Morgan startled and surprised a good many people by the vigor with which he took over the duties of acting chairman last year and the skill he showed at floor management. Until that time he had been a three-days-a-week Congressman; but he evidently is now going to make the job full-time. He had run (I think also owned) a hospital in his hometown, in addition to being Congressman, a heavy load. I believe most of his patients were members of the United Mine Workers, a fact that, in addition to the glass industry, explains his doubts and opposition on reciprocal trade. However, he did a good and apparently even a creative job in handling the Mutual Security Act last year, and what he has done since would tend to suggest he will take charge himself, rather than rely upon someone else, as Thomas Gordon and Robert Chiperfield, his predecessors, did. He is still an enigma. Some people intimately familiar with politics in his district appraise him as a "wonderful candidate" with the good hello, but unable to think of what to do after you've said hi. Others say his summings up are his, and he will make decisions in committee. Some say he will rely upon the staff and the State Department entirely, others that he will not. All one can say is that his past record is largely irrelevant. In district and local matters, he has had the advantage of an exceptionally capable and experienced administrative assistant, John Wiener, a man with twenty-five years of Hill experience. Both of them are reported as "wearing a cloak of anonymity," so you don't know where they do stand, and no one pretends to guess if Wiener will matter on committee affairs or not.

Since Morgan's district is something like Wayne Hays's, there is some danger that Morgan might be more predisposed to be influenced by Hays than would otherwise be the case. The similarities are Slavic population and dying industries. However, the two men are temperamentally so different that Morgan is probably well aware of the low esteem felt for Hays by other members of the committee.

One clue to Morgan's regime may be provided by the manner in which he reconstitutes subcommittee personnel or structure.

Representative Thomas J. O'Brien, Illinois
Fourth-ranking Democrat, Ways and Means

Mr. O'Brien is at present fairly certain to go along with the leadership on reciprocal trade matters. Only a few factories in his district are vocal about foreign competition, and they are not believed to be of any great weight; in any event, the fact that in most of Chicago there is an organization that does work hard and effectively to deliver the vote and gets it in on election day (something in which Chicago differs from most other cities) means that Chicago Congressmen are relatively free from the "pressures" which "beset" and "bedevil" some other Congressmen.

All the Chicago Democrats have usually followed the leadership on both trade and aid; and I know of nothing that is likely to alter Mayor Richard Daley's control of the organization or the general tendency of the organization to support the leadership on such a matter as this. Consequently, with a Congressman with some seniority and alleged local influence there is no reason to expect a change, and O'Brien will probably keep on voting in the future as he has done in the past.

On the other hand, I have never been able to ascertain whether Mr. O'Brien has any views of his own on these topics. I know that I am not unique among scholars and commentators in having more difficulty in getting him to talk, or even to listen to questions, than is common with Congressmen (the late Congressman Cooper of Tennessee is the only prominent Congressman I have found equally tough). If I ever really needed to know Mr. O'Brien's *personal* views on a significant trade-aid issue, I would probably ask Congressman Barratt O'Hara, also from Chicago, who has, for reasons I do not know, great admiration for Mr. O'Brien. Mr. O'Brien is also said to "have great influence in Chicago politics" and among the other Chicago Congressmen. If I found O'Hara unsatisfactory as a source, I suspect it would be necessary to work through the Mayor's office in Chicago in approaching this Congressman; but I see no reason to anticipate that any such need exists or will exist.

Mr. O'Brien is said to be personally a tremendous admirer of Speaker Rayburn, practically putting him in a Christlike category.

Representative Barratt O'Hara, Illinois
Ninth-ranking Democrat, Foreign Affairs

Congressman O'Hara is a man of charm who inspires real affection. He is a man of wide interests and intelligence. He is a man who would generally be sure to take the high road rather than the low road in politics.

Congressman O'Hara is inclined to be committed to mutual security and reciprocal trade. He is proud of the fact (if it is a fact) that he has more Japanese-Americans in his district than any other eastern Congressman. He is aware, unlike most Chicago politicians, of climates of thought and opinion at the University of Chicago, where his brother was for many years professor of literature.

But Congressman O'Hara is certainly not an effective and probably not a reliable member of the committee or the House. He rambles, he seems to possess little ability to discriminate between the significant and the secondary, he wastes his time, and he is unable to distinguish between those occasions when questioning an accepted frame of reference is merely petty and when it is vital. Basically, he probably distrusts the whole doctrine of military commitment as profoundly as any internationalist in the House.

The Independent Voters of Illinois are as powerful in his district as anywhere in the city and would support (they are an affiliate of ADA) both reciprocal trade and mutual security. Mr. O'Hara would be particularly responsive to Japanese-Americans, and he is aware of the more unorthodox and wide-ranging Chicago or ex-Chicago professors such as David Riesman.

Representative John Pilcher, Georgia
Eighth-ranking Democrat, Foreign Affairs

Mr. Pilcher, coming as he does from Georgia, is under the influence and to a considerable degree shares the views of the southeastern textile neo-isolationists (those who attacked Senator George because of his preoccupation, actual or alleged, with international affairs). He impresses some observers as extremely xenophobic, but I would be inclined to infer that he is rather an extremely conscientious man, disposed to distrust rather than hate foreigners, disposed to distrust waste, and inherently "practical" in his point of view. On the basis of what I have been told about him, I would suspect that a presentation of mutual security problems, and to a lesser extent foreign trade problems, not in terms of the idealism or the global considerations with which they are usually introduced so much as the practical business emphasis (another form of idealism but not recognized as such by its holders), would be worth trying. Mr. Pilcher has, I think, some church (Methodist) concerns beyond the average. He knows or thinks he knows a good deal about fertilizers, and one of his objections to last year's mutual security programs was a wasteful fertilizer operation in Korea.

The foregoing indicates that he is one of the members who almost certainly would be worth cultivating, but who would be likely to discourage many people before they should be discouraged. The general rule of interviewing, that you find out how the other guy sees things first before telling him what you think, would apply here in an extreme degree, I'd guess.

Since he has held office in the National Cotton Ginners Association, and his general mercantile business includes cotton ginning, he presumably is aware of the cotton export situation.

He has been a particularly strong opponent of long-term commitments of any sort, but in his case this is more likely a characteristic of the conscientious small-town businessman than absolute undeviating hostility to programs. (Other informed observers quite sharply disagree with me, and interpret him as *per se* antiforeign, antiprogress.)

Representative Armistead Selden, Alabama
Seventh-ranking Democrat, Foreign Affairs

Representative Selden has not been notorious for his concern with or interest in liberal foreign affairs policies. However, in times past his district has elected members quite liberal on such matters, partly no doubt because it is in the agricultural "Black Belt," the old plantation country, dependent upon an export economy. Mr. Selden is, as of now, more responsive to the newer industrial interests. Some informed people say that Mr. Selden would like to be free to be a "northern liberal"; however, it is reported that Mr. Selden is more than normally responsive to the social and ceremonial "advantages" that membership on the Foreign Affairs Committee is supposed to yield, and that therefore he might be more interested in invitations, receptions, etc., than most members, and more impressed by them. Conceivably, as with Wayne Hays, a medal or the like would be useful. An additional straw supporting this report is that he bothers to list in the *Congressional Directory* membership in "Blue Key and ODK leadership fraternities." At any rate, if some basis could be obtained for such action, it would do no harm, but it should be remembered he may sound liberal just to be socially *au fait*. If it involved a trip for him and Mrs. Selden or receptions including her, such a project might be doubly helpful. I have the impression that her family and perhaps she herself before her marriage had more than usual interest in cultural, international, and respectable liberal matters in her hometown (Talladega, Alabama), but I cannot now verify this impression, since it is based upon recollections of fourteen years ago.

Mr. Selden could and should presumably be approached by the Farm Bureau and Cotton Council people—although I have not asked their people about him. They have some who, because of cotton background and general sympathy, would be very likely to help by suggesting the best approaches from a cotton and farm standpoint.

Mr. Selden has an additional source of concern, which might, however, turn out to be an advantage from the standpoint of this memorandum: It is generally believed that Alabama will lose a Congressman in 1962 or 1964, depending on when redistricting occurs, and Selden's seat may be the one eliminated. Three of the four Congressmen from adjoining districts are quite young, which in any case suggests such a difficulty. Selden, who is an attorney, is not necessarily likely to want to go back to Greensboro, and therefore may be more interested in what he may do after the redistricting than many members, who his clients will be, etc.

A possibility to investigate—which is merely a suggestion: Selden's Alabama predecessor on Foreign Affairs, Laurie Battle, was an active and energetic member, with some real concerns about foreign affairs and mutual security. Battle, I believe, does some lobbying around town now.

Representative Richard Simpson, Pennsylvania
Second-ranking Republican, Ways and Means
(Will probably act as ranking minority member of Ways and Means during much of the coming Congress in view of Mr. Reed's ill health.)

Mr. Simpson is a convinced and dedicated protectionist, and a very able man. Although one can imagine circumstances under which he could be influenced, they are not at all likely to develop in this Congress. To him, one of the classic differences between Republicans and Democrats is that Republicans are protectionist.

Although his district does have industries that want protection, Mr. Simpson would be the first to admit that it is his own personal choice and priority that make protection his interest, and under present circumstances there is no more likelihood of changing him than of changing Oscar Strackbein.[8] The efforts of the Taft Committee and the international Chamber of Commerce to show that the "true" interests of his district were in favor of liberal trade merely annoyed and amused him; the report is no doubt still available (it received wide publicity in 1954 and '55) and the data are presumably true and the inferences probably valid, but I would not bother with it. There are several colleges in Mr. Simpson's district where some sentiment for liberal trade exists, but this also annoys rather than convinces him.

I know of nothing to suggest or show that Mr. Simpson is in any particular sense xenophobic or xenophile. Unlike Messrs. Utt and Mason, he could be convinced on some big issue that the national welfare or the welfare of the Republican party demanded temporary action contrary to his protectionist views, and on some small

---

[8]Oscar Strackbein was for many years the leading organizer of small businesses and trade unions, opposed to reciprocal trade concessions.

issue that, though right in substance, it is wrong in procedure; but beyond that, I believe he is not subject to much influence. He guides the tariff lobbyists far more than they guide him.

On the other hand, Mr. Simpson has some good votes on aid programs recorded (the most recent ones), and because of his position on the Republican Campaign Committee he is of far more than usual influence. I would be more than happy if anyone who tried to influence him simply complimented him on the aid votes and hoped he kept them up.

Representative John Watts, Kentucky
Fourteenth-ranking Democrat, Ways and Means

The major economic interests in Representative Watt's district are horses, whisky, tobacco. The tobacco is not, I believe, directly exported; I do not know how far the horses and whisky are. But it is reported by a reasonably reliable informant that when Representative Watts was considering a position on Ways and Means, the tobacco people went to him and said they would support him for this committee if he would vote right on reciprocal trade, etc. He has sometimes in the past voted with coal on the first vote. I am not certain whether there is actually any coal in his district or whether it's simply that some miners live there. A more important factor probably has been his friendship with Representative Carl Perkins, from the adjoining district, who has been heavily dependent upon the UMW. I infer that at one time Mr. Watts wanted to be on the committee, but later changed his mind and was nevertheless "drafted." Since tobacco and whisky are both very heavily concerned with federal tax policy, which is handled by Ways and Means, if I wished to obtain additional information about Mr. Watts I assume that lobbyists for these groups would be a good source. John Fenton, author of *Politics in the Border States* (New Orleans: Hauser Press, 1957), and Jasper Shannon of the University of Kentucky would no doubt have information about factional alignments, etc. It is rumored that in the 1960 primaries Governor Albert B. Chandler will run candidates against every Congressman who isn't with him.

BIBLIOGRAPHIC NOTE

1. A comprehensive and excellent survey of recent literature on Congress has been provided by Robert L. Peabody in the introductory chapter of Ralph K. Huitt and Robert L. Peabody, *Congress: Two Decades of Analysis* (New York: Harper & Row, 1969). No one presently writing a book on Congress can supplant Peabody's useful account.

2. Major omissions in Peabody's survey appear to me to be three:

(a) He largely omits the historical literature on Congress itself. Randall Ripley, in a valuable (but unfortunately unannotated) little paper on the historical research frontier as regards Congress, read at the American Political Science Association meeting, New York, September 1969, treats the possibilities and opportunities here. It is to be hoped he will develop this into a guide to available literature.

(b) Peabody omits, in terms of his definition of the problem, the literature on state politics and legislation, a good deal of which is relevant and useful. For example, almost any citizen can profitably read the chapters of Albert J. Beveridge's *Abraham Lincoln, 1809–1858* (Boston: Houghton Mifflin, 1928) dealing with Lincoln's career and maneuverings in the Illinois state legislature (vol. 1, chaps. 4 and 5, pp. 160–297). Recent critics have claimed that Beveridge had some of the facts wrong; but for our purposes, this is immaterial. Beveridge himself had a long career in Indiana politics, and was himself a United States Senator; whether he describes Illinois legislative politics in the 1830s correctly or not, he does describe federal and Indiana politics as practiced in the early years of the century brilliantly and lucidly (and there have been few changes since then). A more recent and to me fascinating report is that of William Havard and Loren Beth, *Politics of Misrepresentation: Rural-Urban Conflict in the Florida Legislature* (Baton Rouge: Louisiana State University Press, 1962). The title is misleading; the issue of misrepresentation (never in my opinion momentous) has disappeared; but Harvard's and Beth's description of legislative personalities and conflicts is of permanent value and interest.

(c) Naturally, Peabody also does not concern himself with foreign literature or historical literature dealing with British antecedents to our contemporary congressional situation. I find Constantine Melnik and N. C. Leites, *House Without Windows: France*

Selects a President (New York: Harper & Row, 1958), of great interest, both as comparison and as contrast. (Incidentally, many of Leites' observations provoked in me, first, the reaction "That's obvious. That's just political nature," and second, the awareness "But it's not true of the U.S. Congress." I discovered on analysis that I found some of them obvious, because some of them are also true of the Massachusetts legislature, and so Leites helped me see the difference between what I have known as a Bostonian on Beacon Hill and what is true on Capitol Hill.)

A useful and stimulating discussion is James H. Aitchison, "The Speakership of the Canadian House of Commons," in *Canadian Issues: Essays in Honor of Henry F. Angus,* ed. Robert M. Clark (Toronto: University of Toronto Press, 1962), pp. 23–56. It is worth noting that practice has moved in the direction of Aitchison's proposals, and actions in the present Parliament concerning the reelection of Speaker Lucien Lamoreux may establish the precedents he advocates. So here is a legislative study that may have had consequences.

I believe that one of the "works" that has most enlightened me about politics is the *Letters of Horace Walpole.* The most relevant of these are *Walpole's Letters to Horace Mann,* ed. W. S. Lewis and others, 8 vols. (New Haven: Yale University Press, 1954–67), but those wishing a fascinating introduction to real politics and parliamentary conflict should leaf through some of the letters in which Walpole is even more gossipy—for example, his *Letters to the Countess of Upper Ossory,* ed. W. S. Lewis and others, 3 vols. (New Haven: Yale University Press, 1965).

In general, the works of Sir John Neale, Cicely V. Wedgwood, and Sir Lewis Namier on British parliamentary politics from Elizabeth I to George IV, and many responses to some of their work (for instance, by Lewis Wiggin), seem to me the most interesting possible introduction to U.S. congressional politics and among the most valuable means of understanding this topic.

3. Of the books and articles that have appeared since Peabody's on the Congress itself, the outstanding one, to my mind, is John S. Saloma III, *Congress and the New Politics* (Boston: Little, Brown, 1969). Unfortunately, this became available only after I had completed my manuscript; it is a book that needs and deserves careful reflection and study. Its main theme may be described as that of social adaptation and invention. How can Congress accommodate itself to and be useful in the light of new social and

technological developments? What kind of inventions are helpful for Congress as a result of new social awarenesses and technological possibilities? The book also contains some sophisticated analysis, compatible with traditional, preanalytic political philosophy, of the role of Congress.

The title strikes me and others as unfortunate; there is no reference to speak of to the radical New Left, etc. "The New Politics" evidently means the politics of adaptation.

4. Novels provide in some respects a more profound understanding of political and parliamentary politics than "serious" treatises; there is, however, an astounding lack of realistic novels about Washington and the U.S. Congress. There are some excellent novels on state and local legislative politics—excellent as political accounts, however one may rate them as novels. For example, Winston Churchill used his considerable experience in New Hampshire politics in writing *Conistion* (New York: Macmillan, 1906)— see especially the brilliant chapter on "The Woodchuck Session," pp. 182–201—and *Mr. Crewe's Career* (New York: Macmillan, 1908). (Incidentally, in those days a good many New Hampshire legislators were bought, sold, and delivered, as Churchill reports, by the railroads and other interests—a situation much less ambiguous and complex than is true of Congress in 1970, but nevertheless similar in many of its fundamentals.)

I regard Anthony Trollope, along with Horace Walpole, as the source of whatever political awareness I have acquired. His three outstanding novels on politics are *Phineas Finn, Phineas Redux*, and *The Prime Minister*, initially published in the 1870s, now in print in Oxford University Press editions.

5. Part II of this book rests upon a theory of selective attention which, as far as I can trace its history, I owe in part to two neglected articles by David Lindsay Watson, "On the Nature of Mental and Social Organization," *Psychiatry*, 4 (1941): 375–91, and "Selecting Mechanism as a Concept for Psychiatry," *Psychiatry*, 5 (1942): 35–47.

The papers gathered together by Paul Bakan, ed., in *Attention: An Enduring Problem in Psychology* (Princeton, N.J.: Van Nostrand, 1966) suggest at places some sociological analogies or correlates to psychological studies of attention. Bakan says (p. iii): "An enduring problem in psychology may be defined as one that demands to be considered despite the best efforts of theorists to ignore it. This seems to be true of the problem of attention." Note particularly the articles by Donald Broadbent, "Classical Conditioning and Human Watch-Keeping" (pp. 79–94; reprinted from *Psychological Review*, 1953), and by J. Anthony and D. Deutsch, "Attention: Some Theoretical Considerations" (pp. 207–25).

I myself find a good deal of stimulus to thinking about the relation of attention to policy and politics in the larger sense in Sir Geoffrey Vickers' work, notably in his *Art of Judgment: A Study of Policy Making* (New York: Basic Books, 1965).

6. A comprehensive study of Congress would also involve a study of the conception of social organization. An excellent overview of knowledge in this field—especially helpful in understanding Congress as an open system—is Daniel Katz and Robert L. Kahn, *The Social Psychology of Organizations* (New York: Wiley, 1966; see my review of that book in *American Political Science Review*, 62 [1968]:1306–7). It contains a useful and extensive list of references.

7. It is interesting to note that none of the recent literature on Congress, to my knowledge, bears on the problem of greatest interest both to many traditional historians and philosophers and to the most recent generation of college students—the moral roles and obligations of legislators. However, this is an area in which one book is so far superior to all others that no other references need be made. All morally reflective citizens should read T. V. Smith, *The Legislative Way of Life* (Chicago: University of Chicago Press, 1940). (Congressman Smith had formerly been a State Senator in Illinois and was an internationally distinguished professional philosopher.) I personally, were I to teach a course on Congress or the legislative process or the job of a politician, would, generally speaking, regard Congressman Smith's book as the one most significant discussion for the present generation of political science students to master on these topics. It is a pity it appeared a generation ago; had it been published initially today, its impact would be much greater.

INDEX OF NAMES

INDEX OF SUBJECTS

PRINTED IN U.S.A.